Marion Harland, Ella Wheeler Wilcox

Breakfast, dinner and supper

How to cook and how to serve them

Marion Harland, Ella Wheeler Wilcox

Breakfast, dinner and supper
How to cook and how to serve them

ISBN/EAN: 9783744786003

Printed in Europe, USA, Canada, Australia, Japan

Cover: Foto ©Lupo / pixelio.de

More available books at **www.hansebooks.com**

BREAKFAST, DINNER AND SUPPER

HOW TO COOK AND HOW TO SERVE THEM

A COMPREHENSIVE TREATMENT OF THE SUBJECT OF COOKERY, ANCIENT AND MODERN COOKING UTENSILS, ETC., WITH ABUNDANT INSTRUCTIONS IN EVERY BRANCH OF THE ART—SOUPS, FISH, POULTRY, MEATS, VEGETABLES, SALADS BREAD, CAKES, JELLIES, FRUITS, PICKLES, SAUCES, BEVERAGES, CANDIES, SICK ROOM DIET, CANNING, CARVING, SERVING MEALS, MARKETING, ETC.

INCLUDING

VALUABLE RECIPES IN ALL DEPARTMENTS

EDITED BY

A SKILLED CORPS OF PRACTICAL EXPERTS

TO WHICH IS ADDED

Important Departments on the Preparation of Food for Infants and Advice to Housekeepers

BY

MARION HARLAND

TOGETHER WITH CHAPTERS ON INVALID DIET, MARKETING, CARVING, ETC.

WITH A PREFATORY PROEM BY

ELLA WHEELER WILCOX

Profusely Illustrated

NEW YORK
GEORGE J. McLEOD & COMPANY
45 VESEY STREET

PREFACE

How to cook, and how to serve what has been cooked, are vitally important and exceedingly complicated problems. On both these rocks many a household has suffered shipwreck. To buy food and spoil it in the cooking, or to cook food and spoil it in the serving, are either of them deplorable blunders. Nobody is fed and strengthened pleasurably by these failures, but somebody is sure to be irritated, and possibly sickened thereby. Cook good victuals well and serve well-cooked victuals temptingly; then will the family board rival the hotel board in attractiveness, and the family boarder will be well content at home.

How to cook and how to serve, are the two topics discussed in this volume. The suggestions here given are not such as an inexperienced editor might collate and combine in quantity, regardless of quality; but they are the results of long and careful domestic experience in houses where these two arts were studied and practiced. Skilled housekeepers of large experience are responsible for every recipe and hint here given. They have tried and tested these matters of which they write, and happy is the young housekeeper who can profit by their wisdom.

In order to profit thus, care is needed, and much study. This book on a shelf in the kitchen will not act as a charm to prevent burning the beefsteak or toughening the pie-crust. Nor will the mere reading of it transform the careless girl into a thrifty manager of home. The book must be read, studied and obeyed. Do the things here directed and realize the benefits here portrayed. "Practice makes perfect"—provided it be wise practice. Otherwise it spoils everything.

Cook books are numerous, but it is believed this, the latest and best, will surpass them all.

The spaces on the margins of the pages will be found valuable for notes on the recipes of friends.

THE PUBLISHERS

There is no horizontal Stratification of society in this country like the rocks in the earth, that hold one class down below forevermore, and let another come to the surface to stay there forever. Our Stratification is like the ocean, where every individual drop is free to move, and where from the sternest depths of the mighty deep any drop may come up to glitter on the highest wave that rolls.

JAMES A. GARFIELD.

THE WAY TO THE HEART.

By Ella Wheeler Wilcox.

The woman who looks upon man as a sinner,
   Unsaved as to soul and uncertain of heart,
Should learn how to cook and prepare him a dinner,
   And serve it with talent, refinement and art.
Full many a question is solved by digestion;
   Bad morals are caused oftentimes by bad cooks;
And many a riot results from poor diet,
   Conversion may lie in the leaves of cook-books.

About the dull stalk of the thorn tree of duty
   Plant flowers of fragrance and vines of good taste;
Surround the coarse needs of the body with beauty,
   Make common things noble, make vulgar things chaste;
Put art in housekeeping! nor think culture sleeping
   Because the base animal—man, must be fed.
Delsarte should be able to speak in the table;
   "Expression" may lie in a loaf of light bread.

Though hard be the labor, the end recompenses;
   Though weary the journey, reward is the goal.
For the soul of a man must be reached through his senses,
   (As the senses of woman are reached through her soul.)
Speak first to his spirit, he never will hear it;
   Speak first to his body, his soul will reply.
The mortal man fare for, his appetite care for
   And Lo! he will follow your footsteps on high.

ENVOI.

Love born in the boudoir oft dies in the kitchen!
   The failure of marriage, of starts in the soup.
The stomach appeal to, and man's heart you steal to!
   Would you rise to the last; to the first you must stoop.

TABLE OF CONTENTS.

	PAGE.
PREFACE,	3-4
POEM BY ELLA WHEELER WILCOX	9
PART I.—DOMESTIC COOKERY,	15
1. THE ART OF COOKING,	17
2. SOUPS, SOUP STOCK, ETC.,	35
3. FISH, OYSTERS, ETC.,	46
4. POULTRY AND GAME,	61
5. MEATS,	70
i. Beef,	70
ii. Veal,	76
iii. Mutton and Lamb,	82
iv. Pork,	85
6. Vegetables,	91
7. SALADS AND SAUCES	102
8. CROQUETTES AND FRITTERS	111
9. EGGS,	117
10. BREAD, BISCUIT, HOT CAKES, ETC.,	126
i. Bread,	126
ii. Toast,	131
iii. Fancy Breads,	132
iv. Rolls,	134
v. Biscuit, Rusk, and Buns,	136
vi. Muffins and Waffles,	140
vii. Griddle Cakes	142
viii. Yeast and Yeast Cakes,	145
11. PASTRY AND PUDDINGS,	148
12. CREAMS, JELLIES, AND LIGHT DESSERTS,	166
13. CAKES AND CAKE BAKING,	179
14. FRESH FRUITS AND NUTS,	201
15. JELLIES, JAMS, AND PRESERVES,	207

CONTENTS

	PAGE
16. Canned Fruits and Vegetables,	219
17. Pickles and Catsups,	224
18. Beverages,	234
19. Candies,	242
20. Invalid Diet,	248
21. Advice to Housekeepers' by Marion Harland,	254
22. The Family House,	266
23. Made Overs	273
24. Hot Weather Dishes	280
25. Preparation of Foods for Infants' by Marion Harland	285
26. Potted Provisions	292
PART II.—HOUSE MANAGEMENT,	299
1. Marketing,	304
i. Beef,	305
ii. Veal,	307
iii. Mutton	308
iv. Lamb,	310
v. Pork,	310
vi. Venison,	311
vii. Poultry,	312
viii. Vegetables,	312
2. Carving,	315
3. Serving Meals,	326
4. The Bill of Fare.	334
INDEX	349

LIST OF ILLUSTRATIONS.

	PAGE.
Unleavened bread	19
Ancient Egyptian oven	20
Ancient cooking utensils	23
Ancient cooking utensils	24
Ancient cooking utensils	25
Cutting of Beef	305
Cutting of veal	307
Cutting of mutton	309
Cutting of pork	310
Turkey properly trussed	317
Back of a fowl	319
Chicken properly trussed	320
Goose properly trussed	320
Breast of duck	320
Back of duck	320
Bird properly trussed	321
Fore-quarter of lamb	322
Whole roast pig	323
Rabbit properly trussed	324

Domestic Cookery.

THERE is a beautiful legend that tells how Elizabeth of Hungary, having been forbidden by her lord to carry food to the poor, was met by him one day outside the castle walls as she was bearing a lapful of meat and bread to her pensioners. Louis demanding sternly what she carried in her robe, she was obliged to show him the forbidden burden. "Whereupon," says the chronicler, "the food was miraculously changed, for his eyes, to a lapful of roses, red and white, and his mind disabused of suspicion, he graciously bade her pass on withersoever she would."

It would be well for some husbands if "their eyes were holden" in such a way that food served them would seem other and better than it really is. But the sense of taste is a rebellious member—especially in the men. It will cry out against the best appearing dish, if its flavor is not of the best. There is but one way to sure success. The housewife herself must be the angel who casts the spell about the humble board and the lowly fare, and invests them with forms and odors of irresistible attractiveness. This is the true poetry of Domestic Cookery; and blessed is the home where one presides who knows this art, and makes each meal a feast, and every guest a glad participant.

But things do not always take so happy a form. For instance: there was recently a brutal murder in Troy, N. Y., and a paper, reporting the case, clumsily said: "A poor woman was killed yesterday in her own home, while cooking her husband's breakfast in a shocking manner." Quoting this statement, a contemporary remarked: "There are many women who cook their husbands' breakfasts in a shocking manner, but it is seldom that justice overtakes them so summarily." The subject is a serious one to joke over, but the turn given by the commenting paper is bright and suggestive.

The fact is, that by skillful manipulation the plainest fare may be transformed into dishes fit for kings, while by ignorance and inattention the best viands may be rendered unfit for human food. Which turn should housewives attempt to give their own culinary affairs? There can be but one reply. But, be it remembered, that freaks of favoring fortune, such as came to Elizabeth, come only to those who are zealously pursuing the line of helpful duty. There is no royal road to success as a housekeeper or a cook. You must "work your passage," but the way will be smoothed by careful study of pages such as follow, provided the study take shape in wise action.

Remember, too, that the ministry of Domestic Cookery is by no means an unimportant one. It is worthy of the best attention of any housewife.

"The stomach," says an eminent medical authority, "is the mainspring of our system; if it be not sufficiently wound up to warm and support the circulation, the whole business of life will, in proportion, be ineffectually performed; we can neither think with precision, walk with vigor, sit down with comfort, nor sleep with tranquility. There would be no difficulty in proving that it influences (much more than people imagine) all our actions." Dyspepsia is a fearful foe to the human race.

I.—THE ART OF COOKING.

THERE is a *science* and there is an *art* of cooking. The science tells what should be done and why; the art takes hold and does the thing, without, in most cases, knowing any reason why certain methods produce certain results. The one is theoretical, the other practical; the one deals with principles, the other with performances.

The science of cookery proceeds on the basis that man needs certain elements of repair and growth for the various tissues of his body, that these elements exist in nature in various forms, and that the mission of the cook is so to prepare these suitable substances that man may receive them in their most enjoyable and assimilable forms, and thus have his waste repaired and his growth provided for. This basis is solid. On it the whole culinary system is founded. But, from the merely utilitarian idea of repairing waste and supplying force, cookery rises to the supreme height of exquisitely delighting the taste while doing its most important work of feeding the body. Indeed, the art of cooking well, and of serving well-cooked victuals well, is "a fine art" in the best sense of the term. There are *artistes* in this line. Meals may be served artistically. They may become a delight to the most refined natures and a real benefaction to both body and soul.

The great aim of all cooking is to retain all the valuable elements of the food, and to put them into such forms as shall awake desire, stimulate digestion, and secure to the eater, in the readiest and most pleasing way, all the nutriment these viands afford. For instance, in cooking meats it is desirable to retain all the natural juices. To this end, when meat is to be boiled it should be plunged into hot water, which at once renders the outer part measurably impenetrable, and so confines the juices. On the other hand, if the juices are to be drawn out for the production of soup, it must be placed in cold water, and gradually warmed and slowly boiled, so as to allow the exudation of the juices. On the same principle, broiling and roasting, by quickly closing the surface of the meat, retain the juices as well as the odors, and make the meat both juicy and savory. The retention of the fatty substances renders such preparations somewhat less digestible, however, than boiled food or lean meat.

High art in cookery, as elsewhere, demands high rates of expenditure. Instructions on that grade alone would not meet the want of American homes. But high aims in this department are equally commendable with high aims elsewhere. So important a factor in domestic economy as cooking cannot be ignored and should not be treated lightly. Good food, well cooked and well served, goes far to make home happy and its inmates healthy.

The chemical aspect of food and cooking may be left to the chemist and the physiologist. They will perfect the scientific aspects of the case. But the *art* of cooking, which teaches just how and when to do the right things, is for us to learn and to practice day by day. Such is the relation of stomach and brain on the one side, and of stomach and cook on the other side, that the cook becomes the sovereign, to whom many a brain mightier than his own bows in servile allegiance.

What cookery was practiced in the garden of Eden history does not tell. Vegetarians insist that permission to eat animal food was not given until after the flood (Genesis xi, 3, 4), when, by indulgence, man's appetites had become abnormal. If vegetable food only were used in Eden, and that mainly of the nature of fruits, but little cooking was needed, and the simplest forms would suffice amply. Ancient writers say that cooking came into use immediately on the discovery of fire, whenever that was, and that its introduction was in imitation of the natural processes of mastication and digestion.

The first reference of the Bible to cooked food is to "a morsel of bread" (Genesis xviii, 5). Sarah, in this instance, made ready " three measures of fine meal," which she kneaded, and of which she made cakes " upon the hearth." These were, doubtless, the simplest form of unleavened cakes,

UNLEAVENED BREAD, ANCIENT AND MODERN FORMS.

flattened thin and baked upon a hot stone. A tender calf was hastily dressed on this occasion also, but whether by boiling or stewing, by roasting on a hot stone or by broiling over the fire on the point of a stick, is not known. Certainly, the whole dressing required but little time and was not very elaborate. For these same guests Lot baked unleavened bread, and, as the record is, " he made them a feast," quite hurried and simple, no doubt.

When Abraham's servant, searching for a wife for Isaac, reached her father's house, " they did eat and drink," unquestionably in a festive way. Isaac was so fond of venison that he became unduly partial to his son Esau, who excelled as a hunter in capturing game for this dish. The preparation of the meat was in some elaborate style, which Isaac denominated " savory meat," and the eating of it so pleased him that he spoke of it as the meat "that I love," and asked it " that I may eat, and that my soul may bless thee before I die." Irreverent critics may say this was man-like, but reverent ones will pronounce it quite human, and all may conclude that cookery was taking attractive shapes in that early day. So Esau thought, undoubtedly, upon seeing his brother Jacob with a pottage of red lentiles. He was willing to sell out his birthright, with all its high prerogatives, that he might eat of this tempting dish. All these incidents from the book of Genesis indicate that punctuality at the table and systematic forethought for its proper service were undeveloped arts at that time. Many later Biblical references indicate a higher state of culture in these respects, sumptuous fare and great feasts being matters of frequent reference. In the ceremonial law many directions were given concerning the killing and the cooking of animal food.

Ovens are often mentioned in the Bible. In the cities and villages they were located generally in the establishments of bakers (Hosea vii, 4), or in large private establishments. Portable ovens were used by many who lived in a nomadic way. The portable oven was a large earthen jar, widening at the bottom, and having a side opening there by which to extract the ashes and to insert the bread or meat. These are referred to as the possession of every family, in Exodus viii, 3; though in time of destitution, or scarcity of fuel, one oven answered for many families, as Leviticus xxvi, 26, shows. These ovens could be hastily heated by a quick fire of twigs, grasses, etc., which fuel suggested the reference in Matthew vi, 30, to grass, which to-day is in the field and to-morrow is cast into the oven. Loaves or meat were placed inside, and thin cakes upon the outside of these ovens.

ANCIENT EGYPTIAN OVEN.

The remote East, the land of spices, was the first to develop cookery in its higher ranges. Carefully wrought and highly seasoned dishes were first prepared there. Many curious notions are recorded of the various nations in respect to food and cooking. The universal custom in Oriental lands is to cook meat as soon as killed. It never becomes cold, as with us. Goose is a great favorite with the Egyptians. Plutarch says only one class of this nation would eat mutton, and at Thebes it was wholly prohibited. Puddings made from the blood of slaughtered animals were favored by Egyptians but hated by Moslems. Egyptians never ate the head of any animal. Pastry among them was worked into the shapes of animals, and was always sprinkled with caraway and anise.

The Greeks esteemed cookery so highly, that royal personages took pride in preparing their own meals. Homer's poems contain many illustrations of such service. Achilles once personally served up a great feast, its special feature being that smaller meats were garnished with entrails of oxen. It was common at great feasts of the Greeks to dedicate certain dishes to certain gods, and then to eat them in honor of those gods.

In the time of Pericles a class of professional cooks had come into prominence who boasted that they could serve up a whole pig, boiled on one side, roasted on the other, stuffed with cooked birds, eggs, and other delicacies, and yet the whole so neatly done that it could not be discovered where the animal had been opened. Invention was then taxed to invent a new cake, or a new sauce, and he who did it was deemed worthy of high honor. One Greek distinguished himself by devising a new method of curing hams; another devised a cake which took his name and made him famous. In Athenian dishes, assafœtida was a popular ingredient, as were rue and garlick.

To compound one famous dish, certain uninviting parts of sows, asses, hawks, seals, porpoises, star-fish, etc., were used. One visitor to Greece, having eaten a celebrated "black broth," said he had learned why the Spartans were in battle so fearless of death, as the pains of death were preferable to existence on such abominable food. A Greek poet, Archistratus, traveled the world over to study the gastronomic art, and then wrote a poem, "Gastrology," which became the standard among Greek epicures. Greek cooks took special pride in so flavoring and disguising common fish and meat, that epicures even would be deceived by their preparations.

Roman cooking surpassed the Grecian in the more solid dishes, until the decline of the Empire began, when Roman epicures and gluttons came to the front and soon surpassed the world. Fishes, birds, and wines were their chief delicacies, and to secure those of rarest quality the known world was laid under contribution. There is record of a single feast at which were served peacocks from Samos, chickens from Phrygia, kids from Melos, cranes from Ætolia, tunny fishes from Chalcedon, pikes from Pessinus, oysters from Tarentum, mussels from Chios, dates from Egypt, and incidentals from as many more points. Snails were fattened for table uses till their shells would contain a quart; fishes and birds were fed on the choicest dainties to prepare them for human food, while even hogs were fattened on whey and dates.

Lucullus was in the habit of spending fifty thousand denarii (about eight thousand dollars) on each of his sumptuous feasts. Galba's daily breakfasts were each of sufficient cost to feed a hundred families. Vitellius made a single dish of pheasants' brains, peacocks' brains, nightingales' tongues, and livers of the rarest fishes. Its cost was one thousand *sesterces* (about forty thousand dollars). On another occasion two thousand choice fishes and seven thousand rare birds were served by him. It is said his kitchen expenses for four months amounted to twenty-five million dollars.

Heliogabalus had a favorite dish for his own suppers made from the brains of six hundred thrushes. Pork was the choice Roman dish at a later day. It was often served in the famous style already referred to, being half baked,

ANCIENT ROMAN COOKING UTENSILS.
1. Sugar, or Vegetable Boiler.——2. Frying Pan.——3. Measuring Urn.——4. Boiler, on Tripod.

half boiled, and stuffed with birds, eggs, etc. The process of this preparation was long a profound and marvelous secret. It was accomplished, however, by bleeding the animal under the shoulder, removing the intestines by the throat, and refilling by the same passage. The upper side was then baked while the lower lay imbedded in a thick paste of barley meal mixed with wine and oil. The paste was then removed and the lower side boiled in a shallow saucepan.

ANCIENT ROMAN COOKING UTENSILS.
1. Measure for Grain.—2. Kitchen Boiler.—3. Fire Grate.—4. Pitcher, or Urn, for Fluids.

Cooking utensils were elaborately made for the homes of the rich. The finest grades were made of bronze, and usually they were plated with silver. Some articles were of brass, others even of silver. Kitchens were royal apartments then, many of them having marble floors and being decorated with costly paintings. Even the aspirations of our modern "help" would have been gratified fully by the kitchen appointments of those days. Schools of cookery, under the most accomplished professional care, were numerous at that time.

One of the most princely pieces of extravagance ever brought out by good cooking was in the case of Antony. When Cleopatra praised a repast he furnished, Antony at once called the cook and presented him with a city. Another piece of extravagance was when Lucullus entertained

ANCIENT ROMAN COOKING UTENSILS.
1. Bowl.—2. Soup Pot.—3. Grater.—4. Measure for Fluids.—5. Cook's Knife —6. Hashing Knife.

Cicero and Pompey. They three partook of a little feast which cost not less than five thousand dollars. Geta insisted on as many courses at his state dinners as there were letters in the alphabet, and each course was required to contain every viand known, the name of which began with that letter. Alexander the Great once entertained ten thousand guests, all of whom were seated at the tables at one time, and in silver chairs upholstered with purple. Possibly the most extensive "spread" ever made was by the Earl of Warwick when his brother was installed Archbishop of York in 1479. The record of its appointments is as follows: 300 quarters of wheat, 300 tuns of ale, 104 tuns of wine, 1 pipe of spiced wine, 10 fat oxen, 6 wild bulls, 300 pigs, 1,004 sheep, 300 hogs, 3,000 calves, 300 capons, 100 peacocks, 200 cranes, 200 kids, 2,000 chickens, 4,000 pigeons, 4,000 rabbits, 4,000 ducks, 204 bitterns, 400 herons, 200 pheasants, 500 partridge, 5,000 woodcocks, 400 plovers, 100 curlews, 100 quails, 100,000 eggs, 200 roes, 4,000 roebucks, 155 hot venison pasties and 4,000 of them cold, 1,000 dishes of jellies, 2,000 hot custards and 4,000 of them cold, 400 tarts, 300 pikes, 300 bream, 8 seals, and 4 porpoises. The Earl in person was steward; 1,000 servitors, 62 chief cooks, and 515 under cooks and scullions officiated on this monster occasion.

After the fifth century it is said that "cookery, like learning, retired into convents." For several centuries religious houses alone were the abodes of good cooking. In the tenth century the art reappeared among the wealthier citizens of Italy. Discoveries of new countries and the increasing activity of commerce continually enlarged the field for gastronomic delights. Italy, the leader in fine cookery in those days, began to send her methods and her cooks into France, where they received a hearty welcome from Catharine de Medici and her royal spouse. Under these fostering impulses several cities became famous for specialties in food; Hamburg, for example, for hams, Strasburg for sausages, Amsterdam for herrings, Ostend for oysters, Chartres for pies, etc., etc.

The ancient Britons and Saxons knew none of the refinements of the culinary art. Their meal was simple bruised barley; their meat, half-cooked game. The Danes did more at drinking than at eating, at brewing than at baking. The Normans, however, introduced the better styles of food and the cook again loomed up grandly. So great was the excess of these times that the friars of St. Swithin's complained to King Henry II that three of their thirteen regular dinner courses had been withheld from them by their abbot. Cranmer ordered, in 1541, that archbishops should be limited to six dishes of meat daily, bishops to five, and lower orders of clergy to four, or three in certain cases. The poultry to be used was also limited, and the fish.

After the Crusades the higher classes of England imitated the luxurious methods they had learned abroad. Peacocks became a favorite dish. They were usually served with the tail feathers remaining and spread to their fullest extent. In the reign of Elizabeth cooks reached the zenith of their power, many classical scholars willingly espousing this profession.

The early inhabitants of France subsisted chiefly on roots and acorns. After their subjugation by Cæsar they quickly took on the Roman methods, and later the Norman methods, until in the fourteenth century they produced Taillevant, the greatest cook of history. In the reign of Louis XII a company was chartered to make *sauces* and another to cook meats on the *spit*. These were the days when fancy cooking ran toward the impossible. Eggs cooked on the spit, butter fried, roasted, etc., were the surprising delicacies produced by the masters of gastronomy.

In the days of Louis XIV cookery in France was at its height of sumptuousness. A reaction in favor of moderation then began to prevail. Cooks were out of employment. Restaurants then appeared under their care, and they soon found abundant patronage. Carême, of France, is confessedly the greatest of modern French cooks. He has exalted the science of cookery while he has nobly advanced the art.

There are several national or provincial dishes which are well known; for example, the roast beef and plum pudding of England; the sauerkraut of Germany; the salt beef of Holland; the *pillau* of Turkey (made of rice and mutton fat); the macaroni of Italy; the potatoes of Ireland; the oat-meal of Scotland; the pork and beans and the pumpkin pie of New England.

Books on the science and the art of cookery are numerous. The oldest dates from the last half of the fourteenth century. It is from a Frenchman, Le Sage, who has blended moral maxims and culinary recipes in a wonderful manner. The next in order is from Taillevant, already referred to, dated 1392. Scappi, chief cook to Pope Pius V, published a valuable book on cookery in 1570. So have they been multiplied as the years have rolled by, and one who is not an expert in cookery cannot lay his defect at the door of authors or publishers.

But books are not sufficient to elevate a people. There must be instruction, by which the text-books may be expounded and their lessons be illustrated to the masses. The art of cookery must be learned, as are the other arts. There are those who say that domestic cooking should be learned in the home—that the mother should teach the daughters, and that skill and knowledge should thus be handed down from generation to generation. This is a splendid theory; but if the mothers themselves are ignorant and unskillful, what then can be hoped for from the daughters? Then, too, a fixed set of culinary traditions would be handed down in each family by this method, and the children would follow the ways of the parents, irrespective of better ways practiced by their next-door neighbors.

In the face of these facts, it was not at all strange that schools of cookery arose centuries ago; but it is strange that these schools were not extended in their scope, to include others than professional cooks. They aimed merely to provide skilled help for the kitchens of royalty and wealth. This they did to perfection, but the common people knew nothing of the methods whereby their plain fare might be made more toothsome or more beneficial. It has remained for this later day, this utilitarian age, to establish schools designed to furnish good, practical cooks for our homes, and to develop them from our wives and our daughters.

This "cooking-school" movement arose in England. The working classes there were so sadly unskilled in using provision, and provision was so enormously costly, that the question necessarily arose, Is there no way whereby these masses can use what little they have to better advantage? How to make the most of what was in their kitchens was the practical problem. Schools of domestic economy then arose, under the patronage of benevolent persons, to promote the practical solution of this difficulty.

The managers of the South Kensington Museum of Arts, in West London, made the first organized movement in this matter by establishing public lectures on the preparation of food, with platform demonstrations of various culinary operations. But the inadequacy of this course was soon evident. Exposition and illustration were good, but practice was needed. Cookery is like music, in that the only way to do it well is *to do it well*. Lectures on the capabilities of the piano, though supplemented by brilliant illustration, could never make musicians, and the course inaugurated at Kensington Museum was not capable of making cooks. Practice schools soon became an admitted necessity.

To found schools of this character was no easy task. Public sentiment was not up to the need. Teachers, textbooks, and even pupils were wanting. It was unavoidably an expensive method of education, and no great names stood ready to back the movement. But the parties chiefly interested were determined, and they moved onward. The first organized classes for graded instructions and practice in cookery were formed in 1874. These classes were open to all, but especial encouragement was given to those proposing to go out as teachers of this art. In this respect the work was a great success, and large numbers of cooking-schools have been formed in England.

These schools employ a series of printed "lessons," suited for use in all the work in all the various grades. These lessons contained a list of ingredients needed for each dish, with their quantity and cost. Then followed a specification of the several steps to be taken, each distinct in itself and numbered. Nothing was assumed to be known; nothing was here taken for granted, all was clearly specified and, if need be, explained. As trial showed defects in the several lessons, they were carefully revised, and at last text-books were issued. Every pupil learned what to do in each case; then they did it; then they kept on doing it until they could do it to perfection. As at "Dotheboy's Hall," he whose turn it was to spell "scrub" was set to scrub the floor, etc., etc., so at these practice schools, she who studied "Irish stew," made Irish stew, and capped the climax by eating it.

It is surprising that so diversified a company gathered in these schools. An observer of the Kensington Museum establishment says of the attendance: "There were cultivated ladies, the daughters of country gentlemen, old house-keepers, servants, cooks, and colored girls from South Africa, together with a large proportion of intelligent young women who were preparing to become teachers."

It may strike one who goes over these lessons that there is a wearisome attention to trivial details. But it should not be forgotten that the chief difference between good and bad cookery lies just here. It is a prime point in cooking-schools to make each item so prominent that it cannot be overlooked. Strict attention to details is the corner-stone of the culinary art.

Schools of cookery are now numerous in this country. New York, Philadelphia, and all the principal cities have institutions of this character. Text-books are numerous too. Eliza A. Youmans, Juliet Corson, and other ladies have nobly led the van of culinary *artistes*, and their manuals are standards for cooking-schools.

To illustrate the method of the cooking-schools, two "lessons" are here added, both on the making of Cabinet Pudding. The first is from the American edition of *Lessons in Cookery*, the handbook of the London school.

LESSON :—CABINET PUDDING.

Ingredients.—One dozen cherries or raisins, and two or three pieces of angelica. One dozen finger-biscuits and half a dozen ratafias. One ounce of loaf-sugar and fifteen drops of essence of vanilla. Four eggs. One pint of milk.

Time required, about one hour.

To make a *Cabinet Pudding:*

1. Take a *pint-and-a-half mold* and *butter* it inside with your fingers.
2. Take a *dozen raisins* or *dried cherries*, and two or three pieces of *angelica*, and ornament the bottom of the mold with them.
3. Take *one dozen* stale sponge *finger-biscuits** and break them in pieces.
4. Partly fill the mold with pieces of cake and a half a dozen *ratafias.†*
5. Take *four yelks* and *two whites of eggs* and put them in a basin.
6. Add to the eggs one ounce of white sugar, and whip them together lightly.
7. Stir in, by degrees, one pint of milk.
8. Flavor it by adding fifteen drops of essence of vanilla.
9. Pour this mixture over the cakes in the mold.
10. Place a piece of *buttered paper* over the top of the mold.
11. Take a saucepan half full of boiling water, and stand it on the side of the fire.

* To be had at the baker's.
† For sale at all large grocery-houses.

12. Stand the mold in the saucepan, to steam for from three-quarters of an hour to an hour.

<small>N. B.—The water should only reach half way up the mold, or it would boil over and spoil the *pudding*.</small>

13. For serving, turn the pudding carefully out of the mold on to a hot dish."

The other "lesson" is from Miss Corson's *Cooking-school Text-book*. It is the method pursued in the New York Cooking-school and its offshoots.

LESSON:—CABINET PUDDING.

INGREDIENTS.

¼ lb. candied cherries,	20 cents.
2 oz. citron,	4 "
¼ lb. macaroons,	15 "
Sponge cake,	10 "
1 pt. milk,	4 "
½ oz. gelatine,	3 "
1 lemon,	2 "
3 oz. powdered sugar,	2 "
Total,	60 cents.

(1.) Soak the gelatine in two tablespoonfuls of cold water until it is soft, and then put it over the fire in a saucepan with the milk, sugar, and the yellow rind of the lemon cut very thin, and let it heat thoroughly, stirring occasionally until the gelatine and sugar are dissolved. (2.) Cut the citron in thin slices. Butter a plain pudding mold rather thickly with cold butter, and ornament the bottom and sides by placing some of the fruit against them in some pretty shape. (3.) Place the remaining fruit and the cake in the mold in alternate layers, and then strain the milk into the mold. Set it where it will cool and grow firm, which will be in four or five hours, and then turn it out of the mold and serve it cold."

Every city has its leading caterer, who illustrates, when opportunity offers, to what heights the gastronomic art may be carried. On special occasions great " spreads " are made, the cost of which will surprise the uninitiated. From two to five dollars per plate is an ordinary charge for these entertainments. Ten dollars for each guest is by no means unusual. Twenty-five dollars for each guest, the wines included, is a price often charged, and Delmonico, of New York, furnished a dinner to ten persons, the cost of which was estimated to be no less than four hundred dollars each.

The dinner was given by a distinguished yachting-man, who insisted that the five men in waiting should be dressed as sailors. He furnished the suits, new and elegant. The guests drank, or tasted, every vinted liquor that has ever been brought to America—not that they drank every brand of wine, but every grade was represented. They finished with a *pousse cafe* made of eleven liquors.

The bills of fare were a striking feature of the display. Before each plate sat a cut-glass basin, about twenty inches in diameter and four inches deep. Each was nearly filled with water, perfumed with ottar of roses, on the surface of which floated half-open pond lilies. In the basin a perfect model of the yacht owned by the gentleman who gave the dinner was placed. It was cut in red cedar wood, with cabin, rail, wheel for steering, brass work, such as belaying-pins, binnacle, etc., man ropes worked and trimmed with sailor knots, scraped pine masts and booms, rigging of silken cords colored as it would be in the prototype, and sails of satin.

The sails carried the bills of fare. On the flying jib were the words: " Compliments of ————," naming the giver of the dinner; on the jib the date and place; on the foresail was the name of the guest who sat at the place where each little vessel floated; and on the mainsail was the *menu*. As the guest had occasion to consult his bill of fare, he used a little gold oar that rested on the fingers of a silver naiad who peered over the containing glass, and held out both hands to grasp the oar. After the dinner each guest either carried away his bill of fare or had it sent to his home. The bills of fare were supposed to have cost at least one hundred dollars apiece. Of course, the viands spread at such a table were the finest the markets of the world could afford.

An artistic conclusion to an elaborate luncheon in New York is thus described by one who was there: "The last course was quite classic. A Greek would have appreciated it. It would have given him visions of Hybla and Hymettus, and their luxuriant growth of wild thyme. Everything was removed from the table except the ferns in the centre. A glass jug, some small glasses, and a plate of water crackers were brought in. The hostess poured out for each guest a tiny glass of metheglin. Any one who had forgotten the old reputation of this liquor and of what it was made would have been enlightened by seeing the jug. It looked like a honeycomb. Through the wax-looking cells painted upon its surface the liquor appeared like yellow honey. On the stopper was a black and gold bee. The caster, or tray, in which the jug stood was of glass also, covered with white clover and other heather flowers, which give the delicate flavor to Scotch and French honey. Such a finale seems to claim for America mention among those nations which Shakespeare describes as 'exquisite in their drinking.'"

MEMORANDUM
ON
FRIENDS' RECIPES

II.—SOUP STOCK, SOUPS, ETC.

GENERAL SUGGESTIONS ON SOUP STOCK AND SOUP MEAT, HOW TO PREPARE THEM, HOW TO ENRICH THEM, THICKENING SOUP, COLORING SOUP, FLAVORING SOUP, ETC. THIRTY-TWO RECIPES FOR SOUPS AND INCIDENTAL PREPARATIONS.

THE first and great essential to making good soup is *stock*, or good, fresh meat. To make stock, take the liquor left after boiling fresh meat, bones large or small, the large ones being cracked, that the marrow may be extracted, trimmings of meat, bones, and meat left over from a roast or broil, put any or all of these in a large pot or soup-kettle with water enough to cover them. Let them simmer slowly over a steady fire, keep the kettle covered, stir frequently, pour in now and then a cup of cold water, and skim off the scum. If it is fresh meat or bones, commence with cold water; if cooked, with warm water. Bones are as useful as meat in making stock, as they furnish gelatine. A quart of water is usually enough for a pound of meat. Six to eight hours will make stock fit for use. Let it stand over night, then skim off the fat, put the stock into an earthen jar, and it is ready for use.

Fresh meat should be freed from all superfluous skin and fat, which make a soup greasy, rather than rich.

The glutinous substance contained in the bones renders it important that they should be boiled with the meat, as they add to the strength and thickness of the soup. The meat, however, should be cut off the bone and divided into small pieces. Place in cold water over a gentle fire and boil by the long and slow process, that the essence of the meat may

MEMORANDUM ON
FRIENDS' RECIPES

36   *DOMESTIC COOKERY.*

be drawn out thoroughly. When it comes to the boiling point, throw in a little salt to assist the scum to rise; then skim carefully to prevent its becoming turbid. When no more scum accumulates, and the meat is softened so as to readily separate with the use of the fork, it should be strained, the vegetables put it, the seasoning done, and the necessary amount of hot water added if too much has boiled away.

All soup meats are better boiled the day before using, so as to allow the grease to chill over night, when it can readily be removed before putting over the fire again.

The following thickening is almost indispensable to all good soups: A tablespoonful or more of flour mixed to a smooth paste with a little water, and enriched with a teaspoonful of butter, or good beef drippings well stirred in. If it be necessary to add water to a soup, always use boiling water, as cold water injures the flavor. If making a rich soup that requires catsup or wine, let either be added just before the soup is taken from the fire.

Soup may be colored yellow by the use of grated carrots; red with the juice of tomatoes; green with the juice of powdered spinach; brown with carefully scorched flour, kept ready for use. Onions are thought by many to be a necessity in all soups—that their flavor must lurk somewhere, either defined or undefined. Their flavor may be much improved if fried until nicely browned in hot butter before being added to the soup. Potatoes should never be boiled with soup, because they add nothing to its flavor and are themselves injured by the long cooking. They should be boiled separately, and then added.

A most desirable quality in soup is that no one flavor predominate over the others, but, that by a careful blending of the different ingredients it shall contain and harmonize all flavors. Soups and broths should always be strained. It

MEMORANDUM
ON
FRIENDS' RECIPES

makes them more relishable as well as inviting to the eye. A slight acid, like lemon or tomato, gives a peculiar relish to some soups, as do many of the palatable condiments prepared by such manufacturers as Durkee & Co., Annear & Co., Cross & Blackwell, and several others, for this especial purpose. With such helps and a sufficient quantity of *stock* on hand, a choice, rich soup of any variety may be gotten up in thirty minutes.

RECIPES.

Beef Soup.—Boil a shin of beef, or a piece off the shoulder, slowly and thoroughly, the day before desiring to use it; skim well the next day and thin the jelly, if necessary, with water; add a little brandy, a grated carrot, two tablespoonfuls of butter rubbed smooth in brown flour, a little vermicelli, and spices to taste. Two or three eggs may be boiled hard, mashed smooth, and placed in the tureen before turning in the soup.

Beef Soup, No. 2.—Boil a shin of beef of moderate size, crack the bone, remove the tough outside skin, wash, and place in a kettle to boil with six or eight quarts of water. Let it boil about four hours, until it becomes perfectly tender, then take it out of the liquid. Add salt, one pint of tomatoes, two onions cut in small pieces, two turnips cut in quarters, one grated carrot, one large tablespoonful of sugar, a little sweet marjoram and thyme rubbed fine, one red pepper cut in very small pieces, also a celery top or a small quantity of bruised celery seed. This soup may be thickened according to taste either with vermicelli, macaroni, noodles, or drop dumplings.

For an incidental side dish, take the soup meat that has been cut from the bones, chop fine while warm, season with salt and pepper, add one teacup of soup saved out before

MEMORANDUM ON FRIENDS' RECIPES

38   *DOMESTIC COOKERY.*

putting in the vegetables. Pack in a dish, and slice down for tea or lunch when cold.

Beef Soup with Okra.—Cut a round steak in small pieces and fry in three tablespoonfuls of butter, together with one sliced onion, until very brown; put into a soup kettle with four quarts of cold water, and boil slowly an hour; add salt, pepper, and one pint of sliced okra, and simmer three and one-half hours longer. Strain before serving.

Corned Beef Soup.—When the liquor in which corned beef and vegetables have been boiled is cold, remove all the grease that has risen and hardened on the top, and add tomatoes and tomato catsup and boil half an hour—thus making an excellent tomato soup; or add to it rice, or sago, or pearl barley, or turn it into a vegetable soup by boiling in the liquor any vegetables that are fancied. Several varieties of soups may have this stock for a basis and be agreeable to the taste.

Ox-tail Soup.—Chop the ox-tail into small pieces; set on the fire with a tablespoonful of butter, and stir until brown, and then pour off the fat; add broth to taste, and boil gently until the pieces of tail are well cooked. Season with pepper, salt, and three or four tomatoes; boil fifteen minutes and then serve. This soup can be made with water, instead of the stock broth, in which case season with carrot, onion, turnip, and parsley.

Mutton Broth.—After the steaks have been cut from the leg, the lower part is just adapted for a soup. The neck-piece is also very nice. Boil the meat very gently in cold water, adding a turnip, a carrot, and a spoonful of rice. All the fat should be removed. Toward the last, add a little minced parsley. Dumplings are an excellent addition.

Vegetable Soup.—Take two pounds of shin of beef and two pounds of knuckle of veal; remove all the fat and break the bones and take out the marrow; put into a pot with five pints of water; add a teaspoonful of salt, and then cover and let it come to a boil quickly; remove the scum that rises, and set where it will simmer for five hours; one hour before serving, add two young carrots, scraped and cut in slices, half a head of celery, and a small onion cut into squares; in half an hour add one turnip sliced, and in fifteen minutes one cauliflower broken in small pieces.

Bean Soup.—Soak one and a half pints of beans in cold water over night. In the morning drain off the water, wash the beans in fresh water, and put into soup-kettle with four quarts of good beef stock, from which all the fat has been removed. Set it where it will boil slowly but steadily for three hours at the least. Two hours before it is needed for use, slice in an onion and a carrot. Some think it improved by adding a little tomato. If the beans are not liked whole, strain through a colander and send to the table hot.

Black Bean Soup.—Three pounds soup bone, one quart black beans, soaked over night and drained; one onion, chopped fine; juice of one lemon. Pepper, salt, and Durkee's Challenge Sauce to taste. Boil the soup bone, beans, and onions together six hours; strain, and add seasoning. Slice lemon and put on top when served.

Tomato Soup.—Take a knuckle of veal, a bony piece of beef, a neck of mutton, or almost any piece of meat you may happen to have; set it over the fire in a small quantity of water, cover it closely, and boil very gently, to extract the juices of the meat. When nearly done, add a quantity of peeled tomatoes, and stew till the tomatoes are done; add salt and pepper to your taste. This is a very cheap, healthful, and easily made soup.

Tomato Soup, No. 2.—Take one quart of tomatoes. When boiling, add one teaspoonful of soda, two pulverized soda

MEMORANDUM ON
FRIENDS' RECIPES

DOMESTIC COOKERY.

crackers, one pint of hot water, one pint of milk, salt, and pepper; strain through a colander and serve hot.

Green Pea Soup.—Boil the empty pods of a half-peck of green peas in one gallon of water one hour; strain them out; add four pounds of beef cut into small pieces, and boil slowly for an hour and a half longer. Half an hour before serving add the shelled peas, and twenty minutes later half a cup of rice flour, salt, pepper, and a little chopped parsley. After adding the rice flour stir frequently so as to prevent scorching.

Dried Split Pea Soup.—One gallon of water, one quart of soaked split peas, half a pound of salt pork, one pound of beef. Put over the fire, seasoning with salt and pepper, celery salt, salpicant, curry powder, marjoram, or savory; let it boil slowly for two hours, or until the quantity of liquor does not exceed two quarts. Pour into a colander and press the peas through with a spoon. Fry two or three slices of stale bread in butter till brown, scatter them in the soup after it is placed in the tureen.

Corn Soup.—Cut the corn from the cob, and to a pint of corn allow one quart of hot water; boil an hour and press through a colander; put into a saucepan an ounce of butter and a tablespoonful of flour, being careful to stir well to prevent it being lumpy; then add the corn pulp, a little cayenne pepper, salt, a pint of boiling milk, and half a pint of cream.

Onion Soup.—Slice ten medium-sized onions and fry brown in butter with a tablespoonful and a half of flour; put into a saucepan, and stir in slowly four or five pints of milk and water (about one-third water); season to taste, and add a teacupful of grated potato; set in a kettle of boiling water, and cook ten minutes; add a cup of sweet cream and serve quickly.

MEMORANDUM
ON
FRIENDS' RECIPES

SOUP STOCK, SOUPS, ETC.

Mock-turtle Soup.—Scald a calf's head and wash it clean; boil it in a large pot of water for half an hour, cut all the skin off, and take the tongue out. Take the broth made of a knuckle of veal, put in the tongue and skin, with one onion, half-ounce of cloves, half-ounce of mace, half a nutmeg, all kinds of sweet herbs chopped fine, and three anchovies. Stew till tender; then take out the meat, and cut it in pieces two inches square; cut the tongue, previously skinned, in slices; strain the liquor through a sieve; melt half a pound of butter in a stewpan; put in it half a pound of flour and stir it till smooth—if at all lumpy, strain it; add the liquor, stirring it all the time; then put to the meat the juice of two lemons, or one bottle of Madeira wine, if preferred; season rather highly with pepper, salt, and cayenne pepper; put in a few meat balls and eight eggs boiled hard. Stew gently one hour, and serve in a tureen; if too thick, add more liquor before stewing the last time.

Mock-turtle Soup. No. 2.—Take a calf's head and about two pounds of delicate fat pork. Put both into a soup-kettle, with two onions, sweet herbs, celery, pepper, and mace. Fill the kettle with water, and boil very gently till the meat is tender. Take out the head and the pork, return the bones of the head into the soup; let it stew several hours longer; and, when cold, take off the fat, strain the soup, and thicken; add the juice of a lemon and half a pint of white wine. Cut up the head and pork into pieces; warm them up in the soup, adding some choice meat balls made from finely minced, savory meat. The pork will be found quite an addition to the soup and a substitute for the fat of the turtle.

Gumbo Soup.—Cut up two chickens, two slices of ham, and two onions into dice; flour them, and fry the whole to a light brown; then fill the frying-pan with boiling water, stir

MEMORANDUM ON FRIENDS' RECIPES

it a few minutes, and turn the whole into a saucepan containing three quarts of boiling water; let it boil forty minutes, removing the scum. In the meantime soak three pods of okra in cold water twenty minutes; cut them into thin slices, and add to the other ingredients; let it boil one hour and a half. Add a quart of canned tomatoes and a cupful of boiled rice half an hour before serving.

Southern Gumbo Soup.—Cut up one chicken, and fry it to a light brown, also two slices of bacon; pour on them three quarts of boiling water; add one onion and some sweet herbs tied in a bag; simmer them gently three hours and a half; strain off the liquor, take off the fat, and then put the ham and chicken (cut into small pieces) into the liquor; add half a teacup of sliced okra, also half a teacup of boiled rice. Boil all half an hour, and just before serving add a glass of wine and a dozen oysters with their juice.

Julienne Soup.—Scrape two carrots and two turnips, and cut in pieces an inch long; cut slices lengthwise about one-eighth of an inch thick; then cut again, so as to make square strips; put them in a saucepan, with two ounces of butter, three tablespoonfuls of cabbage chopped fine, and half an onion chopped; set on the fire and stir until half fried; add broth as you wish to make thick or thin; boil until done; salt to taste; skim off the fat, and serve; it takes about two hours to prepare this soup properly. It can be served with rice or barley.

Macaroni or Vermicelli Soup.—Two small carrots, four onions, two turnips, two cloves, one tablespoonful salt, pepper to taste. Herbs—marjoram, parsley, and thyme. Put any cooked or uncooked meat and its bones in enough water to cover them; when they boil, skim them and add the vegetables. Simmer three or four hours, then strain through a colander and put back in the saucepan to reheat.

MEMORANDUM
ON
FRIENDS' RECIPES

Boil one-half pound macaroni until quite tender, and place in the soup tureen, and pour the soup over it—the last thing. Vermicelli will need to be soaked a short time only—not to be boiled.

White Soup.—Boil a knuckle of veal for three hours. Add a quarter of a pound of macaroni, and when done, a pint of cream. Season with lemon-peel and mace.

Turkey Soup.—Take the turkey bones and boil three-quarters of an hour in water enough to cover them; add a little summer savory and celery chopped fine. Just before serving, thicken with a little browned flour, and season with pepper, salt, and a small piece of butter.

Chicken Soup.—To the broth in which chickens have been boiled for salad, etc., add one onion and eight or ten tomatoes; season with pepper and salt; add Challenge Sauce or Salpicant, if desired; boil thirty minutes; add two well-beaten eggs just before sending to the table.

Lobster Soup.—To boil a lobster, put it in a fish-kettle and cover it with cold water, cooking it on a quick fire. Remove the small bladder found near the head, and take out a small vein found immediately under the shell all along the back of the lobster, and use the rest. Two lobsters will make soup for six or eight persons, and salad also. All the under shell and small claws are pounded in a mortar to make the soup; when pounded, put it into a pan and set it on the fire with broth or water. The meat is cut in small pieces, to be added afterward. The soup is left on the fire to boil gently for half an hour; then put it in a sieve and press it with a masher to extract the juice. To make it thicker, a small piece of parsnip can be added and mashed with the rest into a pan, so that all the essence is extracted in that way from the lobster. When you have strained it put a little

MEMORANDUM
ON
FRIENDS' RECIPES

DOMESTIC COOKERY.

butter with it and add as much broth as is required; put some of the meat in the tureen and pour the soup over it.

Clam Soup.—Wash the clams free from grit; boil them in a pint of water till they will come from the shells easily. Take a small quantity of the liquor, add some milk, thicken it with a little flour, and add the clams. Split crackers are very nice added.

Portable Soup.—Boil a knuckle of veal, also the feet, a shin of beef, a cowheel or any other bones of meat which will produce a stiff jelly, in a large kettle, with as much water as will cover them. Let it stand a long time over the fire before it boils. Skim it most thoroughly, until the broth appears entirely clear. Then fill up the kettle with hot water, and boil it eight hours, or until it has evaporated so as to be somewhat thick. Run it through a hair sieve, set it in a cool place where it will harden very quickly. Skim off every particle of fat, and return it to a saucepan; skim and stir continually, so that it may not scorch, and all the previous labor be lost, until it becomes a very thick syrup. As soon as it can be no longer done in this way, transfer it to a deep jar, and set into a kettle of water, hot, but not boiling, until it jellies very thick. This will keep good many months, if packed dry in tin canisters. This is the concentrated essence of soup, and is a most convenient article of use, either at home in an emergency or in traveling, and especially at sea. To make a pint of soup, cut off a piece as large as a walnut, dissolve it in the boiling water, and it is ready for use.

Fluid Beef.—Among the advanced preparations of the day meat extracts are taking a high place. One of the finest of these preparations is "Johnston's Fluid Beef." It contains all the nutritive constituents of the beef, and is readily available for soups, sandwiches, beef tea, etc. For medical uses, traveling, picnics, etc., it is very convenient. To

SOUP STOCK, SOUPS, ETC.

use for soups and beef tea, add a teaspoonful to a cup of boiling water and season to taste; or as a sandwich paste, it may be used on toast, with or without butter. Put up in cans of various sizes, from two ounces to one pound, which can be left open without injury to contents.

RECIPES INCIDENTAL TO SOUPS.

Meat Balls for Soup.—Take fresh cooked meat or fowl and chop fine; season with pepper, salt, and herbs, and a little lemon; mix together with an egg; roll in bread-crumbs, and fry in hot lard.

Browned Flour for Soups.—Dredge the bottom of a spider well with flour, and shake it over hot coals, letting it brown gradually, but not burn. Keep it in a dry place, in a tin canister, without wholly closing the lid. It is very convenient to have it already prepared, although when used fresh it is much nicer.

Home-made Noodles—a substitute for Vermicelli.—Wet with the yelks of four eggs as much fine, dry, sifted flour as will make them into a firm but very smooth paste. Roll it out as thin as possible, and cut it into bands of about an inch and a quarter in width. Dust them lightly with flour, and place four of them one upon the other. Cut them in the finest possible strips, separate them with the point of a knife, and spread them on the pie-board so that they may dry a little before they are used. Drop them gradually into the boiling soup, and in five minutes they will be done.

Drop Dumplings.—Take prepared flour, add a little beef drippings or lard, well rubbed through, and moisten to a soft dough. With floured hands pinch off very small pieces and form into balls by rolling in the palm of the hand. In boiling dumplings of any kind, put them in the water one at a time. If they are put in together they will blend with each other.

MEMORANDUM
ON
FRIENDS' RECIPES

MEMORANDUM
ON
FRIENDS' RECIPES

III.—FISH, OYSTERS, Etc.

HINTS CONCERNING FISH—TESTS OF FRESHNESS, HOW TO CLEAN, HOW TO DRESS, HOW TO BOIL FISH, HOW TO BAKE FISH, HOW TO BROIL FISH, HOW TO FRY FISH, ETC. FIFTY-THREE RECIPES FOR COOKING FISH, OYSTERS, ETC., AND FOR INCIDENTAL PREPARATIONS.

FISH should be eaten as soon as possible after being taken from the water. In every kind of fish, the brightness of the eyes, redness of the gills, firmness of the flesh, and stiffness of the fins are indications of freshness. Fish should be thoroughly cleaned as soon as practicable. Great care should be taken to remove every atom of blood, to rinse carefully, and not to soak them longer than necessary. Fish are dressed in a variety of ways to suit different tastes—boiled, baked, broiled, and fried. The most ordinary methods are broiling or frying. In boiling, large fish should be wrapped in a cloth previously floured to prevent sticking, tied with a string, and covered with from two to three inches of cold water already salted; from six to ten minutes per pound will generally be found sufficient for boiling. Remove from the fire the moment it is done, and place upon a sieve to drain.

In baking fish, cleanse and wipe dry; fill to taste; sew together; place in a dripping-pan; season with salt and pepper; add sufficient water to baste with, or if a filling of oysters is used, baste with the liquor off them. The space between the fish and the sides of the pan may be filled with slices of raw potatoes one-quarter of an inch thick, and serve fish and potatoes together. A large fish will bake in an hour.

FISH, OYSTERS, ETC.

MEMORANDUM ON FRIENDS' RECIPES

For broiling, thoroughly cleanse and dry; split open so that the backbone will be flat in the middle; season with salt and pepper, and place on a buttered gridiron over a clear fire with the inside downward until it begins to brown, then turn over. When done, serve on a hot dish and butter liberally.

Fish may be very nicely fried in hot lard with only a seasoning of salt and pepper, and a little flour dredged over it, or it may be spread with beaten eggs and rolled in cracker or bread crumbs before frying. Challenge sauce, Worcestershire sauce, and similar condiments upon fish will be found to give a most delicate and piquant flavoring.

RECIPES.

Broiled Shad.—Scrape, split, wash, and dry the shad on a cloth; season with pepper and salt; grease the gridiron well; as soon as it is hot lay the shad on to broil with the inside downward. One side being well browned, turn it. It should broil a quarter of an hour or more, according to thickness. Butter well and send to table hot.

Baked Shad.—Many people are of the opinion that the very best method of cooking a shad is to bake it. Stuff it with bread-crumbs, salt, pepper, butter, and parsley, and mix this up with beaten yelk of egg; fill the fish with it, and sew it up or fasten a string around it. Pour over it a little water and some butter, and bake as you would a fowl. A shad will require from an hour to an hour and a quarter to bake.

Halibut Cutlets.—Cut your halibut steaks an inch thick, wipe them with a dry cloth, and season with salt and cayenne pepper. Have ready a pan of yelk of eggs well beaten and a dish of grated bread-crumbs. Put some fresh

MEMORANDUM
ON
FRIENDS' RECIPES

48   *DOMESTIC COOKERY.*

lard or beef drippings in a frying-pan and hold it over the fire till it boils. Dip your cutlets in the egg, and then in the bread-crumbs. Fry a light brown; serve up hot. Salmon or any large fish may be fried in the same manner.

Baked Cod or Halibut.—Use a piece of fish from the middle of the back, weighing four, five, or six pounds. Lay the fish in very cold salt-and-water for two hours; wipe dry; make deep gashes in both sides at right angles with the backbone, and rub into these, as well as coat it all over with, a force-meat made of the crumbs, pork, herbs, onion, and seasoning, made to adhere by raw egg. Lay in the baking-pan and pour over it the drawn butter (which should be quite thin), season with the anchovy sauce, lemon juice, pepper, and a pinch of parsley. Bake in a moderate oven nearly an hour—or even more if the piece be large—basting frequently lest it should brown too fast. Add a little butter-and-water when the sauce thickens too much. When the fish is done, remove to a hot dish, and strain the gravy over it. A few capers or chopped green pickles are a pleasant addition to the gravy.

Boiled Halibut.—Take a small halibut, or what you require from a large fish. Put it into the fish-kettle, with the back of the fish undermost; cover it with cold water, in which a handful of salt and a bit of saltpetre the size of a hazel-nut have been dissolved. When it begins to boil skim it carefully, and then let it just simmer till it is done. Four pounds of fish will require half an hour nearly to boil it. Drain it, garnish with horse-radish or parsley. Egg sauce, or plain melted butter, are served with it.

Boiled Rockfish.—After the fish has been nicely cleaned, put it into a pot with water enough to cover it, and throw in salt in the proportion of half a teaspoonful to a pound of fish. Boil it slowly until the meat is tender and easily separates from the bones. A large fish will require an hour to cook. When done, serve on a hot dish, and have a few hard-boiled eggs, cut in thin slices, laid around it and over it. Eat with egg-sauce.

White Fish.—This fish may be broiled, fried, or baked. To bake it, prepare a stuffing of fine bread-crumbs, a little salt pork chopped very fine ; season with sage, parsley, pepper, and salt. Fill the fish with the stuffing, sew it up, sprinkle the outside with salt, pepper, and flour, and bake. In frying white fish, pour off the fat as it accumulates, as it is apt to be too fat when served.

Broiled Salmon.—The steaks from the centre of the fish are best. Sprinkle with salt and pepper, spread on a little butter, and broil over a clear but slow fire.

Smoked Salmon, Broiled.—Take a half pound of smoked salmon and parboil it ten minutes ; lay in cold water for the same length of time ; wipe dry and broil over a clear fire. Add two tablespoonfuls of butter while hot ; season with cayenne and the juice of half a lemon ; pile in a "log-cabin" square upon a hot plate, and serve with dry toast.

Boiled Salmon.—A piece weighing six pounds should be rubbed with salt, tied carefully in a cloth, and boiled slowly for three-quarters of an hour. It should be eaten with egg or caper sauce. If any remain after dinner, it may be placed in a deep dish, a little salt sprinkled over, and a teacupful of boiling vinegar poured upon it. Cover it closely, and it will make a nice breakfast dish.

Baked Salmon with Cream Sauce.—Butter a sheet of foolscap paper on both sides, and wrap the fish up in it, pinning the ends securely together. Lay in the baking-pan, and pour six or seven spoonfuls of butter-and-water over it. Turn another pan over all, and steam in a moderate oven

MEMORANDUM
ON
FRIENDS' RECIPES

MEMORANDUM
ON
FRIENDS' RECIPES

DOMESTIC COOKERY.

from three-quarters of an hour to an hour, lifting the cover, from time to time, to baste and assure yourself that the paper is not burning. Meanwhile, have ready in a saucepan a cup of cream, in which you would do well to dissolve a bit of soda a little larger than a pea. This is a wise precaution whenever cream is to be boiled. Heat this in a vessel placed within another of hot water; thicken with a heaping teaspoonful of corn-starch; add a tablespoonful of butter, pepper and salt to taste, a liberal pinch of minced parsley, and when the fish is unwrapped and dished, pour half the dressing slowly over it, sending the rest to table in a boat. If you have no cream, use milk, and add a beaten egg to the thickening.

Salmon Steaks or Cutlets Fried.—Cut slices from the middle of the fish one inch thick: wipe dry, and salt slightly; dip in egg, then in cracker crumbs; fry very quickly in hot butter; drain off every drop of grease, and serve upon a hot dish. Sprinkle green parsley in bunches over it. The French use the best salad-oil in this recipe instead of butter.

Pickled Salmon.—Soak salt salmon twenty-four hours, changing the water frequently; afterward pour boiling water around it, and let it stand fifteen minutes; drain off and then pour on boiling vinegar with cloves and mace added.

Fried Perch.—Scale and clean them perfectly; dry them well, flour and fry them in boiling lard. Serve plenty of fried parsley round them.

Fried Trout.—Wash, drain, and split; roll in flour, season with salt; have some thin slices of salt pork in a pan, and when very hot put in the fish and fry to a nice brown.

Stewed Trout.—Clean and wash the fish with care, and wipe it perfectly dry; put into a stewpan two tablespoonfuls of butter, dredge in as it melts a little flour, grate half a nutmeg, a few blades of mace, a little cayenne, and a teaspoonful of salt; mix it all together; then lay in the fish, let it brown slightly; pour over some veal gravy, a lemon thinly sliced; stew very slowly for forty minutes; take out the fish, and add two glasses of wine to the gravy. Lay the fish on a hot dish, and pour over it some of the gravy. Serve the rest in a sauce-tureen.

Fried Catfish.—Catfish must be cooked quite fresh—if possible, directly out of the water. The larger ones are generally coarse and strong; the small-sized fish are the best. Wash and clean them, cut off their heads and tails, remove the upper part of the backbone near the shoulders, and score them along the back with deep gashes or incisions. Dredge them with flour, and fry them in plenty of lard, boiling fast when the catfish are put into the pan. Or you may fry them in the drippings or gravy saved from roast beef or veal. They are very nice dipped in a batter of beaten egg and grated bread-crumbs, or they may be done plain, though not in so nice a way, with Indian meal instead of bread-crumbs. Drain off the lard before you dish them. Touch each incision or cut very slightly with a little cayenne before they go to table.

Fried Eels.—After skinning, emptying, and washing them as clean as possible, cut them into short pieces, and dry them well with a soft cloth. Season them with fine salt and cayenne, flour them thickly, and fry them in boiling lard; when nicely browned, drain and dry them, and send to the table with plain melted butter and a lemon, or with fish-sauce. Eels are sometimes dipped into batter and then fried, or into egg and dried bread-crumbs, and served with plenty of crisped parsley.

Fish Chowder.—Take a fresh haddock, of three or four pounds, clean it well, and cut in pieces of three inches

MEMORANDUM
ON
FRIENDS' RECIPES

MEMORANDUM ON FRIENDS' RECIPES

DOMESTIC COOKERY.

square. Place in the bottom of your dinner-pot five or six slices of salt pork, fry brown, then add three onions sliced thin, and fry those brown. Remove the kettle from the fire, and place on the onions and pork a layer of fish. Sprinkle over a little pepper and salt, then a layer of pared and sliced potatoes, a layer of fish and potatoes, till the fish is used up. Cover with water, and let it boil for half an hour. Pound six biscuits or crackers fine as meal, and pour into the pot; and, lastly, add a pint of milk; let it scald well, and serve.

New England Chowder.—Take a good haddock, cod, or any other solid fish, cut it in pieces three inches square; put a pound of fat, salt pork, cut into strips, into the pot; set it on hot coals and fry out the grease; take out the pork, but leave the grease in the bottom of the pot, and put in a layer of fish, over that a layer of sliced onions, over that a layer of fish, with slips of the fried pork, then another layer of onions and a few sliced raw potatoes, and so on alternately until your fish is all in; mix some flour with as much water as will fill the pot; season to suit your taste, and boil for half an hour; have ready some pilot bread, soaked in water, and throw them into your chowder five minutes before taking off; serve in a tureen.

Fish-balls.—Two cupfuls cold boiled codfish, fresh or salted. Chop the fish when you have freed it of bones and skin; work in one cupful of mashed potatoes, and moisten with a half cup of drawn butter with an egg beaten in. Season to taste. Have them soft enough to mold, yet firm enough to keep in shape. Roll the balls in flour, and fry quickly to a golden-brown in lard or clean dripping. Take from the fat so soon as they are done; lay in a colander or sieve and shake gently, to free them from every drop of grease. Turn out for moment on white paper to absorb any lingering drops, and serve on a hot dish.

FISH, OYSTERS, ETC.

Stewed Oysters.—Take one quart of oysters; put the liquor (a teacupful for three persons) in a stewpan, and add half as much more water, salt and pepper to taste, and let it boil. Have your oysters ready in a bowl, and the moment the liquor boils, pour in all your oysters, say ten for each person, or six will do. Now, watch carefully, and as soon as it begins to boil take out your watch, count just thirty seconds, and take your oysters from the stove. You will have your big dish ready, with one and a half tablespoonfuls of cream or milk for each person. Pour your stew on this and serve immediately. Never boil an oyster in milk.

Maryland Stewed Oysters.—Put the juice into a saucepan and let it simmer, skimming it carefully; then rub the yelks of three hard-boiled eggs and one large spoonful of flour well together, and stir into the juice. Cut in small pieces quarter of a pound of butter, half a teaspoonful of whole allspice, a little salt, a little cayenne, and the juice of a fresh lemon; let all simmer ten minutes, and just before dishing add the oysters. This is for two quarts of oysters.

Panned Oysters.—Have ready several small pans of block tin, with upright sides. Cut stale bread in thin slices, then round them to a size that will just fit in the bottoms of your pans. Toast these quickly to a light brown, butter, and lay within your tins. Wet with a great spoonful of oyster liquid, then, with a silver fork, arrange upon the toast as many oysters as the pans will hold without heaping them up. Dust with pepper and salt, put a bit of butter on top, and set the pans, when all are full, upon the floor of a quick oven. Cover with an inverted baking-pan to keep in steam and flavor, and cook until the oysters "ruffle." Eight minutes in a brisk oven should be enough. Send very hot to the table in tins in which they were roasted. Next to roasting in the shell, this mode of cooking oysters best preserves their native flavor.

MEMORANDUM
ON
FRIENDS' RECIPES

MEMORANDUM
ON
FRIENDS' RECIPES

DOMESTIC COOKERY.

Roasted Oysters.—Take oysters in the shell; wash the shells clean, and lay them on hot coals; when they are done they will begin to open. Remove the upper shell, and serve the oysters in the lower shell, with a little melted butter poured over each, and season to taste.

Oyster Toast.—Select fifteen plump oysters; mince them, and season with mixed pepper and a pinch of nutmeg, beat the yelks of four eggs and mix them with half a pint of cream. Put the whole into a saucepan and set it over the fire to simmer till thick; stir it well, and do not let it boil, lest it should curdle. Toast five pieces of bread, and butter them; when your dish is near the boiling-point, remove it from the fire and pour it over the toast.

Cream Oysters.—Fifty shell oysters, one quart sweet cream; butter, pepper, and salt to suit taste. Put the cream and oysters in separate kettles to heat, the oysters in their own liquor, and let them come to a boil; when sufficiently cooked, skim; then take them out of the liquid and put them into a dish to keep warm. Put the cream and liquid together. Season to taste, and thicken with powdered cracker. When sufficiently thick, stir in the oysters.

Broiled Oysters.—Drain select oysters in a colander. Dip them one by one into melted butter, to prevent sticking to the gridiron, and place them on a wire gridiron. Broil over a clear fire. When nicely browned on both sides, season with salt, pepper, and plenty of butter, and lay them on hot buttered toast, moistened with a little hot water. Serve very hot. Oysters cooked in this way and served on broiled beefsteak are delicious.

Fried Oysters.—Select the largest and finest fresh oysters, put them into a colander and pour over a little water to rinse them; then place them on a clean towel and dry them. Have ready some grated bread-crumbs, seasoned with

FISH, OYSTERS, ETC.

pepper and salt, and plenty of yelk of egg beaten till very light; and to each egg allow a large teaspoonful of rich cream or of the best fresh butter. Beat the egg and cream together. Dip each oyster first into the egg and cream, and then into the crumbs. Repeat this twice, until the oysters are well coated all over. Have ready boiling, in a frying-pan, an equal mixture of fresh butter and lard. It must very nearly fill the frying-pan, and be boiling fast when the oysters go in, otherwise they will be heavy and greasy. Fry them of a yellow brown on both sides, and serve hot.

Oyster Salad, see Salads.

Spiced or Pickled Oysters.—Put into a porcelain kettle one hundred and fifty large oysters with the liquor; add salt, and simmer till the edges roll or curl; skim them out; add to the liquor one pint of white wine vinegar, one dozen blades mace, three dozen cloves, and three dozen peppercorns; let it come to a boil, and pour over the oysters. Serve with slices of lemon floating in saucer.

Oyster Omelette.—Allow for every six large oysters or twelve small ones one egg; remove the hard part and mince the rest very fine; take the yelks of eight eggs and whites of four, beat till very light, then mix in the oysters; season and beat up thoroughly; put into a skillet a gill of butter, let it melt; when the butter boils, skim it and turn in the omelette; stir until it stiffens; fry light brown; when the under side is brown, turn on to a hot platter. To brown the upper side, hold a red-hot shovel over it.

Scalloped Oysters, No. 1.—Open the shells, setting aside for use the deepest ones. Have ready some melted butter, *not* hot, seasoned with minced parsley and pepper. Roll each oyster in this, letting it drip as little as may be, and lay in the shells, which should be arranged in a baking-pan Add

---

MEMORANDUM
ON
FRIENDS' RECIPES

MEMORANDUM
ON
FRIENDS' RECIPES

to each a little lemon juice, sift bread-crumbs over it, and bake in a quick oven until done. Serve in the shells.

Scalloped Oysters, No. 2.—Cover the bottom of a baking-dish (well buttered) with a layer of crumbs, and wet these with cream, put on spoonful by spoonful. Pepper and salt, and strew with minute bits of butter. Next, put in the oysters, with a little of their liquor. Pepper them, stick bits of butter in among them, and cover with dry crumbs until the oysters are entirely hidden. Add more pieces of butter, very small, and arrange thickly on top. Set in the oven, invert a plate over it to keep in the flavor, and bake until the juice bubbles up to the top. Remove the cover, and brown on the upper grating for two or three minutes. Serve in the bake-dish.

Oyster Pie.—Line a dish with a puff paste or a rich biscuit paste, and dredge well with flour; drain one quart of oysters; season with pepper, salt, and butter, and pour into the dish; add some of the liquor; dredge with flour, and cover with a top crust, leaving a small opening in the centre. Bake in a quick oven.

Oyster Patties.—Put one quart of oysters in a saucepan, with liquor enough to cover them, set it on the stove and let them come to a boil; skim well, and stir in two tablespoonfuls of butter, a little pepper, and salt. Line some patty-pans with puff-paste, fill with oysters, cover with paste, and bake twenty minutes in a hot oven. The upper crust may be omitted, if desired.

Oyster Macaroni.—Boil macaroni in a cloth to keep it straight. Put a layer in a dish seasoned with pepper, salt, and butter, then a layer of oysters, until the dish is full. Mix some grated bread with a beaten egg, spread over the top, and bake.

Oyster Sauce, see Sauces.

MEMORANDUM ON FRIENDS' RECIPES

FISH, OYSTERS, ETC.

Boiled Lobster.—If purchased alive, lobsters should be chosen by weight (the heaviest are the best) and their liveliness and briskness of motion. When freshly boiled they are stiff, and their tails turn strongly inward; when the fish appear soft and watery, they are stale. The flesh of the male lobster is generally considered of the finest flavor for eating, but the hen lobster is preferred for sauce and soups, on account of the coral.

To properly boil lobsters, throw them living into a kettle of fast-boiling salt and water, that life may be destroyed in an instant. Let them boil for about half an hour. When done, take them out of the kettle, wipe them clean, and rub the shell with a little salad-oil, which will give a clear red appearance. Crack the large claws without mashing them, and with a sharp knife split the body and tail from end to end. The head, which is never eaten, should also be separated from the body, but laid so near it that the division is almost imperceptible. Dress in any way preferred.

Deviled Lobster.—Procure a live, heavy lobster; put it in a pot of boiling water, with a handful of salt to it. When done and cold, take out all the meat carefully, putting the fat and coral on separate plates; cut the meat in small pieces, rub the coral to a paste; stir the fat in it, with a little salt, cayenne, chopped parsley, essence of anchovies, and salad-oil, or melted butter and lemon juice; cut the back of the lobster-shell in two, lengthwise; wash clean; stir the lobster and sauce well together; fill the shells; sprinkle bread-crumbs and a few bits of butter over the top; set in the oven until the crumbs are brown.

Stewed Lobster.—A middling-sized lobster is best; pick all the meat from the shells and mince it fine; season with a little salt, pepper, and grated nutmeg; add three or four spoonfuls of rich gravy and a small bit of butter. If you

MEMORANDUM
ON
FRIENDS' RECIPES

have no gravy, use more butter and two spoonfuls of vinegar; stew about twenty minutes.

Lobster Salad, see Salads.

Lobster Croquettes, see Croquettes.

Lobster Sauce, see Sauces.

Lobster Patties.—Proceed as in oyster patties, but use the meat of a cold boiled lobster.

Terrapins.—Put the terrapins into a pot of boiling water, where they must remain until they are quite dead. You then divest them of their outer skin and toe-nails; and, after washing them in warm water, boil them again until they become quite tender, adding a handful of salt to the water. Having satisfied yourself of their being perfectly tender, take off the shells and clean the terrapins very carefully, removing the sandbag and gall without by any means breaking them. Then cut the meat into small pieces and put into a saucepan, adding the juice which has been given out in cutting them up, but *no water*, and season with salt, cayenne, and black pepper to your taste, adding a quarter of a pound of good butter for each terrapin and a handful of flour for thickening. After stirring a short time, add four or five tablespoonfuls of cream, and a half pint of good Maderia to every four terrapins, and serve hot in a deep dish. A very little mace may be added and a large tablespoonful of mustard; just before serving, add the yelks of four hard-boiled eggs. During the stewing, particular attention must be paid to stirring the preparation frequently; and terrapins cannot possibly be served too hot.

Mock Terrapin.—Take half a calf's liver, season and fry it brown; chop it into dice, not too small; flour it thickly, and add a teaspoonful of mixed mustard, a little cayenne pepper, two hard-boiled eggs chopped fine, a lump of but-

FISH, OYSTERS, ETC.

ter the size of an egg, and a teacupful of water. Let it boil a minute or two. Cold veal will do as well as liver.

Scalloped Crabs.—Put the crabs into a kettle of boiling water, and throw in a handful of salt. Boil from twenty minutes to half an hour. Take them from the water when done and pick out all the meat; be careful not to break the shell. To a pint of meat put a little salt and pepper; taste, and if not enough add more, a little at a time, till suited. Grate in a very little nutmeg, and add one spoonful of cracker or bread crumbs, two eggs well beaten, and two tablespoonfuls of butter (even full); stir all well together; wash the shells clean, and fill each shell full of the mixture; sprinkle crumbs over the top and moisten with butter, then bake until nicely browned on top.

Soft-shell Crabs.—Season with pepper and salt; roll in flour, then in egg, then in bread-crumbs, and fry in hot lard. Serve hot with rich condiments.

Stewed Clams.—Chop the clams and season with pepper and salt; put in a saucepan butter the size of an egg, and when melted add a teaspoonful of flour; add slowly the clam liquor and then the clams, and cook three minutes; then add half a pint of cream, and serve.

Deviled Clams.—Chop fifty clams very fine; take two tomatoes, one onion chopped equally fine, a little parsley, thyme, and sweet marjoram, a little salt, pepper, and bread-crumbs, adding the juice of the clams until the mixture is of the consistency of sausage; put it in the shells with a lump of butter on each; cover with bread-crumbs, and bake one-half hour.

Clam Chowder.—Forty-five clams chopped, one quart of sliced potatoes, one-half pint sliced onions. Cut a few slices salt pork, fry to a crisp, chop fine. Put in kettle a little fat

MEMORANDUM ON FRIENDS' RECIPES

MEMORANDUM
ON
FRIENDS' RECIPES

DOMESTIC COOKERY.

from the pork, a layer of potatoes, clams, onions, a little pepper and salt; another layer of chopped pork, potatoes, etc., until all are in. Pour over all the juice of the clams. Cook three hours, being careful not to burn. Add a teacupful of milk just before serving.

Scallops.—Wipe dry; dip separately into seasoned egg, then into cracker dust, and fry in hot lard.

RECIPES INCIDENTAL TO FISH.

Bread Stuffing for Fish.—Take about half a pound of stale bread and soak in water, and when soft press out the water; add a very little chopped suet, pepper, salt, a large tablespoonful of onion minced and fried, and, if preferred, a little minced parsley; cook a trifle, and after removing from the fire add a beaten egg.

Bread Stuffing, No. 2.—Bread-crumbs with a little chopped parsley and pork, salt, pepper, and butter. Fill up the fish, sew it closely, then bake.

Cleaning a Shad.—Scale and scrape it carefully; split it down the back and remove the contents, reserving the roe or melt. Wash well and cook as desired.

Soaking Salt Fish.—Very salt fish should be soaked several hours in three or four changes of warm water. Place the skin side up, so that salt crystals may fall away from the under or meat side. Wipe carefully and clean, then soak for an hour in very cold water.

Fish in Season.—As a rule, fish are in best condition just before they spawn, and many are so while they are full of roe, as smelts, mackerel, and shad. As soon as spawning is over, they become unfit for food, some of them becoming positively unwholesome. In season, the flesh is firm and it boils white; when it boils to a bluish hue, the fish are not in season, or are stale.

IV.—POULTRY AND GAME.

GENERAL REMARKS ON POULTRY AND GAME—HOW TO SELECT, PREPARATION FOR BOILING, FOR ROASTING, ETC. THIRTY-ONE RECIPES FOR POULTRY AND GAME.

POULTRY should invariably be selected young, plump, and well fed, but not too fat. If old and tough, fowls are never as savory when cooked as if they be young and tender. This applies especially to ducks and geese. The flesh of young fowls will be firm and fleshy to the touch, and heavy in proportion to their size; the skin should be clear, white, and finely grained, the toes pliable and easily broken when bent back, the end of the breast-bone also pliable. All kinds of poultry, turkeys especially, are improved by hanging a day or two, unless the weather should be exceedingly sultry. Dark-legged fowls are best for roasting, while the white-legged ones should be chosen for boiling.

In preparing fowls for boiling, some persons soak fowls an hour or two in skimmed-milk and then sew them in a floured cloth. This tends to preserve them of a nice color, but it may be dispensed with by carefully skimming them while over the fire.

In dressing poultry, care should be taken not to break the gall; a thorough cleansing in every part also is necessary. The hairs should be singed off with a well-lighted piece of paper, holding the fowl before a hot fire. All the pin-feathers should be carefully and entirely removed, as also the oil-bag at the end of the back. The legs should be cut off at the first joint next to the feet. The inside should be

MEMORANDUM
ON
FRIENDS' RECIPES

MEMORANDUM
ON
FRIENDS' RECIPES

DOMESTIC COOKERY.

washed and rinsed several times in cold water, after everything has been removed. Remove extra fat, as it tends to make the gravy greasy. The heart should be slit open and cleansed, also the gizzard, and both should be put by themselves to soak in water.

Roasted or broiled poultry of all kinds should be thoroughly cooked and handsomely browned. It is not easy to state exactly the time required for the different sorts to be well done. Experience and practice are the only sure guides.

RECIPES.

Roast Turkey.—A young turkey, weighing not more than eight or nine pounds, is the best. Wash and clean thoroughly, wiping dry, as moisture will spoil the stuffing. Take one small loaf of bread grated fine, rub into it a piece of butter the size of an egg, one small teaspoonful of pepper and one of salt; a sprinkling of sweet marjoram, summer savory, or sage, if liked. Rub all together, and fill the turkey, sewing up so that the stuffing cannot cook out. Always put the giblets under the side of the fowl, so they will not dry up. Rub salt, pepper, and butter on the outside; put into dripping-pan with one teacupful of water, basting often, turning the fowl till brown all over; bake about two hours; take out the giblets and chop fine. After taking out the turkey, put a large tablespoonful of flour into the pan and stir until brown. Put the giblets into a gravy-boat, and pour over them the gravy.

Boiled Turkey.—Stuff the turkey as for roasting. A very nice dressing is made by chopping half a pint of oysters and mixing them with bread-crumbs, butter, pepper, salt, thyme, and wet with milk or water. Baste about the turkey a thin cloth, the inside of which has been dredged with flour, and put it to boil in cold water with a teaspoonful of salt.

POULTRY AND GAME.

in it. Let a large turkey simmer for three hours; skim while boiling. Serve with oyster sauce, made by adding to a cupful of the liquor in which the turkey was boiled the same quantity of milk and eight oysters chopped fine; season with minced parsley; stir in a spoonful of rice or wheat flour wet with cold milk; a tablespoonful of butter. Boil up once and pour into a tureen.

Boned Turkey.—Boil a large turkey in as little water as possible until the meat falls from the bones; remove all the bones and skin; pick the meat into small pieces, and mix dark and light together; season with pepper and salt; put into a mold and pour over it the liquor, which must be kept warm, and press with a heavy weight.

Roast Chicken.—Having selected your chickens in view of the foregoing hints, proceed, in the matters of cleansing, filling, and preparing for the oven, precisely as directed in the case of roast turkey. As the roasting goes on, baste and turn as may be needful to secure a rich brown all over the fowls. Prepare the gravy as in the former case.

Stewed Chicken.—Clean and cut the chicken into joints; put it in a saucepan with the giblets; stew in just enough water to cover it until tender; season with pepper, salt, and butter; thicken with flour; boil up once and serve with the gravy poured over it.

Broiled Chicken.—Only young, tender chickens are nice broiled. After cleaning and washing them, split down the back, wipe dry, season with salt and pepper, and lay them inside down on a hot gridiron over a bed of bright coals. Broil until nicely browned and well cooked through, watching and turning to prevent burning. If chickens are large steaming them for one-half hour before placing on the gridiron will better insure their being cooked through.

MEMORANDUM
ON
FRIENDS' RECIPES

MEMORANDUM
ON
FRIENDS' RECIPES

DOMESTIC COOKERY.

Fricasseed Chickens.—Cut them in pieces, and put in the stewpan with salt and pepper; add a little water, and let them boil half an hour; then thicken the gravy with flour; add butter and a little cream, if you have it. Catsup is an additional relish to the gravy.

Smothered Chicken.—Dress your chickens; wash and let them stand in water half an hour to make them white; cut them open at the back; put into a baking-pan, sprinkle salt and pepper over them, putting a lump of butter here and there; cover tightly with another pan the same size, and bake one hour; baste often with butter.

Fried Chicken.—Prepare the chicken as for stewing; dry it, season with salt and pepper, dredge with flour, and fry brown in hot butter or lard; take it out, drain, and serve with Challenge Sauce, or some other savory condiment, or pour into the gravy left in the frying-pan a cup of milk, thicken with flour, add a little butter, and season with Salpicant; boil once and pour over the chicken, or serve separately.

Chickens Fried with Rice.—Take two or three chickens, cut them up, and half fry them; then boil half a pint of rice in a quart of water, leaving the grains distinct, but not too dry; stir one large tablespoonful of butter in the rice while hot; let five eggs be well beaten into the rice, with a little salt, pepper, and nutmeg, if the last is liked; put the chickens into a deep dish, and cover with the rice; brown in an oven not too hot.

Chicken Pie.—Line the sides of a deep pie-dish with a good puff paste. Have your chicken cooked, as for a fricassee, seasoned with salt and pepper and a little chopped parsley. When they are nearly cooked, lay them in a pie-dish with half a pound of salt pork cut into small squares, and some of the paste also cut into half-inch pieces; pour

POULTRY AND GAME.

in a part of the chicken gravy, thicken with a little flour, and cover the dish with the paste cover. Cut a hole the size of a dollar in the cover, and cover it with a piece of dough. When baking, remove this piece occasionally and examine the interior. Brush egg over the top crust of the pie, and bake in a quick oven. Should the pie become dry pour in more of the gravy. Pigeon pie or any other bird pie may be made by the above recipe.

Chicken Pot-pie.—Cut and joint a large chicken. Cover with water, and let it boil gently until tender. Season with salt and pepper, and thicken the gravy with two tablespoonfuls of flour mixed smooth in a piece of butter the size of an egg. Have ready nice, light bread dough; cut with a biscuit-cutter about an inch thick; drop this into the boiling gravy, having previously removed the chicken to a hot platter; cover, and let them boil from one-half to three-quarters of an hour. To ascertain whether they are done, stick them with a fork; if it comes out clean, they are done. Lay them on the platter with the chicken, pour over the gravy, and serve.

Pressed Chicken.—Boil three chickens until the meat comes off the bones; then, removing all bones, etc., chop, not very fine; add a piece of butter as large as an egg, salt and pepper to season well. Have about a pint of the broth, into which put one-half box gelatine until dissolved; then put back the chopped chicken and cook until the broth is evenly absorbed. Press under a weight in a pan until cold. Veal may be treated in a similar manner with very excellent results.

Jellied Chicken.—Boil a chicken in as little water as possible, until the meat falls from the bones; chop rather fine, and season with pepper and salt; put in a mold a layer of

MEMORANDUM
ON
FRIENDS' RECIPES

MEMORANDUM
ON
FRIENDS' RECIPES

DOMESTIC COOKERY.

the chopped meat, and then a layer of hard-boiled eggs cut in slices; then layers of meat and egg alternately until the mold is nearly full; boil down the liquor left in the pot one-half; while warm, add one-quarter of an ounce of gelatine, and when dissolved pour into the mold over the meat. Sit in a cool place over night to jelly.

Roast Goose and Duck.—A goose should always be parboiled, as it removes the rank taste and makes it more palatable. Clean, prepare, and roast the same as turkey, only adding to the force-meat a large onion chopped fine. Ducks do not require parboiling (unless very old), otherwise they are cooked the same as geese.

Canvas-back Duck.—Having picked, singed, and drawn it well, wipe it carefully, so as to have it clean without washing. Truss it, leaving the head on, to show its quality. Place it in a moderately hot oven for at least three-quarters of an hour; serve it hot, in its own gravy, on a large chafing-dish. Currant jelly should be on the table.

Roast Pigeons.—Clean, wash, and stuff the same as poultry; lay them in rows in a dripping-pan with a little water. Unless they are very fat, baste with butter until they are half done, afterward with their own gravy.

Roast Snipe.—Clean and truss, but do not stuff. Lay in rows in the dripping-pan, sprinkle with salt, and baste well with butter, then with butter and water. When they begin to brown, cut as many slices of bread as there are birds. Toast quickly, butter, and lay in the dripping-pan, a bird upon each. When the birds are done, serve upon the toast, with the gravy poured over it. The toast should lie under them while cooking at least five minutes, during which time the birds should be basted with melted butter seasoned with pepper. The largest snipe will not require above twenty minutes to roast. Or, dip an oyster in melted butter, then in bread-crumbs, seasoned with pepper and salt, and put in each bird before roasting. Small birds are especially delicious cooked in this way.

Roast Partridges, Pheasants, or Quails.—Pluck, singe, draw, and truss them; season with salt and pepper; roast for about half an hour in a brisk oven, basting often with butter. When done, place on a dish together with bread-crumbs fried brown and arranged in small heaps. Gravy should be served separately in a tureen.

Quail on Toast.—Clean, wash, slit down the back, sprinkle with salt and pepper, and lay them on a gridiron, the inside down. Broil slowly; when nicely browned, butter well. Serve with cream gravy on toast. Omitting the cream, gravy, and toast, you have the ordinary broiled quail. Pigeons, woodcock, and small birds may be broiled in the same manner, and are delicious and nourishing for invalids.

Fried Rabbit.—After the rabbit has been thoroughly cleaned and washed, put it into boiling water and let it boil for about ten minutes; drain, and when cold, cut it into joints; dip into beaten egg, and then into fine bread-crumbs, seasoned with salt and pepper. When all are ready, fry them in butter over a moderate fire fifteen minutes; thicken the gravy with an ounce of butter and a small teaspoonful of flour. Serve hot.

Roast Rabbit.—Dress nicely and fill with a dressing made of bread-crumbs, a little onion, sage, pepper, and salt, and a small piece of butter; tie a piece of salt pork over it; put into a dripping-pan with a little water in a quick oven; baste often; serve with currant jelly.

Broiled Steaks of Venison.—Heat the gridiron, grease it well, lay on the steaks; broil quickly, without scorching,

MEMORANDUM
ON
FRIENDS' RECIPES

MEMORANDUM
ON
FRIENDS' RECIPES

68   *DOMESTIC COOKERY.*

turning them two or three times; season with salt and pepper. Have butter melted in a well-heated platter, into which lay steaks, hot from the gridiron, turning them over several times in the butter, and serve hot with currant jelly on each steak. It is well to set the platter into another containing boiling water.

Game or Poultry in Jelly.—Take a knuckle of veal weighing two pounds; a slice of lean ham; one shallot, minced; a sprig of thyme and one of parsley; six pepper-corns (white) and one teaspoonful of salt, with three pints of cold water. Boil all these together until the liquor is reduced to a pint; strain without squeezing, and set to cool until next day. It should then be a firm jelly. Take off every particle of fat. Then take one package gelatine, soaked in one cupful cold water for three hours; one tablespoonful of sugar; two tablespoonfuls strained lemon juice, and two tablespoonfuls of currant jelly, dissolved in cold water, and strained through a muslin cloth. Pour a quart of *boiling* water over the gelatine, stir for a moment, add the jellied "stock," and when this is dissolved, add sugar, lemon juice, and coloring. Stir until all are mixed and melted together, and strain without shaking or squeezing through a flannel bag until quite clear. Have ready several hard-boiled eggs, and the remains of roast game, roast or boiled poultry, cut in neat, thin slices, and salted slightly. Wet a mold with cold water, and when the jelly begins to harden, pour some in the bottom. Cut the whites of the eggs in pretty shapes—stars, flowers, rings, leaves—with a keen penknife, and arrange these on the lowest stratum of jelly, which should be thin, that the forms may be visible. Add more jelly, and on this lay slices of meat, close together. More jelly, and proceed in this order until the mold is full. Set in a cool place to harden, and then turn out upon a flat dish. A mold with smooth, upright sides, is best for this purpose.

POULTRY AND GAME.

RECIPES INCIDENTAL TO POULTRY, GAME, ETC.

Gravy for Poultry.—Boil the giblets very tender; chop fine; then take the liquor in which they are boiled, thicken with flour; season with salt, pepper, and a little butter; add the giblets and dripping in which the turkey was roasted.

Plain Stuffing.—Take stale bread, cut off all the crust, rub very fine, and pour over it as much melted butter as will make it crumble in your hands; salt and pepper to taste. See also under "Roast Turkey."

Potato Stuffing.—Take two-thirds bread and one-third boiled potatoes grated, butter size of an egg, pepper, salt, one egg; mix thoroughly.

Oyster Stuffing.—By substituting oysters for potatoes in the above, you have oyster filling. See also under "Boiled Turkey."

Stuffing for Boiled Chicken.—One cupful of bread-crumbs, one tablespoonful of butter, one egg, half a teaspoonful of salt, and one tablespoonful of sweet marjoram. Mix well; stuff and sew in.

Capons.—Young male fowls, prepared by early gelding, and then nicely fattened, are the finest delicacies in the poultry line. They may be known by a small head, pale comb, which is short and withered, the neck feathers longer than usual, smooth legs, and soft, short spurs. They are cooked as ordinary chickens.

Keeping Game.—Game is rendered more tender, and its flavor is improved by keeping. If wrapped in a cloth saturated with equal parts of pyroligneous acid and water, it will keep many days. If in danger of tainting, clean, rub well with salt, and plunge into boiling water, letting it run through them for five minutes; then hang in a cold place. If tainted, put them in new milk over night. Always hang them up by the neck.

MEMORANDUM ON FRIENDS' RECIPES

MEMORANDUM ON
FRIENDS' RECIPES

V.—MEATS.

I.—BEEF.

HOW TO SELECT BEEF; CHOICE ROASTING PIECES, STEAKS, BOILING PIECES, SOUP PIECES, ETC. HOW TO ROAST, BROIL, AND BOIL BEEF. NINETEEN RECIPES FOR COOKING BEEF.

GOOD beef may be known by its color. That of a deep, healthy red, fine, smooth, open grain, veined with white, being the best. The fat should be oily, smooth, and inclined to white, rather than yellow, as yellow fat is a sure sign of inferior quality.

The sixth, seventh, and eighth ribs and the sirloin are considered the choicest cuts for roasting. The inside of the sirloin and the rump are the most tender for steaks, though here is a point where individual taste may be exercised. By some epicures what is known as the pin-bone steak is regarded as superior to any other. The round, buttock, shin, or brisket may be boiled or stewed. The neck or shoulder is generally used for soups, gravy, etc.

In roasting beef it is necessary to have a brisk fire. The roast must be well seasoned with salt and pepper and dredged with flour. Baste it frequently. About fifteen minutes is required for roasting every pound of beef.

To broil meats well, have the gridiron hot and the bars well greased before putting on the meat.

In boiling beef, or indeed any fresh meat, plunge it into boiling water, that the outer parts may contract, and so retain the internal juices. Salt meats should be put on in cold water, that the salt may be extracted in the cooking. In boiling meats, it is important to keep the water constantly

MEATS.

boiling, otherwise the meat will absorb the water. Be careful to add boiling water only, if more is needed. Cold water will check the process of cooking and spoil the flavor. Remove the scum as soon as the boiling commences. Allow about twenty minutes boiling for each pound of fresh meat, and from one-half to three-quarters of an hour for all salt meats, except ham, which requires but fifteen minutes to the pound. The more gently all meats boil the more tender they will be. Slow boiling makes meat far better.

RECIPES.

Roast Beef.—The best roasting-pieces are the middle ribs and the sirloin. The ends of the ribs should be removed from the flank, and the latter folded under the beef and securely fastened with skewers. Rub a little salt into the fat part; place the meat in the dripping-pan with a pint of stock or water; baste freely, and dredge with flour half an hour before taking the joint from the oven. Should the oven be very hot, place a buttered paper over the meat to prevent it scorching while yet raw. When the paper is used it will need very little basting. Or, turn the rib side up toward the fire for the first twenty minutes. The time it will take in cooking depends upon the thickness of the joint and the length of time the animal has been killed. Skim the fat from the gravy and add a tablespoonful of prepared brown flour to the remainder.

Roast Beef with Yorkshire Pudding.—Take a large rib roast; rub salt and pepper over it, and dredge with flour. Place on a rack in a dripping-pan, with very little water, until it is heated thoroughly; baste frequently. When nicely browned on the upper side, turn and baste. About three-quarters of an hour before it is done, take out the meat, pour off most of the dripping, put the batter for the

MEMORANDUM
ON
FRIENDS' RECIPES

MEMORANDUM
ON
FRIENDS' RECIPES

DOMESTIC COOKERY.

pudding in the bottom of the pan, allowing the drippings from the beef to drop into it. When the pudding is done, return the meat and finish roasting. Add some hot water to the dripping and thicken with flour for the gravy.

For the batter of this pudding, take half a cup of butter, three cups of flour, three eggs, one cup of milk, and two teaspoonfuls of baking powder.

Beef a la Mode.—Take a round of fresh beef, extract the bone, and take away the fat. For a round weighing ten pounds, make a seasoning or stuffing as follows: Half a pound of beef suet; half a pound of grated bread-crumbs; the crumbled yelks of three hard-boiled eggs; a little bundle of sweet marjoram, the leaves chopped; another of sweet basil; four onions minced small; a large tablespoonful of mixed mace and nutmeg powdered. Season lightly with salt and cayenne. Stuff this mixture into the place from whence you took out the bone. Make a number of deep cuts about the meat, and stuff them also. Skewer the meat into a favorable shape, and secure its form by tying it round with tape. Put it into a tin bakepan, and pour over it a pint of port wine. Put on the lid, and bake the beef slowly for five or six hours, or till it is thoroughly done. If the meat is to be eaten hot, skim all the fat from the gravy, into which, after it is taken off the fire, stir in the beaten yelks of two eggs. Minced oysters may be substituted for onions.

Spiced Beef.—Boil a shin of beef weighing ten or twelve pounds, until the meat falls readily from the bones. Pick the meat to pieces, and mash the gristle very fine, rejecting all parts that are too hard to mash. Set away the liquor in which the beef has boiled till it is cold; then take off all the fat. Boil the liquor down to a pint and a half. Roll a dozen crackers very fine, and add them to the meat. Then return the meat to the liquor, and heat it all. Add salt and pepper to taste, half a teaspoonful of cloves, half a teaspoon-

MEMORANDUM
ON
FRIENDS' RECIPES

ful of cinnamon, half a teaspoonful of parsley chopped fine, and a little powdered nutmeg. Let it boil up once, and put into a mold or deep dish, with a weight adjusted to press it down. When it is entirely cold, cut into thin slices.

Savory Beef.—Take a shin of beef from the hind-quarter, saw it into four pieces, put it into a pot, and boil it until the meat and gristle drop from the bones; chop the meat very fine, put it in a dish, and season it with a little salt, pepper, clove, and sage, to your taste; pour in the liquor in which the meat was boiled, and place it away to harden. Cut in slices and eat cold.

Minced Beef.—Cut cold roast beef into thin slices; put some of the gravy into a stewpan, a bit of butter rolled in flour, pepper and salt, and boil it up. Add a little catsup, and put in the minced slices, and heat them through, but do not let it boil. Put small slices of toast in the dish, and cover with the meat.

Deviled Beef.—Take slices of cold roast beef, lay them on hot coals, and broil; season with pepper and salt, and serve while hot, with a small lump of butter on each piece.

Curried Beef.—Take about two ounces of butter and place them in a saucepan with two small onions cut up into slices and let them fry till they are of a light brown; then add a tablespoonful and a half of curry powder, and mix it up well. Now cut up the beef into pieces about an inch square; pour in from a quarter to a third of a pint of milk, and let it simmer for thirty minutes; then take it off and place it in a dish with a little lemon juice. While cooking stir constantly, to prevent burning. Send it to table with a wall of mashed potatoes or rice around it.

Beef Hash.—Chop fine cold steak or roast beef, and cook in a little water; add cream or milk, and thicken with flour; season to taste, and pour over thin slices of toast.

MEMORANDUM
ON
FRIENDS' RECIPES

DOMESTIC COOKERY.

Beef Stew.—Cut cold beef into small pieces, and put into cold water; add one tomato, a little onion, chopped fine; pepper and salt, and cook slowly; thicken with butter and flour, and pour over toast.

Boiled Corned Beef.—Put four or five pounds of lean corned meat into a pot with plenty of water. The water should be hot. The same care should be taken in skimming as for fresh meat. Allow half an hour for every pound of meat after it has begun to boil. The excellence of corned beef depends very much upon its being boiled gently and long. If it is to be eaten cold, lay it, when boiled, into a coarse earthen dish or pan, and over it a clean board about the size of the meat; upon this put a heavy weight. Salt meat is much improved by pressing.

Stewed Shin of Beef.—Wash, and set it on to stew in sufficient cold water to keep it just covered until done. When it boils, take off the scum, and put an ounce and a quarter of salt to the gallon of water. It is usual to add a few cloves and some black pepper, slightly bruised and tied up loosely in a fold of muslin, two or more onions, a root of celery, a bunch of savory herbs, four or five carrots, and as many turnips, either whole or sliced; if to be served with the meat, the last two will require a little more than the ordinary time of boiling, but otherwise they may be simmered with the meat from the beginning. Give the beef from four to five hours' gentle stewing, and serve it with part of its own liquor thickened and flavored, or quite plain.

Boiled Tongue.—Soak the tongue over night, then boil four or five hours. Peel off the outer skin and return it to the water in which it was boiled to cool. This will render it juicy and tender.

Baked Heart.—Wash carefully and stuff nicely; roast or bake and serve with gravy, which should be thickened with

MEMORANDUM
ON
FRIENDS' RECIPES

MEATS.

some of the stuffing. It is very nice hashed, with a little port wine added.

Broiled Beefsteak.—Have the choice steaks cut three-quarters of an inch thick; grease the gridiron and have it well heated. Put the steak over a hot, clear fire. When the steak is colored, turn it over, which must be done without sticking a fork into it and thus letting out the juice. It should be quite rare or pink in the centre, but not raw. When cooked sufficiently, lay on a hot platter and season with pepper and salt; spread over the top some small bits of butter, and serve immediately. Salt extracts the juices of meats in cooking. Steaks ought not to be salted until they have been broiled.

Beefsteak with Onions.—Take a nice rumpsteak, and pound it with a rolling-pin until it is quite tender; flour and season; put it into a frying-pan with hot lard and fry it. When well browned on both sides, take it up and dredge with flour. Have about two dozen onions ready boiled; strain them in a colander and put them in a frying-pan, seasoning with pepper and salt; dredge in a little flour, and add a small lump of butter; place the pan over the fire and stir the onions frequently, to prevent their scorching. When they are soft and a little brown, return the steak to the pan, and heat all together. Place the steak on a large dish, pour the onions and gravy over it, and send to the table hot.

Beefsteak and Tomatoes.—Stew a dozen good-sized tomatoes one hour, with salt and pepper. Then put in a pound of tender beefsteak, cut in small pieces, and boil fifteen minutes longer. Lay buttered toast in a deep dish, pour on the steak and tomato, and you have a most relishing and healthful dish.

Stuffed Beefsteak.—Take a rump steak about an inch thick. Make a stuffing of bread and herbs, and spread it over the steak. Roll it up, and with a needle and coarse thread sew

MEMORANDUM
ON
FRIENDS' RECIPES

76   *DOMESTIC COOKERY.*

it together. Lay it in an iron pot on one or two wooden skewers, and put in water just sufficient to cover it. Let it stew slowly for two hours—longer if the beef is tough; serve it in a dish with the gravy turned over it. To be carved crosswise, in slices, through beef and stuffing.

Beefsteak Pudding.—Prepare a good suet crust, and line a cake tin with it; put in layers of steak, with onions, tomatoes and mushrooms chopped, a seasoning of pepper, salt, and cayenne, and half a teacupful of water before closing it. Bake from an hour and a half to two hours, and serve hot.

II.—VEAL.

CHOOSING VEAL, FOR ROASTING, FOR STEWING; THE HEAD, FEET, KIDNEYS, SWEET-BREADS, ETC.; GENERAL USEFULNESS. TWENTY-ONE RECIPES FOR COOKING VEAL.

VEAL should be fat, finely grained, white, firm, and not overgrown. When large, it is apt to be coarse and tough, and if too young, it lacks flavor and is less wholesome. It is more difficult to keep than any meat except pork, and should never be allowed to acquire the slightest taint before it is dressed.

The fillet, the loin, the shoulder, and the best end of the neck, are the parts preferred for roasting; the breast and knuckle are more usually stewed or boiled. The head and feet of the calf are valuable articles of food, both for the nutriment which the gelatinous parts of them afford, and for the greater variety of modes in which they may be dressed. The kidneys, with the rich fat that surrounds them, and the sweet-breads especially, are well-known delicacies; the liver and the heart also are very good eating; and no meat is so generally useful for rich soups and gravies as veal.

MEATS. 77

The best veal is from calves not less than four, or more than six weeks old. If younger it is not wholesome. If older its character begins to change materially from the calf's use of grasses and other food.

RECIPES.

Roast Veal.—Take a loin or fillet of veal; make a stuffing as for roast turkey; fill the flat with the stuffing, and sew it firmly to the loin; rub the veal with salt, pepper, and flour, and put it into a pan with a little water. While roasting, baste frequently, letting it cook until thoroughly done. Allow two hours for a roast weighing from six to eight pounds. When done, remove the threads before sending to the table; thicken the gravy with a little flour. Veal should be rather overdone.

Pot-roasted Fillet.—Remove the bone and fill the cavity with a force-meat made of bread-crumbs, a very little salt, pork chopped fine, sage, pepper, salt, and ground cloves. Lay in the pot a layer of slices of salt pork; put in the fillet, fastened with skewers, cover with additional pork, pour over it a pint of good stock, cover down close, and let it cook slowly two or three hours; then take off the cover and let it brown. Serve hot.

Boiled Fillet.—A small and delicately white fillet should be selected for this purpose. Bind it round with tape, after having washed it thoroughly; cover it well with cold water, and bring it gently to a boil; clear off carefully the scum as it rises, and be very cautious not to allow the water to become smoked. Let the meat be *gently simmered* for three hours and a half to four and a half, according to its weight. Send it to table with rich white sauce.

Veal Stew.—Cut four or five pounds of veal into strips; peel a dozen large potatoes, and cut them into slices; place a layer of sliced salt pork with salt, pepper, sage, and onion

MEMORANDUM
ON
FRIENDS' RECIPES

MEMORANDUM
ON
FRIENDS' RECIPES

78   *DOMESTIC COOKERY.*

on the bottom of the pot, then a layer of potatoes, then a layer of the veal nicely seasoned. Use up the veal thus. Over the last layer of veal put a layer of the pork, and over the whole a layer of potatoes. Pour in water till it covers the whole; cover the pot closely; heat it rapidly for a few minutes, and then let it simmer two hours.

Veal Hash.—Take a teacupful of boiling water in a saucepan, stir into it an even teaspoonful of flour wet in a tablespoonful of cold water, and let it boil five minutes; add one-half teaspoonful of black pepper, as much salt, and two tablespoonfuls of butter, and let it keep hot, but not boil. Chop the veal fine and mix with half as much stale breadcrumbs. Put into a pan and pour the gravy over it, then let it simmer ten minutes. Serve this on buttered toast.

Veal Pie.—Line a pudding-dish with good pie crust; into this put a layer of veal cut into small slices from the neck, or other less valuable part; make a second layer of hard-boiled eggs sliced thin; butter and pepper this layer. Add a layer of sliced ham, or salt pork, squeezing a few drops of lemon juice on the ham. Add more veal, as before, with eggs, ham, etc., till the dish is nearly full. Pour over a cupful of stock and cover with a stout crust. Bake in a moderate oven for two hours.

Veal Pot Pie.—Make a crust of a dozen mashed potatoes, two tablespoonfuls of butter, half a teacup of milk or cream, a little salt, and flour enough to stiffen it nicely. Fry half a dozen slices of salt pork, then cut up the veal and boil these together, in but little water, till the veal is almost done. Peel and slice a dozen potatoes quite thin, and roll the dough about half an inch thick and cut it into strips. Now build in your pot a layer of crust, meat, potatoes; then sprinkle with salt and pepper. Then another set of layers, and top off with crust. Pour on the liquor in which the meat was cooked, and let all simmer for half an hour, or until the top crust is cooked. Brown the crust by holding over it a red-hot shovel.

Veal Loaf.—Take a piece of butter the size of an egg, three pounds of raw veal, one heaping teaspoonful of salt, one of pepper, and two raw eggs. Chop the veal fine and mix all together, and put in about two tablespoonfuls of water. Mold this into a loaf, then roll it in eight tablespoonfuls of rolled crackers, and pour over it three tablespoonfuls of melted butter; place in a pan and bake two hours. To be sliced off when cold, and served at luncheon or tea.

Veal with Oysters.—Cut the veal in small, thin slices, place it in layers in a jar with salt, pepper, and oysters. Pour in the liquor of the oysters, set the jar in a kettle of boiling water, and let it stew till the meat becomes very tender.

Veal with Rice.—Pour over a small knuckle of veal rather more than sufficient water to cover it; bring it slowly to a boil; take off all the scum with great care; throw in a teaspoonful of salt, and when the joint has simmered for about half an hour, throw in from eight to twelve ounces of well-washed rice, and stew the veal gently for an hour and a half longer, or until both the meat and rice are perfectly tender. A seasoning of cayenne and mace in fine powder, with more salt, should it be required, must be added twenty or thirty minutes before they are served. For a superior stew, good veal broth may be substituted for the water.

Veal with Peas.—A quart or more of full-grown green peas, instead of rice, added to the veal, prepared as above, as soon as the scum has been cleared off, will make a most excellent stew. It should be well seasoned with white pepper, and the mace should be omitted.

Cutlets in Cracker.—Pound the cutlet and season, cut the edges into good shape; take one egg, beat it a little, roll the cutlet in it, then cover thoroughly with rolled crackers.

MEMORANDUM
ON
FRIENDS' RECIPES

MEMORANDUM
ON
FRIENDS' RECIPES

80   DOMESTIC COOKERY.

Have a lump of butter and lard mixed hot in your skillet, put in the meat and cook slowly. When nicely browned stir in one spoonful of flour for the gravy; add half a pint of sweet milk, and let it come to a boil. Salt and pepper.

Cutlets, Broiled.—Trim evenly; sprinkle salt and pepper on both sides; dip in melted butter, and place upon the gridiron over a clear fire; baste while broiling with melted butter, turn over three or four times; serve with melted butter, or tomato sauce.

Pressed Veal.—Put four pounds of veal in a pot; cover with water; stew slowly until the meat drops from the bone, then take out and chop fine; let the liquor boil down until there is a cupful; put in a small cupful of butter, a tablespoonful of pepper, a little allspice, and a' beaten egg; stir this through the meat; slice a hard-boiled egg; lay in a mold, and press in the meat; when put upon the table garnish with celery tops or parsley.

Minced Veal.—Heat a cupful of well-thickened gravy to a boil; add two tablespoonfuls of cream or rich milk, one tablespoonful of butter, pepper and salt, parsley to taste, a small onion, and three eggs well beaten. When these are stirred in, add the cold minced meat, salted and peppered. Let it heat thoroughly, but not boil.

Veal Scallops.—Mince the meat very small, and set it over the fire; season with grated nutmeg, pepper and salt, and a little cream. Then put it into scallop-shells, and cover with crumbs of bread, over which put bits of butter, and brown at a quick fire. Serve hot, with catsup or mushroom sauce.

Calf's Liver or Heart.—Cut the liver in slices, plunge into boiling water for an instant, wipe dry, season with pepper and salt, dredge with flour, and fry brown in lard. Have it perfectly done. Serve in gravy, made with either milk or water. Calf's heart dressed in this way is also very palatable.

MEATS.

Broiled Sweet-breads.—Parboil and blanch the sweet-breads by putting them first into hot water and keeping it at a hard boil for five minutes, then plunging it into ice-cold water somewhat salted. Allow them to lie in this ten minutes, wipe them very dry, and with a sharp knife split in half, lengthwise. Broil over a clear, hot fire, turning whenever they begin to drip. Have ready upon a deep plate melted butter, well salted and peppered, mixed with catsup or Challenge sauce. When the sweet-breads are done to a fine brown lay them in this preparation, turning them over several times; cover and set them in a warm oven. Serve on fried bread or toast in a chafing-dish, a piece of sweet-bread on each. Pour on the hot butter and send to table.

Stewed Sweet-breads.—Parboil, blanch, and cut into small pieces; boil fifteen minutes in milk; stir into this chopped parsley, a little butter, and cornstarch to thicken. Serve hot.

Broiled Kidneys.—Skin the kidneys carefully, but do not slice or split them. Lay for ten minutes in warm (not hot) melted butter, rolling them over and over, that every part may be well basted. Broil on a gridiron over a clear fire, turning them every minute. Unless very large, they should be done in about twelve minutes. Sprinkle with salt and pepper, and lay on a hot dish, with butter upon each.

Calf's Tongue.—Of all the tongue preparations, calf's tongue is regarded as best. To pickle them, use for each a quarter pound of salt, one ounce of saltpetre, and a quarter pound of sugar. Rub the tongues daily with this, allowing them to lie in pickle for two weeks, after which they will be ready for smoking or boiling. If used without smoking, they require no soaking, but should simmer several hours till perfectly done, when the skin will peel off readily. If soaking is needed, lay them first in cold water and then in tepid water for two hours each; then boil till done.

MEMORANDUM
ON
FRIENDS' RECIPES

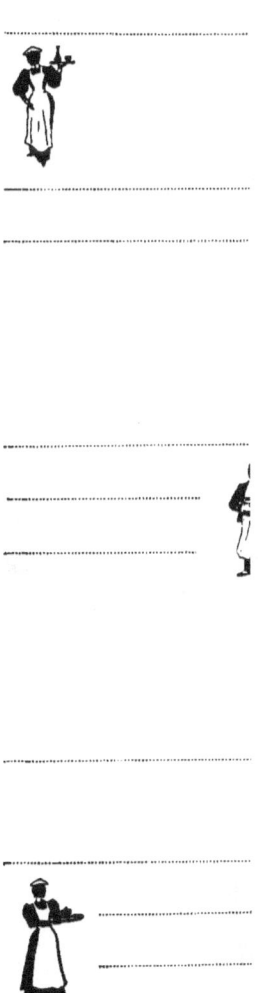

MEMORANDUM
ON
FRIENDS' RECIPES

III.—MUTTON AND LAMB.

CHOOSING MUTTON AND LAMB, FOR ROASTING, FOR BOILING; CUTLETS, SUITABLE VEGETABLES, ETC. THIRTEEN RECIPES FOR MUTTON AND LAMB.

THE best mutton is small-boned, plump, finely grained, and short legged; the lean of a dark, rather than of a bright hue, and the fat white and clear; when this is yellow, the meat is rank, and of bad quality. The leg and the loin are the desirable joints; and the preference would probably be given to the latter, but for the superabundance of its fat, which renders it a somewhat wasteful part.

The parts for roasting are the shoulder, saddle, or chine, the loin, and haunch. The leg is best boiled, unless the mutton is young and very tender. The neck is sometimes roasted, but it is more generally boiled; the scrag, or that part of it which joins the head, is seldom used for any other purpose than making broth, and should be taken off before the joint is dressed. Cutlets from the thick end of the loin are commonly preferred, but they are frequently taken from the best end of the neck and from the middle of the leg.

Lamb should be eaten very fresh. In the fore-quarter, the vein in the neck should be blue, otherwise it is stale. In the hind-quarter the fat of the kidney will have a slight odor if not quite fresh. Lamb soon loses its firmness if stale.

New potatoes, asparagus, green peas, and spinach, are the vegetables to be eaten with roast lamb.

RECIPES.

Roast Mutton.—Wash the meat well, sprinkle with pepper and salt, dredge with flour, and put in the dripping-pan, with a little water in the bottom. Baste often with the drippings, skim the gravy well, and thicken with flour.

Boiled Leg of Mutton.—Cut off the shank-bone, trim the knuckle, and wash the mutton; put it into a pot with salt, and cover with boiling water. Allow it to boil a few minutes; skim the surface clean, draw your pot to the side of the fire, and simmer until done. Time, from two to two hours and a half. Do not *try* the leg with a fork to determine whether it is done. You lose the juices of the meat by so doing. Serve with caper sauce, or drawn butter, well seasoned. The liquor from this boiling may be converted into soup with the addition of a ham-bone and a few vegetables boiled together.

Mutton Dressed like Venison.—Skin and bone a loin of mutton, and lay it into a stewpan with a pint of water, a large onion stuck with a dozen cloves, half a pint of port wine, and a spoonful of vinegar; add, when it boils, a little thyme and parsley, and some pepper and salt; let it stew three hours, and turn it often. Make some gravy of the bones, and add it at intervals to the mutton.

Broiled Mutton Chops.—Trim off a portion of the fat, or the whole of it, unless it be liked; heat the gridiron, rub it with a bit of the mutton suet, broil over a brisk fire, and turn often until they are done, which, for the generality of eaters, will be in about eight minutes, if the chops are not more than half an inch thick, which they should not be. Add salt and pepper with melted butter, and serve on a hot plate.

Mutton and Green Peas.—Select a breast of mutton not too fat, cut it into small, square pieces, dredge it with flour, and fry to a fine brown in butter; add pepper and salt, cover it with water, and set it over a slow fire to stew, until the meat is perfectly tender. Take out the meat, skim off all the fat from the gravy, and just before serving add a quart of young peas, previously boiled with the strained gravy, and let the whole boil gently until the peas are entirely done.

MEMORANDUM
ON
FRIENDS' RECIPES

MEMORANDUM
ON
FRIENDS' RECIPES

DOMESTIC COOKERY.

Irish Stew.—Blanch three pounds of mutton chops **by dipping** them first in boiling water, for two or three minutes, and then into ice-cold water. Place them on the bottom of a clean stewpan, barely covering them with cold water. Bring them slowly to a boil; add one teaspoonful of salt; skim clean; add a little parsley, mace, and a few peppercorns. Simmer twenty minutes; add a dozen small onions whole, and two tablespoonfuls of flour mixed well with cold water. Let it simmer for an hour; add a dozen potatoes pared and cut to about the size of the onions. Boil till these are done; then dish, placing the chops around the edge of the plate, and pouring the onions and potatoes into the centre. Strain the gravy, add three tablespoonfuls of chopped parsley, and pour over the stew.

Boiled Leg of Lamb.—Choose a ewe leg, as there is more fat on it; saw off the knuckle, trim off the flap, and the thick skin on the back of it; soak in warm water for three hours, then boil gently (time according to size). Serve with oyster sauce. (See Sauces.)

Roast Lamb.—Wash well, season with pepper and salt, put in the dripping-pan with a little water. Baste often with the dripping; skim the gravy well and thicken with flour.

Lamb Stewed in Butter.—Select a nice loin, wash well, and wipe very dry; skewer down the flap, and lay it in a close-shutting and thick stewpan, or saucepan, in which three ounces of good butter have been just dissolved, but not allowed to boil; let it simmer slowly over a very gentle fire for two hours and a quarter, and turn it when it is rather more than half done. Lift it out, skim, and pour the gravy over it; send to table with brown gravy, mint sauce, and a salad.

Saddle of Lamb.—This is a dainty joint for a small party. Sprinkle a little salt over it, and set it in the dripping-pan, with a few small pieces of butter on the meat; baste it occasionally with tried-out lamb-fat; dredge a little flour over it a few minutes before taking from the oven. Serve with currant-jelly and a few choice early vegetables. Mint-sauce may be served with the joint, but in a very mild form. (See Sauces.)

Broiled Lamb Chops.—Trim off most of the fat; broil over a brisk fire, turning frequently until the chops are nicely browned. Season with pepper and salt, and baste with hot butter. Serve on a buttered dish.

Breaded Lamb Chops.—Grate plenty of stale bread, season with salt and pepper, have ready some well-beaten egg, have a spider with hot lard ready, take the chops one by one, dip into the egg, then into the bread-crumbs; repeat it, as this will be found an improvement; then lay the chops separately into the boiling lard, fry brown, and then turn. To be eaten with currant jelly.

Lamb Steaks, Fried.—Dip each steak into well-beaten egg, cover with bread-crumbs or corn-meal, and fry in butter or new lard. Mashed potatoes and boiled rice are a necessary accompaniment. The gravy may be thickened with flour and butter, adding a little lemon juice; pour this hot upon the steaks, and place the rice in spoonfuls around the dish to garnish it.

IV.—PORK.

PORK REQUIRES CAREFUL CHOOSING; NEEDS THOROUGH COOKING. NINETEEN RECIPES FOR COOKING PORK.

PORK, more than any other meat, requires to be chosen with the greatest care. The pig, from its gluttonous habits, is particularly liable to disease, and if killed and eaten when in an unhealthy condition, those who partake of it will probably pay dearly for their indulgence. Dairy-fed pork is the best.

MEMORANDUM ON FRIENDS' RECIPES

MEMORANDUM
ON
FRIENDS' RECIPES

DOMESTIC COOKERY.

If this meat be not thoroughly well-done, it is disgusting to the sight and poisonous to the stomach. "In the gravy of pork, if there is the least tint of redness," says an eminent medical authority, "it is enough to appall the sharpest appetite. Other meats under-done may be unpleasant, but pork is absolutely uneatable."

RECIPES.

Roast Pig.—A fat pig about three weeks old is best for a roast. Wash it thoroughly inside and out; chop the liver fine with bread-crumbs, onions, parsley, pepper, salt, and potatoes boiled and mashed; make it into a paste with butter and egg. Put this stuffing into the pig and sew it up; put in a baking-pan with a little water and roast over a bright fire, basting well with butter; rub frequently also with a piece of lard tied in a clean rag. When thoroughly done, lay the pig, back up, in a dish, and put a red apple or pickled-mango in its mouth. Make a dressing with some of the stuffing, with a glass of wine and some of the dripping. Serve with the roast pig, and also in a gravy-boat.

Roast Pork.—Choose for roasting, the loin, the leg, the saddle, the fillet, the shoulder, or the spare-rib. The loin of young pork is roasted with the skin on, and this should be scored in regular strips of about a quarter inch wide before the joints are laid to the fire. The skin of the leg also should be cut through in the same manner. This will prevent blistering, and render it more easy to carve. In beginning the roasting the meat should be placed at some distance from the fire, in order that it may be heated through before the skin hardens. The basting should be constant. The cooking must be thorough and the meat well-browned before removed from the fire.

Roast Spare-rib.—Spare-rib should be well rubbed with salt and pepper before it is roasted. If large and thick, it

MEATS. 87

will require two or three hours to roast; a very thin piece may be roasted in an hour. Lay the thick end to the fire. When you put it down to roast, dust on some flour, and baste with a little butter. The shoulder, loin, and chine are roasted in the same manner.

Leg of Pork Roasted.—Parboil a leg of pork, take off the skin, and then roast; baste with butter, and make a savory powder of finely minced or dried or powdered sage, ground black pepper, salt, and some bread-crumbs rubbed together through a colander; add to this a little very finely minced onion; sprinkle the meat with this when it is almost done; put a half pint of gravy into the dish.

Baked Pork Tenderloins.—Split the tenderloin lengthwise nearly through; stuff with a filling of bread-crumbs, pepper, salt, and sweet marjoram. Tie a string around it, to keep the filling in, and bake in a hot oven for half an hour, basting well as the cooking proceeds.

Pork Cutlets.—Cut them about half an inch thick from a delicate loin of pork, trim into neat form, and take off part of the fat, or the whole of it when it is not liked; dredge a little pepper or cayenne upon them, and broil (or fry) over a clear and moderate fire from fifteen to eighteen minutes, sprinkle a little fine salt upon them just before they are dished. They may be dipped into egg and then into bread-crumbs mixed with minced sage, then finished in the usual way. When fried, flour them well, and season with salt and pepper. Serve with gravy made in the pan.

Boiled Ham.—The soaking which must be given to a ham before it is boiled depends both on the manner in which it has been cured and on its age. If highly salted, hard, and old, a day and night, or even longer, may be requisite to open the pores sufficiently and to extract a portion of the salt. The water must be several times changed during the steeping. After the ham has been scraped or brushed as

MEMORANDUM
ON
FRIENDS' RECIPES

MEMORANDUM
ON
FRIENDS' RECIPES

clean as possible, pare away lightly any part which may be blackened or rusty. Lay it into a suitable kettle and cover it plentifully with cold water; bring it *very slowly* to boil, and clear off the scum, which will be thrown up in great abundance So soon as the water has been cleared from this, draw the pot to the edge of the stove, that the ham may be simmered slowly but steadily, until it is tender. On no account allow it to boil fast. When it can be probed very easily with a sharp skewer, lift it out, strip off the skin, and return the ham to the water to cool.

Baked Ham.—A ham of sixteen pounds must be boiled three hours, then skin and rub in half a pound of brown sugar, cover with bread-crumbs, and bake well for two hours.

Glazed Ham.—Take a cold-boiled ham from which the skin has been removed, and brush it well all over with beaten egg. To a cup of powdered cracker allow enough rich milk or cream to make into a thick paste, salt it, and work in a teaspoonful of melted butter. Spread this evenly, a quarter of an inch thick, over the ham, and set to brown in a moderate oven.

Ham and Eggs.—Cut the ham in very thin slices, and fry long enough to cook the fat, but not long enough to crisp the lean. A very little boiling water may be put into the frying-pan to secure the ham moist and tender. Remove the ham when it is done, break eggs gently into the pan, without breaking the yelks, and fry till done, about three minutes. The eggs will not require to be turned. Cut off the uneaven edges, place the eggs around the ham, and pour in the gravy.

Ham or Tongue Toast.—Toast a thick slice of bread and butter it on both sides. Take a small quantity of remains of ham or tongue, grate it, and put it in a stewpan with **two**

MEATS.

hard-boiled eggs chopped fine, and mixed with a little butter, salt, and cayenne; heat it quite hot, then spread thickly upon the buttered toast. Serve while hot.

Broiled Salt Pork.—Cut the pork in thin slices. Put a little water in the pan, and when it has boiled three minutes pour it off; dredge the pork with flour and brown it.

Bacon Broiled or Fried.—Cut evenly into thin slices, or *rashers;* pare from them all rind and rust; curl them round; fasten them with small, slight skewers, then gently fry, broil, or toast them; draw out the skewers before they are sent to table. A few minutes will dress them either way. They may be cooked without being curled. The slow cooking is necessary that the meat may be well done without being dried or hardened.

Fried Sausage.—Sausages should be used while quite fresh. Melt a piece of butter or dripping in a clean frying-pan; when just melted, put in the sausages, shake the pan for a minute, and keep turning them; do not break or prick them; fry them over a very slow fire till they are nicely browned; when done, lay them on a hair-sieve before the fire to drain the fat from them. The secret of cooking sausages well is to let them heat very gradually. If so done the skins will not burst if they are fresh. The common practice of pricking them lets the gravy out, which is undesirable.

Baked Sausages.—The most wholesome way to cook sausages is to bake them. Place them in a baking-pan in a single layer, and bake in a moderate oven; turn them over when half done, that they may be equally browned. Serve with pieces of toast between them, having cut the toast about the same size as the sausage, and moistened it with a little of the sausage fat.

Sausage Meat.—Many prefer to use sausage meat in bulk.

MEMORANDUM
ON
FRIENDS' RECIPES

MEMORANDUM ON FRIENDS' RECIPES

DOMESTIC COOKERY.

Small portions of the meat should be packed lightly together and fried slowly until nicely browned. When done, drain through a hair-sieve. Do not pack hard. It will make the sausages tough.

Scrapple.—Boil a hog's head one day, and let it stand five or six hours, or all night. Slip out the bones and chop fine; then return the meat to the liquor; skim when cold; warm and season freely with pepper, salt, sage, and sweet herbs. Add two cupfuls of buckwheat-meal and one cupful of corn-meal. Put into molds, and when cold cut into slices and fry for breakfast.

Boiled Pork.—The shoulder or leg are regarded as the most economical pieces for boiling. They should be well salted first, by about ten days' pickling. Boil precisely as ham is boiled, but not for so long a time, about three hours sufficing to thoroughly cook an ordinary sized leg of pork. After it has come to the boiling point, let the process proceed slowly as possible. Peel off the skin when done and spot the surface with dashes of red and black pepper, or with allspice, or garnish with parsley.

Souse.—Pigs' feet and ears may be soused by cleaning thoroughly, soaking in salt and water several days, and then boiling till the bones can be picked out with ease and the skin peeled off. Cover the meat and gelatinous substance with boiling vinegar, highly spiced with peppercorns and mace. This may be eaten cold or the meat may be fried after dipping in egg and cracker.

Pig's head may be prepared the same way, the meat being chopped fine and mixed with pounded crackers. Mix with herbs, spices, salt, and pepper to taste, and a small quantity of vinegar. Press into a mold, or a jar, and cut in slices To be eaten cold.

MEMORANDUM
ON
FRIENDS' RECIPES

VI.—VEGETABLES.

VEGETABLES SHOULD BE FRESH—HOW TO WASH AND PRESERVE—HOW TO COOK WELL, AND IMPORTANCE OF SO DOING—SUITABLE POTS FOR COOKING VEGETABLES—VEGETABLES SUITABLE TO CERTAIN MEATS. FIFTY-FIVE RECIPES FOR COOKING VEGETABLES.

ALL vegetables should be used when fresh as possible. Wash them thoroughly, and allow them to lie in cold water until ready to be used.

Great care must be taken to remove gravel and insects from heads of lettuce, cabbage, and cauliflower. To do this, lay them for half an hour or more in a pan of strong brine, placing the stalk ends uppermost. This will destroy the small snails and other insects which cluster in the leaves, and they will fall out and sink to the bottom.

Strong-flavored vegetables, like turnips, cabbage, and greens, require to be put into a large quantity of water. More delicate vegetables, such as peas, asparagus, etc., require less water. As a rule, in boiling vegetables, let the water boil before putting them in, and let it continue to boil until they are done. Nothing is more indigestible than vegetables not thoroughly cooked. Just when they are done must be ascertained to a certainty in each particular case, without depending upon any general directions.

Never let boiled vegetables stand in the water after coming off the fire; put them instantly into a colander over a pot of boiling water, and let them remain there, if you have to keep them back from the table.

An iron pot will spoil the color of the finest greens; they should be boiled by themselves in a tin, brass, or copper vessel.

MEMORANDUM
ON
FRIENDS' RECIPES

DOMESTIC COOKERY.

Potatoes are good with all meats. Carrots, parsnips, turnips, greens, and cabbage belong with boiled meats; beets, peas, and beans are appropriate to either boiled or roast.

RECIPES.

Boiled White Potatoes.—Peel off a strip about a quarter of an inch wide, lengthwise, around each potato. Put them on in cold water, with a teaspoonful of salt in it. Let them boil fifteen minutes, then pour off half the water and replace it with cold water. When the edge of the peel begins to curl up they are done. Remove them from the pot, cover the bottom of a baking-tin with them, place them in the oven, with a towel over them, for fifteen minutes, leaving the oven door open. Then serve with or without the skins.

The use of cold water in boiling potatoes, as in this recipe, is exceptional. Hot water is generally used, but for this purpose cold seems preferable.

Roasted White Potatoes.—Select the largest and finest potatoes for roasting. Wash them thoroughly and put in the oven with their skins on. Roast about one hour, turning them occasionally with a fork. When done, send them to the table hot, and in their skins.

Potatoes Roasted with Meats.—To roast potatoes with beef, poultry, and other meats, peel the potatoes, lay them in a pan, and cook them in the gravy. It is quite proper to roast both white and sweet of potatoes in the same pan.

Mashed Potatoes.—Steam or boil pared potatoes until soft, in salted water; pour off the water and let them drain perfectly dry; sprinkle with salt and mash; have ready hot milk or cream, in which has been melted a piece of butter; pour this on the potatoes, and stir until white and very light. A solid, heavy masher is not desirable. An open wire tool is much better.

VEGETABLES.

Stewed Potatoes.—Take sound raw potatoes, and divide each into four parts, or more, if they be very large. Put them into the stewpan; add salt, pepper, and a piece of fresh butter; pour in milk, with a little cream, just to keep the potatoes from burning. Cover the saucepan, and allow the potatoes to stew until thoroughly soft and tender.

Fried Potatoes.—Boil some good and large potatoes until nearly done; set them aside a few minutes; when sufficiently cool, slice or chop them; sprinkle them with pepper and salt, and fry in butter or fresh lard until they are of a light brown color. Serve hot.

Saratoga Potatoes.—Peel and slice the potatoes on a slaw-cutter, into cold water; wash them thoroughly, and drain; spread between the folds of a clean cloth, rub and pat until dry. Fry a few at a time in boiling lard; salt as you take them out. Saratoga potatoes are very nice when eaten cold. They can be prepared three or four hours before needed, and if kept in a warm place they will be crisp and nice. They may be used for garnishing game and steaks.

Potato Cakes.—Mash thoroughly a lot of potatoes just boiled; add a little salt, butter and cream; fry brown on both sides, after making into little cakes.

Boiled Sweet Potatoes.—Take large, fine potatoes, wash clean; boil with the skins on in plenty of water, but without salt. They will take at least one hour. Drain off the water, and set them for a few minutes in a tin pan before the fire, or in the oven, that they may be well dried. Peel them before sending to the table.

Roasted Sweet Potatoes.—Sweet potatoes are roasted in the same manner as white, but they require a little longer time.

Fried Sweet Potatoes.—Choose large potatoes, half boil them, and then, having taken off the skins, cut the potatoes in slices and fry in butter, or in nice drippings.

MEMORANDUM
ON
FRIENDS' RECIPES

MEMORANDUM
ON
FRIENDS' RECIPES

94   *DOMESTIC COOKERY.*

Stewed Tomatoes.—Pour boiling water on the tomatoes to be used, and then peel and slice them. Stew them gently, without adding any water, fifteen minutes; then add some pulverized cracker or bread crumbs, sufficient to thicken it a little, and salt and pepper to your taste. Stew fifteen minutes longer, and add a large piece of butter.

The thickening suggested is not essential. Many prefer the pure tomatoes. Try both ways and adopt the more pleasing.

Broiled Tomatoes.—Cut large tomatoes in two, from side to side, not from top to bottom; place them on a gridiron, the cut surface down; when well seared, turn them and put on butter, salt, and pepper; then cook with the skin side down until done.

Fried Tomatoes.—Cut the tomatoes in slices without skinning; pepper and salt them well; then sprinkle a little flour over them and fry in butter until browned. Put them on a hot platter; then pour milk or cream into the butter and juice, and when this is boiling hot, pour it over the tomatoes.

Tomatoes Baked Whole.—Select a number of sound, ripe tomatoes. Cut a round hole in the stem side of each, and stuff it with bread-crumbs, nicely peppered and salted; cover the bottom of the pan with the tomatoes, the opened side upward; put in a very little water, dredge with flour, and bake till brown. Serve hot.

Baked Sliced Tomatoes.—Skin the tomatoes, slice in small pieces; spread a thick layer in the bottom of a pudding dish; cover with a thin layer of bread-crumbs, and sprinkle salt, pepper, and a few small pieces of butter over them; add another layer of tomatoes, then of crumbs, etc., until the dish is filled; sprinkle over the top a layer of fine rolled crackers; bake one hour. Canned tomatoes, put up whole, may be used nicely this way.

VEGETABLES.

Tomatoes a la Creme.—Pare and slice ripe tomatoes; one pound of fresh ones or a quart can; stew until perfectly smooth, season with salt and pepper, and add a piece of butter the size of an egg. Just before taking from the fire, stir in one cup of cream, with a tablespoonful of flour stirred smooth in a part of it; do not let it boil after the flour is put in. Have ready in a dish some pieces of toast; pour the tomatoes over this and serve.

Boiled Green Corn.—Take off the outside leaves and the silk, letting the innermost leaves remain on until after the corn is boiled, which renders the corn much sweeter. Boil for half an hour in plenty of water, drain, and after fully removing the leaves, serve.

Baked Corn.—Grate one dozen ears of sweet corn, one cup of milk, a small piece of butter; salt to taste, and bake in a pudding dish for one hour.

Corn Fritters, see Fritters.

Lima Beans.—Shell, wash, and put into boiling water; when boiled tender, drain and season them. Dress with cream, or with a large lump of butter, and let the whole simmer for a few moments before serving.

Succotash.—Take ten ears of green corn and one pint of Lima beans; cut the corn from the cob, and stew gently with the beans until tender. Use as little water as possible. Season with butter, salt, and pepper—milk, if you choose. If a few of the cobs are stewed in the succotash, it will improve the flavor, as there is great sweetness in the cob.

String Beans.—Remove the strings of the beans with a knife, and cut off both ends. Cut each bean into three pieces, boil tender, add butter when they are done, pepper and salt, and serve hot.

Boiled Beans.—Dried beans must soak over night in soft water; put them in a strong bag, leaving room for them to

MEMORANDUM
ON
FRIENDS' RECIPES

MEMORANDUM
ON
FRIENDS' RECIPES

DOMESTIC COOKERY.

swell; let them boil in a plenty of water until done; hang up the bag that all the water may drain off; then season with butter, pepper, and salt to the taste.

Baked Beans.—Put the beans to soak early in the evening, in a dish that will allow plenty of water to be used. Change the water at bed-time. Next morning early, parboil two hours; pour off nearly all the water; take raw pork, scored on top; put the beans in a *deep dish*, a stoneware jar is very nice, the pork in the middle, sinking it so as to have it just level with the surface. Add half a teaspoonful of soda, two tablespoonfuls of molasses, and bake at least six hours. As the beans bake dry, add more water, a little at a time, until the last hour, when it is not necessary to moisten them.

Boiled Green Peas.—The peas should be young and freshly shelled; wash and drain them carefully; put them into fast-boiling, salted water; when quite tender drain, and add pepper, butter, and a little milk. Serve hot.

Boiled Asparagus.—Scrape the stems of the asparagus lightly, but make them very clean, throwing them into cold water as you proceed. When all are scraped, tie them in bunches of equal size; cut the hard ends evenly, that all may be of the same length, and put into boiling water. Prepare several slices of delicately browned toast half an inch thick. When the stalks are tender, lift them out and season with pepper and salt. Dip the toast quickly into the liquor in which the asparagus was boiled, and dish the vegetable upon it, the points, or the butts, meeting in the centre of the dish. Pour rich melted butter over it, and send to the table hot.

Boiled Beets.—Wash, but do not cut them, as cutting destroys the sweetness; let them boil from two to three hours, or until they are perfectly tender; then take them up, peel and slice them, and pour vinegar, or melted butter, over them, as may be preferred.

VEGETABLES.

Boiled Turnips.—Pare and cut into pieces; put them into boiling water well salted, and boil until tender; drain thoroughly and then mash and add a piece of butter, pepper, and salt to taste. Stir until they are thoroughly mixed, and serve hot.

Boiled Onions.—Skin them carefully and put them to boil; when they have boiled a few minutes, pour off the water, add clean cold water, and then set them to boil again. Pour this away also, and add more cold water, when they may boil till done. This change of waters will make them white and clear, and very mild in flavor. After they are done, pour off all the water, and dress with a little cream, salt, and pepper to taste.

Fried Onions.—Peel and slice fresh, solid onions very evenly, then fry them in a pan of hot butter till slightly browned.

Boiled Leeks.—Trim off the coarser leaves of young leeks, cut them into equal lengths, tie them in small bunches, and boil in plenty of water, previously salted. Serve on toast, and send melted butter to the table with them.

Boiled Squash.—Remove the seeds; boil till very tender; then press out all the water through a colander, and mash, with butter, pepper, and salt.

Fried Squash.—Pare the squash, cut in slices, dip in egg seasoned with pepper and salt, then into cracker dust, and fry to a nice brown.

Boiled Parsnips.—Scrape thoroughly, then wash and boil in a little water well salted. When done, dress with butter and a little pepper, or drawn butter, if desired.

Fried Parsnips.—Having boiled your parsnips, split open the largest ones, season with pepper and salt, dredge a little flour over them, and fry to a light brown.

MEMORANDUM
ON
FRIENDS' RECIPES

MEMORANDUM
ON
FRIENDS' RECIPES

98   *DOMESTIC COOKERY.*

Fried Egg-plant.—Pare and cut in slices quarter of an inch thick; sprinkle with salt; cover and let stand for an hour. Pour off the juice or water which exudes; wipe each slice dry; dip first in beaten egg, then in rolled cracker or bread crumbs. Season with pepper and salt, and fry brown in butter. Serve very hot.

Fried Egg-plant No. 2.—Put into water and boil until soft, then cut in two and scoop out all the inside; season; take a tablespoonful of the remaining pulp at a time, dip in egg and bread-crumbs, and fry in hot lard. Serve hot.

Baked Egg-plant.—Boil them till somewhat tender, in order to remove the bitter flavor. Then slit each one down the side, and take out the seeds. Have ready a stuffing made of grated cracker, butter, minced herbs, salt, pepper, nutmeg, and beaten yelk of eggs. Fill with this the cavity left by the seeds, and bake the plants in a hot oven. Serve with well-seasoned gravy poured around them in the dish.

Boiled Cabbage.—Strip off the loose or withered leaves, and wash well; then split in two, or if the head be very large, into four pieces, and put into boiling water with some salt; let it boil slowly, skimming carefully and frequently. When done, strain through a colander. Serve in a vegetable-dish and lay inside, among the leaves, some bits of butter; season with pepper, and serve while hot.

Boiled Cauliflower.—Trim off all the outside leaves; wrap in a cloth and put into boiling water well salted; boil until tender, and then serve with drawn butter.

Cabbage a la Cauliflower.—Cut the cabbage fine, as for slaw; put it into a stewpan, cover with water, and keep closely covered; when tender, drain off the water; put in a small piece of butter, with a little salt, one-half a cupful of cream, or one cupful of milk. Leave on the stove a few minutes before serving.

VEGETABLES.

Boiled Spinach.—Boil the spinach in plenty of water, drain, and press the moisture from it; chop it small, put it into a clean saucepan, with a slice of fresh butter, and stir the whole until well mixed and very hot. Smooth it in a dish, and send it quickly to table.

Boiled Greens.—Turnip-tops, mustard-tops, cabbage-leaves, beet-tops, cowslips, dandelions, and various similar articles are much relished in the spring, boiled in salt and water or with salt pork. When done sufficiently they will sink to the bottom.

Stewed Celery.—Clean the heads thoroughly; take off the coarse, green, outer leaves; cut the stalks into small pieces, and stew in a little broth; when tender, add some rich cream, a little flour, and butter enough to thicken the cream. Season with pepper, salt, and a little nutmeg, if that is agreeable.

Boiled Artichokes.—Soak the artichokes and wash them in several waters; cut the stalks even; trim away the lower leaves, and the ends of the other leaves; boil in salted water with the tops downward, and let them remain until the leaves can be easily drawn out. Before serving, remove the surrounding leaves, and send the remainder to the table with melted butter.

Broiled Mushrooms.—In order to test mushrooms, sprinkle salt on the gills; if they turn *yellow*, they are poisonous; if they turn *black*, they are good. When satisfied at this point, pare, and cut off the stems, dip them in melted butter, season with salt and pepper, broil them on both sides over a clear fire, and serve on toast.

Stewed Mushrooms.—Being sure you have the genuine mushrooms, put them in a small saucepan, season with pepper and salt, add a spoonful of butter and a spoonful or two of gravy from roast meat, or, if this be not at hand, the

MEMORANDUM
ON
FRIENDS' RECIPES

MEMORANDUM
ON
FRIENDS' RECIPES

DOMESTIC COOKERY.

same quantity of good, rich cream; shake them about over the fire, and when they boil they are done.

Boiled Rice.—Wash a cupful of rice in two or three waters; let it lie for a few minutes in the last water, then put it into three quarts of fast-boiling water, with a little salt; let it boil twenty minutes, then turn into a colander, drain, and serve, using such sauce or dressing as may be desired.

Boiled Hominy.—Soak one cupful of fine hominy over night in three cupfuls of water, and salt to taste; in the morning turn it into a quart pail; then put the pail into a kettle of boiling water, cover tightly, and steam one hour; add one teacupful of sweet milk, and boil fifteen minutes additional, then serve hot.

Stewed Macaroni.—Break the macaroni into small pieces, wash it, and put into salted hot water; cook about twenty minutes; drain, and put in a vegetable dish a layer of macaroni, sprinkle with grated cheese, bits of butter, pepper and salt; proceed in this manner until the dish is full, but omit the cheese at the last. Set the dish in the oven for a few minutes, and let it get thoroughly *hot*.

Baked Macaroni.—For baked macaroni, proceed as in stewed, but, when prepared fully as above, pour a few spoonfuls of milk over the top, and bake half an hour.

Macaroni with Tomatoes.—Have water boiling in a large saucepan; throw into it macaroni, broken, but not too short; let it cook twenty to thirty minutes, pour over it some cold water, and strain it quite dry; cut an onion into small dice, throw it into cold water and squeeze it dry in a cloth; put some olive oil, butter, or clarified fat into a saucepan; the oil, of course, is best. Throw into it the onion, and let it cook, shaking occasionally, until the onion is almost melted away. Have some cooked tomatoes ready to add to this

VEGETABLES.

MEMORANDUM ON FRIENDS' RECIPES

sauce. If it is too thick, add some cold water by teaspoonfuls at a time. Let all simmer for ten minutes longer. Sprinkle some grated cheese over your macaroni, which must be piping hot, in a dish. Pour the sauce over this and serve. A quarter of a pound of macaroni makes a large dish, and takes about a third of a can to half a can of tomatoes.

Sliced Cucumbers.—Peel and slice the cucumbers as thin as possible; lay the slices in salted water for an hour; then pour off the water; cover them with vinegar, half a teaspoonful of pepper, and salt as may be necessary.

Stewed Oyster-plant.—Cut off the tops of a bunch of salsify, or oyster-plant, close to the root; scrape and wash well, and slice lengthwise or round; stew until tender in salted water; drain and put in a stewpan, cover with milk; to one pint of salsify add a tablespoonful of butter rolled in flour; season with salt and pepper; let it stew a few minutes and add a little vinegar, if liked.

Mock Fried Oysters.—Scrape one bunch of salsify, and boil until tender; mash through a colander, add one beaten egg, a small piece of butter, salt and pepper to taste; drop by the spoonful into hot lard and fry brown.

MEMORANDUM
ON
FRIENDS' RECIPES

VII.—SALADS AND SAUCES.

SALADS DEFINED—HOW DRESSED, COMBINED, AND SERVED SAUCES DEFINED—THEIR USES AND COMPOSITION. HOW TO PREPARE INGREDIENTS FOR SALADS, WHAT VEGETABLES TO EMPLOY, FRESHNESS, EXCELLENCE, ETC. FORTY-SIX RECIPES FOR SALADS AND SAUCES.

UNDER the head of salads all preparations of uncooked herbs or vegetables is placed. They are usually dressed with salt, vinegar, oil, and spices. Sometimes they are combined with meat or shell fish, as chicken, veal, lobster, etc. They are used chiefly as relishes with other food.

Sauces are generally used to impart a relish to articles of food. Sometimes vegetables are employed as the basis of sauces, but they are compounded chiefly of savory condiments, that they may add zest to eating.

Meat or fish used in salads should not be minced, but rather picked apart, or cut in pieces of moderate size. Cabbage, celery, asparagus, cauliflower, water-cress, and all kinds of lettuce are the vegetables best adapted for use in salads. They must be used when quite fresh and crisp, and all the ingredients used in their dressing must be of the best quality and flavor.

All condiments are in some sense sauces, but the term is usually confined to those which are the result of compounding a variety of articles.

RECIPES.

Coldslaw.—With a sharp knife, or, better, with a knife made for the purpose, cut up into fine shavings a firm head of cabbage; sprinkle with as much salt and pepper as you deem necessary; beat up the yelk of one egg, add a lump of butter the size of a walnut, a gill of cream, the same quantity of vinegar, a tablespoonful of sugar, an even teaspoonful of mustard, and a pinch of bruised celery seed. Heat these condiments together, without boiling, and pour over the sliced cabbage; then toss it with a fork until thoroughly mixed. Allow time for it to cool before serving.

Coldslaw, No. 2.—Take equal parts of chopped cabbage and the green stalks of celery. Season with salt, pepper, and vinegar.

Maryland Coldslaw.—Halve the cabbage and lay it in cold water for one hour; shave down the head into small slips with a sharp knife. Put in a saucepan a cup of vinegar, and let it boil; then add a cup of cream, with the yelks of two eggs, well beaten; let it boil up, and pour over the cabbage. As soon as the cabbage is cut it should be sprinkled with a little salt and pepper.

Cabbage Salad.—Take one head of fine, white cabbage, minced fine; three hard-boiled eggs; two tablespoonfuls of salad oil; two teaspoonfuls white sugar; one teaspoonful salt; one teaspoonful pepper; one teaspoonful made mustard; one teacupful vinegar. Mix and pour upon the chopped cabbage.

Lettuce Salad.—Take a good-sized head of lettuce and pull the leaves apart. Wash them a moment, then shake off the water and dry the leaves. Examine them carefully, wipe off all grit, and reject those that are bruised. Take the yelks of two hard-boiled eggs; add one-half teaspoonful of mixed mustard, and mix to a paste with a silver fork; then add slowly, mixing carefully, about one-half a cup of vinegar, one teaspoonful of sugar, and salt to taste; cut the lettuce small as may be desired with a sharp knife, and pour the dressing over it; garnish with hard-boiled eggs.

MEMORANDUM
ON
FRIENDS' RECIPES

DOMESTIC COOKERY.

Potato Salad.—Steam and slice the potatoes; add a very little raw onion chopped very fine, and a little parsley, and pour over the whole a nice salad dressing. Serve either warm or cold, as may be preferred.

Potato Salad, No. 2.—Cut up three quarts of boiled potatoes, *while hot*, into neat pieces; add a tablespoonful of chopped parsley, a tablespoonful of chopped onion, a teaspoonful of pepper, and one of salt; also add a cupful of oil, and mix; then add a cupful of warm stock, a wineglassful of vinegar (from the mixed-pickle bottle); mix the ingredients together carefully, and do not break the potatoes any more than is absolutely unavoidable. Set the whole in the ice-box and serve cold. The onion and parsley may be omitted, and boiled root celery added, or a little stalk celery chopped fine.

Chicken Salad.—Boil a small chicken until very tender. When entirely cold, remove the skin and fat, cut the meat into small bits, then cut the white part of the stalks of celery into pieces of similar size, until you have twice as much celery as meat. Mix the chicken and celery together; pour on Durkee's Salad Dressing, and stir all thoroughly. Cold veal used in place of chicken will also make a very excellent salad.

Chicken Salad, No. 2.—Take three chickens, boil until very tender; when cold, chop them, but not too fine; add twice the quantity of celery cut fine, and three hard-boiled eggs sliced. Make a dressing with two cups of vinegar, half a cup of butter (or two tablespoonfuls of oil), two eggs beaten, with a large tablespoonful of mustard, saltspoonful of salt, two tablespoonfuls of sugar, tablespoonful of pepper, or a little cayenne pepper; put the vinegar into a tin pan and set in a kettle of boiling water; beat the other ingredients together thoroughly and stir slowly into the vinegar until it thickens. Cool it and pour over the salad just before serving.

SALADS AND SAUCES.

Lobster Salad.—To a three-pound lobster take the yelk of one raw egg beaten very lightly; then take the yelks of three hard-boiled eggs (cold), and add to the raw yelk, beating all the time; add, a few drops at a time, one-half bottle of the finest olive oil, stirring all the while; then add one and a half tablespoonfuls of the best English mustard, salt and pepper to taste; beat the mixture until light and add a tablespoonful of strong vinegar. Cut the lobster into small pieces and mix with it salt and pepper; pour over it the dressing just before sending to the table; garnish with the white of boiled eggs, celery tops, and the small claws.

Salmon Salad.—For a pound can of salmon, garnished with lettuce, make a dressing of one small teacupful of vinegar, butter half the size of an egg, one teaspoonful of mustard, one-half teaspoonful of cayenne pepper, one-half teaspoonful of salt, one teaspoonful of sugar, two eggs. When cold, add one-half teacupful of cream and pour over the salmon.

Mixed Mustard.—One tablespoonful of mustard, one teaspoonful of sugar, one saltspoonful of salt, enough vinegar to blend into a paste.

Plain Horse-radish is grated and merely covered with sharp vinegar.

Horse-radish Sauce.—Take one tablespoonful of grated horse-radish, a dessertspoonful of mustard, half a teaspoonful of sugar; then add vinegar, and stir it smooth. Serve in a sauce-tureen.

Tomato Sauce.—Stew one-half dozen tomatoes with a little chopped parsley; salt and pepper to taste; strain, and when it commences to boil add a tablespoonful of flour, stirred smooth with the same quantity of butter. When it boils it is ready to take up.

MEMORANDUM
ON
FRIENDS' RECIPES

MEMORANDUM
ON
FRIENDS' RECIPES

DOMESTIC COOKERY.

Tomato Sauce, No. 2.—Halve the tomatoes and squeeze out the seeds and watery pulp. Stew the solid portions gently with a little gravy or strong broth until they are entirely softened. Strain through a hair sieve and reheat with additional gravy, a little cayenne pepper and salt. Serve hot.

Green Tomato Sauce.—Cut up two gallons of green tomatoes; take three gills of black mustard seed, three tablespoonfuls of dry mustard, two and a half of black pepper, one and a half of allspice, four of salt, two of celery seed, one quart each of chopped onions and sugar, and two and a half quarts of good vinegar, a little red pepper to taste. Beat the spices and boil all together until well done.

Chili Sauce.—Take ten pounds of ripe tomatoes, peeled and sliced; two pounds of peeled onions chopped fine; seven ounces of green peppers finely chopped, without the seeds; six ounces of brown sugar; four ounces salt; a pint and a half of vinegar. Boil all together in a porcelain-lined kettle for several hours, until thick as desired; put up in tight cans or jars, and use with soups and gravies.

Celery Sauce.—Pick and wash two heads of celery; cut them into pieces one inch long, and stew them in a pint of water, with one teaspoonful of salt, until the celery is tender. Rub a large spoonful of butter and a spoonful of flour well together; stir this into a pint of cream; put in the celery, and let it boil up once. Serve hot with boiled poultry.

Mint Sauce.—Wash the sprigs of mint, let them dry on a towel, strip off the leaves, and chop them very fine; put in a sauce-boat with a cupful of vinegar and four lumps of sugar; let it stand an hour, and before serving stir all together. Mint sauce, if bottled, will keep a long time, and be just as good, if not better, than when freshly made.

Asparagus Sauce.—Take a dozen heads of asparagus; two teacupfuls drawn butter; two eggs; the juice of half a

SALADS AND SAUCES.

lemon; salt and white pepper. Boil the tender heads in a very little salt water. Drain and chop them. Have ready a pint of drawn butter, with two raw eggs beaten into it; add the asparagus, and season, squeezing in the lemon juice last. The butter must be hot, but do not cook after putting in the asparagus heads. This is a delightful sauce for boiled fowls, stewed fillet of veal, or boiled mutton.

Mushroom Sauce.—Pick, rub, and wash a pint of young mushrooms, and sprinkle with salt to take off the skin. Put them into a saucepan with a little salt, a blade of mace, a little nutmeg, a pint of cream, and a piece of butter rolled in flour; boil them up and stir till done.

Caper Sauce.—Make a drawn butter sauce, and add two or three tablespoonfuls of French capers; remove from the fire and add a little lemon juice.

Cranberry Sauce.—Cover a quart of cranberries with water and let it simmer gently till thoroughly cooked. Strain the skins out through a colander, and add to the juice two cupfuls of sugar; let it simmer again for fifteen minutes, and pour into a mold previously wet in cold water.

Strawberry Sauce.—Rub half a cupful of butter and one cupful of sugar to a cream; add the beaten white of an egg and one cupful of strawberries thoroughly mashed.

Lemon Sauce.—One-half a cupful of butter, one cupful of sugar, yelks of two eggs, one teaspoonful of corn-starch. Beat the eggs and sugar until light; add the grated rind and juice of one lemon. Stir the whole into three gills of boiling water until it thickens sufficiently for the table.

Lemon Sauce, No. 2.—One large tablespoonful of butter, one small tablespoonful of flour, one cupful of sugar, grated rind and juice of one lemon.

MEMORANDUM
ON
FRIENDS' RECIPES

MEMORANDUM ON FRIENDS' RECIPES

DOMESTIC COOKERY.

Vanilla Sauce.—Put half a pint of milk in a small sauce pan over the fire; when scalding hot add the yelks of three eggs, and stir until it is as thick as boiled custard; remove the saucepan from the fire, and when cool add a tablespoonful of extract of vanilla and the beaten whites of two eggs.

Venison Sauce.—Mix two teaspoonfuls of currant jelly, one stick of cinnamon, one blade of mace, grated white bread, ten tablespoonfuls of water; let the whole stew till thoroughly cooked, when done serve with venison steak.

Anchovy Sauce.—Stir two or three teaspoonfuls of prepared essence or paste of anchovy, into a pint of melted butter; let the sauce boil a few minutes, and flavor with lemon juice.

Lobster Sauce.—Break the shell of the lobster into small pieces. Pour over these one pint of water or veal-stock and a pinch of salt; simmer gently until the liquid is reduced one-half. Mix two ounces of butter with an ounce of flour, strain the liquid upon it and stir all, over the fire, until the mixture thickens, but do not let it boil. Add two tablespoonfuls of lobster meat chopped fine, the juice of half a lemon, and serve.

Oyster Sauce.—Strain fifty oysters; put the juice into a saucepan; add one pint of new milk; let it simmer, and then skim off whatever froth may rise. Rub a large spoonful of flour and two of butter together; stir this into the liquor; add a little salt and pepper. Let this simmer five minutes, but do not add the oysters till just as they are to be sent to the table, as oysters much cooked are hard. For turkeys, etc., this is a splendid dressing.

Plain French Dressing.—A plain French dressing is made simply of salt, pepper, oil, and vinegar. Three tablespoonfuls of oil to one of vinegar, saltspoon heaping full of salt, an even saltspoonful of pepper mixed with a little cayenne.

SALADS AND SAUCES.

Mayonnaise Sauce.—Work the yelks of two raw eggs to a smooth paste, and add two saltspoonfuls of salt, half a saltspoonful of cayenne, a saltspoonful of dry mustard, and a teaspoonful of oil; mix these thoroughly and add the strained juice of half a lemon. Take what remains of half a pint of olive oil and add it gradually, a teaspoonful at a time, and every fifth teaspoonful add a few drops of lemon juice until you have used two lemons and the half-pint of oil.

Mayonnaise Sauce, No. 2.—Rub the yelks of three hard-boiled eggs with the yelk of one raw egg to a smooth paste; add a heaping teaspoonful of salt, two saltspoonfuls of white pepper, and two saltspoonfuls of made mustard; mix thoroughly and work a gill of oil gradually into the mixture, alternated with a teaspoonful of vinegar, until you have used three tablespoonfuls of vinegar. Should the sauce appear too thick, add a wineglassful of cream.

Butter Sauce.—Mix well together two tablespoonfuls of butter, some chopped parsley, juice of half a lemon, salt, and pepper. For broiled meat or fish.

Brown Butter Sauce.—Put butter into a frying-pan and let it stand on the fire until very brown; then add a little parsley and fry a moment longer.

Drawn Butter Sauce.—Take one-quarter pound of butter; rub with it two teaspoonfuls of flour. When well mixed, put into a saucepan with one-half pint of water; cover it, and set the saucepan into a larger one full of boiling water. Shake it constantly till completely melted and beginning to boil; season with salt and pepper.

Boiled Egg Sauce.—Add to half a pint of drawn butter sauce two or three hard-boiled eggs, chopped.

MEMORANDUM
ON
FRIENDS' RECIPES

MEMORANDUM
ON
FRIENDS' RECIPES

110　　　　　　　*DOMESTIC COOKERY.*

White Sauce.—Thicken half a pint of new milk with a little flour or arrowroot. After it has boiled, stir in slowly about two ounces of fresh butter, cut into small pieces. Continue to stir until the butter is completely dissolved. Add a few thin strips of lemon rind, a little salt, and pounded mace.

White Sauce, No. 2.—Boil a few thin strips of lemon peel in half a pint of good veal gravy just long enough to give it their flavor. Stir in a thickening of arrowroot, or flour and butter; add salt and a quarter of a pint of boiling cream.

Cream Sauce.—Beat the yelks of three eggs, three tablespoonfuls of white sugar, and vanilla flavor. Turn on it a pint of boiling milk, and stir well.

Brandy Sauce.—Four ounces of sugar and two ounces of butter, well creamed together; then beat an egg into it, with two ounces of brandy.

Wine Sauce.—Take one pint bowl of white sugar, not quite a quarter of a pound of butter, one glass of wine, one grated nutmeg, and a tablespoonful of warm water; beat together steadily for half an hour.

Hard Sauce.—One cupful butter, three cupfuls sugar; beat very hard, flavoring with lemon juice; smooth into shape with a knife dipped into cold water.

Sauces in General.—Worcestershire, Challenge, Annear, and other sauces in the market have each their specially good points. Trial of them should be made and the best used.

VIII.—CROQUETTES AND FRITTERS.

CROQUETTES DEFINED; FRITTERS DEFINED; USES OF BOTH TWENTY-FOUR RECIPES FOR CROQUETTES AND FRITTERS.

THE term *croquette* (pronounced cro-ket) is from a French verb, meaning "to crunch." It designates all that class of preparations made of minced meat, or other ingredients, highly seasoned and fried in bread-crumbs.

Fritters, like croquettes, are fried, but they are made of batter containing other ingredients, as taste may dictate. Both these preparations are used as accessories of the dinner or tea table rather than as principal dishes.

RECIPES.

Rice Croquettes.—Put a quarter of a pound of rice into a pint of milk. Let it simmer gently until the rice is tender and the milk absorbed. It must then be boiled until thick and dry, or it will be difficult to mold. Add three tablespoonfuls of sugar, one of butter, one egg, and flavor to taste with vanilla or cinnamon; beat thoroughly for a few minutes, and when cold form into balls or cones, dip these into beaten egg, roll lightly in bread-crumbs, and fry in hot butter.

Hominy Croquettes.—To a cupful of cold boiled hominy (small grained) add a tablespoonful of melted butter and stir hard; moisten by degrees with a cupful of milk, beating to a soft, light paste. Put in a teaspoonful of white sugar and a well-beaten egg. Roll into oval balls with floured hands, dip in beaten egg, then in cracker-crumbs, and fry in hot lard.

MEMORANDUM
ON
FRIENDS' RECIPES

MEMORANDUM
ON
FRIENDS' RECIPES

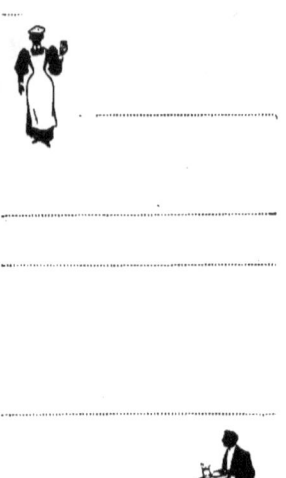

DOMESTIC COOKERY.

Potato Croquettes.—Season cold mashed potatoes with pepper, salt, and nutmeg. Beat to a cream, with a tablespoonful of melted butter to every cupful of potato. Add two or three beaten eggs and some minced parsley. Roll into small balls; dip in beaten egg, then in bread-crumbs, and fry in hot lard.

Oyster-Plant Croquettes.—Wash, scrape, and boil the oyster-plant till tender; rub it through a colander, and mix with the pulp a little butter, cream, salt, cayenne, and lemon juice; mix the ingredients thoroughly together to a smooth paste, and set the dish in the ice-box to get cold; then shape it into small cones, dip them in beaten egg, roll in crumbs, and fry crisp and brown.

Chicken Croquettes.—Add to the quantity of minced chicken about one-quarter the quantity of bread-crumbs, also one egg well beaten to each cupful of meat; pepper, salt, and chopped parsley to taste, add the yelks of two hard-boiled eggs rubbed smooth. Add gravy or drawn butter to moisten it, make into cones or balls, roll in cracker-dust or flour, and fry in hot lard.

Veal Croquettes.—Make these the same as chicken croquettes, by substituting for the chicken cold minced veal and ham in equal parts. The salt may be omitted, as the ham usually supplies it sufficiently. Turkey, duck, or the remains of any cold game or meat may be used in the same way with very satisfactory results.

Oyster Croquettes.—Take the hard ends of the oysters, leaving the other end for a soup or stew; scald them, then chop fine, and add an equal weight of potatoes rubbed through a colander; to one pound of this combination add two ounces of butter, one teaspoonful of salt, half a teaspoonful of pepper, half a teaspoonful of mace, and one-half gill of cream, make in small rolls, dip them in egg and grated bread, fry in deep, hot lard.

CROQUETTES AND FRITTERS.

Lobster Croquettes.—Chop the lobster very fine; mix with pepper, salt, bread-crumbs, and a little parsley; moisten with cream and a small piece of butter; shape with your hands; dip in egg, roll in bread-crumbs, fry in hot lard.

Plain Fritters.—Take one pint of flour, four eggs, one pint of boiling water, and one teaspoonful of salt. Stir the flour into the boiling water gradually, and let it boil three minutes, stirring constantly. Remove from the fire and stir in the yelks of the eggs, afterward the whites, they having been well beaten. Drop this batter by large spoonfuls into boiling lard and fry to a light brown. Serve hot powdered with white sugar.

Bread Fritters.—Grate stale bread until you have a pint o. crumbs; pour a pint of boiling milk upon these, a tablespoonful of butter having been dissolved in it, and let the whole stand for an hour. Then beat up the mixture and flavor with nutmeg. Stir in gradually a quarter pound of white sugar, two tablespoonfuls of brandy, six well-beaten eggs, and currants enough to flavor the whole. The currants should be washed, dried, and floured. Drop by large spoonfuls into boiling lard and fry to a light brown. Serve with wine and powdered sugar.

Potato Fritters.—Break open four nicely baked potatoes; scoop out the insides with a spoon, and mix with them a wineglassful of cream, a tablespoonful of brandy, two tablespoonfuls of powdered sugar, the juice of one lemon, half a teaspoonful of vanilla extract, and well-beaten yelks of four and the whites of three eggs; beat the batter until it is quite smooth; drop large tablespoonfuls of the mixture into boiling fat and fry to a light brown; dust them with powdered sugar and send to table hot.

Corn Fritters.—Scrape twelve ears of corn, mix with two

MEMORANDUM
ON
FRIENDS' RECIPES

MEMORANDUM
ON
FRIENDS' RECIPES

114　　　　　　　　*DOMESTIC COOKERY.*

eggs, one and one-half cups of milk, salt and pepper to taste and flour enough to hold all together. Fry in hot fat.

Hominy Fritters.—Two teacupfuls of cold boiled hominy; stir in one teacupful of sweet milk and a little salt, four tablespoonfuls of sifted flour, and one egg; beat the white separately and add last; drop the batter by spoonfuls in hot lard and fry to a nice brown.

Rice Fritters.—Boil a quarter of a pound of rice in milk till it is tender, then mix it with a pint of milk, two eggs, one cup of sugar, a little salt and cinnamon, and as much flour as will make a thick batter. Fry them in thin cakes and serve with butter and white powdered sugar.

Parsnip Fritters.—Boil four good-sized parsnips in salted water until tender; drain them, beat them to a pulp, and squeeze the water from them as much as possible; bind them together with a beaten egg and a little flour. Shape into cakes and fry in hot lard.

Fruit Fritters.—The following recipe will serve for many kinds of fruit or vegetable fritters: Make a batter of ten ounces of flour, half a pint of milk, and two ounces of butter; sweeten and flavor to taste; stir in the whites of two eggs well beaten; dip the fruit in the batter and fry. Small fruit and vegetables should be mixed with the batter.

Apple Fritters.—Take one egg, two tablespoonfuls of flour, a little sifted sugar and ginger, with milk enough to make a smooth batter; cut a good sized apple into slices and put them into the batter. Put them into a frying-pan, with the batter which is taken up in the spoon. When fried, drain them on a sieve and sift on powdered sugar.

Currant Fritters.—Take two cupfuls dry, fine bread-crumbs, two tablespoonfuls prepared flour, two cups of milk, one-half pound currants, washed and well dried; five eggs whipped very light and the yelks strained, one-half cup powdered sugar, one tablespoonful butter, one-half teaspoonful mixed cinnamon and nutmeg. Boil the milk and pour over the bread. Mix and put in the butter. Let it get cold. Beat in, next, the yelks and sugar, the seasoning, flour, and stiff whites, finally the currants dredged white with flour. The batter should be thick. Drop great spoonfuls into the hot lard and fry. Drain them and send hot to table. Eat with a mixture of wine and powdered sugar.

Oyster Fritters.—Take one and one-half pints of sweet milk, one and one-fourth pounds of flour, four egg (the yelks having been beaten very thick); add milk and flour; stir the whole well together, then beat the whites to a stiff froth and stir them gradually into the batter; take a spoonful of the mixture, drop an oyster into it, and fry in hot lard; let them be a light brown on both sides.

Clam Fritters.—Take a dozen chopped clams, one pint of milk, three eggs. Add liquor from the clams, with salt and pepper, and flour enough to produce thin batter. Fry in hot lard.

Cream Fritters.—Take one cup of cream, the whites of five eggs, two full cups prepared flour, one saltspoonful of nutmeg, a pinch of salt. Stir the whites into the cream in turn with the flour, put in nutmeg and salt, beat all hard for two minutes. The batter should be rather thick. Fry in plenty of sweet lard, a spoonful of batter for each fritter. Drain and serve upon a hot, clean napkin. Eat with jelly sauce. Do not cut them open, but break or pull them apart.

French Fritters.—Take two cupfuls of flour, two teaspoonfuls of baking powder, two eggs, milk enough for stiff batter, and a little salt. Drop into boiling lard and fry light brown. Serve with cream and sugar or sauce.

MEMORANDUM
ON
FRIENDS' RECIPES

MEMORANDUM
ON
FRIENDS' RECIPES

116   DOMESTIC COOKERY.

Spanish Fritters.—Cut stale bread into small, round slices about an inch thick; soak them in milk, and then dip them into well-beaten egg which has been sweetened to taste. Sprinkle thickly with cinnamon and fry in hot lard.

Venetian Fritters.—Take three ounces of whole rice, wash and drain into a pint of cold milk. Let it come slowly to a boil, stirring often, and let it simmer till quite thick and dry. Add two ounces of powdered sugar, one of fresh butter, a pinch of salt, the grated rind of half a lemon. Let the whole cool in the saucepan, and while still a little warm mix in three ounces of currants, four ounces of chopped apples, a teaspoonful of flour, and three well-beaten eggs. Drop the batter in small lumps into boiling fat, allowing them to fry till the under side is quite firm and brown; then turn and brown the other side. When done, drain through a hair sieve, and powder with white sugar when about to serve.

IX.—EGGS.

NUTRITIOUS VALUE OF EGGS—TEST OF FRESHNESS—PACKING EGGS—PRESERVING EGGS. TWENTY-EIGHT WAYS OF COOKING EGGS.

HIGH chemical authorities agree that there is more nutriment in an egg than in any substance of equal bulk found in nature or produced by art. They are much used for food the world over, and few articles are capable of more varied employment.

The freshness of an egg may be determined in various ways. In a fresh egg, the butt end, if touched on the tongue, is sensibly warmer than the point end. If held toward the light and looked through ("candled"), a fresh egg will show a clear white and a well-rounded yelk. A stale egg will appear muddled. Probably the surest test is to put the eggs into a pan of cold water. Fresh eggs sink quickly; bad eggs float; suspicious ones act suspiciously, neither sinking nor floating very decidedly. Of all articles of food, doubtful eggs are most certainly to be condemned.

On the packing of eggs, the following conclusions may be regarded as established among egg-dealers: By cold storage, temperature forty to forty-two degrees Fahrenheit, kept uniform, with eggs packed properly or in cases, they will keep in good condition from six to nine months; but they must be used soon after being taken out of the cold storage, as they soon spoil. Eggs become musty from being packed in bad material. They will become musty in cases, as a change of temperature causes the eggs to sweat and the wrapping-paper to become moist and taint the eggs.

MEMORANDUM
ON
FRIENDS' RECIPES

MEMORANDUM
ON
FRIENDS' RECIPES

DOMESTIC COOKERY.

Well-dried oats, a year old, makes the best packing. Eggs become " mixed " by jarring in shipping. Fresh eggs mix worse than those kept in cold storage. Eggs which have been held in cold storage in the West should be shipped in refrigerator cars in summer. Eggs will keep thirty days longer if stood on the little end than in any other position. They must be kept at an even temperature and in a pure atmosphere. Eggs laid on the side attach to the shell and are badly injured. To prevent imposition as to the freshness of the eggs, the egg gatherers should " candle " them when they get them from the farmers. Eggs keep better in the dark than in the light.

Methods of preservation for domestic purposes are, to pack them in bran or salt, the small end down ; to grease them with linseed oil, or dip them in a light varnish. For extra long keeping, slack one pound of lime in a gallon of water ; when this is entirely cold, place it in a jar and fill with fresh eggs. Do not agitate the contents when eggs are removed from the jar. Eggs kept so will continue good for a year.

The French method of preserving eggs is to dissolve beeswax and olive oil and anoint the eggs all over. If left undisturbed in a cool place, they will remain good for two years.

RECIPES.

Boiled Eggs.—Put into a saucepan of *boiling* water with a tablespoon, being careful not to break or crack them. Boil steadily three minutes, if you want them soft ; ten, if hard.

Another way is to put them on in cold water, and let it come to a boil. The inside, white and yelk, will be then of the consistency of custard.

Still another way is to put them in water, heated to the boiling point, and let them stand from five to seven minutes without boiling. If desired for salad, boil them ten minutes ;

then throw them in cold water; roll them gently on a table or board, and the shell can be easily removed. Wire egg racks, to set in boiling hot water with the eggs held in place, are exceedingly convenient.

Boiled Eggs, with Sauce.—Boil hard, remove the shell, set in a hot dish, and serve with seasoning and sauce to taste.

Poached Eggs.—Have the water well salted, but do not let it boil hard. Break the eggs separately into a saucer, and slip them singly into the water; when nicely done, remove with a skimmer, trim neatly, and lay each egg upon a small thin square of buttered toast, then sprinkle with salt and pepper. Some persons prefer them poached rather than fried with ham; in which case substitute the ham for toast.

Poached Eggs with Ham Sauce.—Mince fine two or three slices of boiled ham, a small onion, a little parsley, pepper, and salt; stew together for a quarter of an hour; put the poached eggs in a dish, squeeze over them the juice of a lemon, and pour on the sauce hot but not boiling.

Poached Eggs a la Creme.—Nearly fill a clean frying-pan with water boiling hot; strain a tablespoonful of vinegar through double muslin, and add to the water with a little salt. Slip your eggs from the saucer upon the top of the water (first taking the pan from the fire). Boil three minutes and a half; drain, and lay on buttered toast in a hot dish. Turn the water from the pan and pour in half a cupful of cream or milk. If you use the latter, thicken with a very little corn-starch. Let it heat to a boil, stirring to prevent burning, and add a great spoonful of butter, some pepper, and salt. Boil up once and pour over the eggs. Or better still, heat the milk in a separate saucepan, that the eggs may not have to stand. A little broth improves the sauce.

MEMORANDUM
ON
FRIENDS' RECIPES

MEMORANDUM
ON
FRIENDS' RECIPES

DOMESTIC COOKERY.

Steamed Eggs.—Butter a tin plate and break in your eggs; set in a steamer; place over a kettle of boiling water, and steam until the whites are cooked; they are more ornamental when broken into patty tins, as they keep their form better; the whites of the eggs, when cooked in this manner, are tender and light, and not tough and leathery, as if cooked by any other process.

Eggs in this style can be eaten by invalids, and are very much richer than by any other method.

Whirled Eggs.—Put a quart of water, slightly salted, into a saucepan over the fire, and keep it at a fast boil. Stir with wooden spoon or ladle in one direction until it whirls rapidly. Break six eggs, one at a time, into a cup and drop each carefully into the centre, or vortex, of the boiling water. If kept at a rapid motion, the egg will become a soft, round ball. Take it out carefully with a perforated spoon, and put it on a slice of buttered toast laid upon a hot dish. Put a bit of butter on the top. Set the dish in the oven to keep warm, and proceed in the same way with another egg, having but one in the saucepan at a time. When all are done, dust lightly with salt and pepper and send up *hot*.

Eggs a la Mode.—Remove the skin from a dozen tomatoes, medium size, cut them up in a saucepan, add a little butter, pepper, and salt; when sufficiently boiled, beat up five or six eggs, and just before you serve, turn them into a saucepan with the tomato, and stir one way for two minutes, allowing them time to be well done.

Baked Eggs.—Mix finely chopped ham and bread-crumbs in about equal proportions, season with salt and pepper, and moisten with milk and a little melted butter; half fill your small patty pans with the mixture, break an egg over the top of each, sprinkle with fine bread-crumbs, and bake; serve hot.

EGGS.

Baked Eggs, No. 2.—Butter a clean, smooth saucepan, break as many eggs as will be needed into a saucer, one by one, and if found good, slip each into the saucepan. No broken yelk must be allowed, nor must they crowd so as to risk breaking the yelk after put in. Put a small piece of butter on each, and sprinkle with pepper and salt. Set into a well-heated oven, and bake till the whites are set. If the oven is rightly heated, it will take but a few minutes, and the cooking will be far more delicate than fried eggs.

Eggs sur le Plat.—Melt butter on a stone-china or tin plate. Break the eggs carefully into this; dust lightly with pepper and salt, and put on top of the stove until the whites are well set. Serve in the dish in which they are baked.

Scrambled Eggs.—Put into a frying-pan enough butter to grease it well; slip in the eggs carefully without breaking the yelks; add butter, and season to taste; when the whites begin to set, stir the eggs from the bottom of the pan, and continue stirring until the cooking is completed. The appearance at the end should be *marbled*, rather than *mixed*.

Scrambled Eggs with Ham.—Put into a pan, butter, a little pepper and salt, and a little milk; when hot, drop in the eggs, and with a knife cut the eggs and scrape them from the bottom as the whites begin to set; add some cold ham chopped fine, and when done, serve in a hot dish.

Toasted Eggs.—Cover the bottom of an earthenware or stone-china dish with rounds of delicately toasted bread, or with rounds of stale bread dipped in beaten egg and fried quickly to a golden-brown in butter or nice dripping. Break an egg carefully upon each, and set the dish immediately in front of a glowing fire. Toast over this as many slices of *fat* salt pork or ham as there are eggs in the dish, holding the meat so that it will fry very quickly and all the dripping fall upon the eggs. When these are well set, they are done. Turn the dish several times while toasting the

MEMORANDUM
ON
FRIENDS' RECIPES

MEMORANDUM ON FRIENDS' RECIPES

DOMESTIC COOKERY.

meat, that the eggs may be equally cooked. Do not send the pork to table, but pepper the eggs lightly and remove with the toast to the dish in which they go to the table.

Egg Toast.—Beat four eggs, yelks and whites, together thoroughly; put two tablespoonfuls of butter into a saucepan and melt slowly; then pour in the eggs and heat, without boiling, over a slow fire, stirring constantly; add a little salt, and when hot spread on slices of nicely browned toast and serve at once.

Egg Baskets.—Boil quite hard as many eggs as will be needed. Put into cold water till cold, then cut neatly into halves with a thin, sharp knife; remove the yelk and rub to a paste with some melted butter, adding pepper and salt. Cover up this paste and set aside till the filling is ready. Take cold roast duck, chicken, or turkey, which may be on hand, chop fine and pound smooth, and while pounding mix in the paste prepared from the yelks. As you pound, moisten with melted butter and some gravy which may have been left over from the fowls; set this paste when done over hot water till well heated. Cut off a small slice from the end of the empty halves of the whites, so they will stand firm, then fill them with this paste; place them close together on a flat, round dish, and pour over the rest of the gravy, if any remains, or make a little fresh. A few spoonfuls of cream or rich milk improves this dressing.

Fricasseed Eggs.—Boil six eggs hard; when cold, slice with a sharp knife. Have ready some slices of stale bread, fried to a nice brown in butter or drippings. Put a cupful of good broth in drawn butter over the fire, season it with pepper, salt, and a trace of onion; let it come to a boil. Dip the slices of egg first into raw egg, then into cracker dust or bread-crumbs, and lay them gently into the gravy upon the side of the range. Do not let it actually boil, lest the eggs should break, but let them lie thus in the gravy at least five minutes. Place the fried bread upon a platter, lay the sliced eggs evenly upon this, pour the gravy over all, and serve hot.

Curried Eggs.—Boil six or eight fresh eggs quite hard, and put them aside until they are cold. Mix well together from two to three ounces of good butter, and from three to four dessertspoonfuls of currie-powder; shake them in a stewpan, or thick saucepan, over a clear but moderate fire for some minutes, then throw in a couple of mild onions finely minced, and fry gently until they are soft; pour in by degrees from half to three-quarters of a pint of broth or gravy, and stew slowly until they are reduced to pulp; mix smoothly a small cup of thick cream with two teaspoonfuls of wheaten or rice flour; stir them to the currie, and simmer the whole until the raw taste of the thickening is gone. Cut the eggs into half-inch slices, heat them through in the sauce without boiling them, and send to the table as hot as possible.

Plain Omelet.—Beat thoroughly yelks of five eggs, and a dessertspoonful of flour, rubbed smooth in two-thirds of a cupful of milk. Salt and pepper to taste, and add a piece of butter the size of a hickory-nut. Beat the whites to a stiff froth, pour the mixture into the whites, and without stirring pour into a hot, buttered omelet pan. Cook on top of the range for five minutes; then set pan and all into the oven to brown the top nicely.

Baked Omelet.—Beat the yelks of six eggs, and add the whites of three eggs beaten very light; salt and pepper to taste, and a tablespoonful of flour mixed in a cup of milk. Pour into a well-buttered pan and put into a hot oven; when thick, pour over it the whites of three eggs beaten light; then brown nicely, without allowing the top to become crusted. Serve immediately.

MEMORANDUM
ON
FRIENDS' RECIPES

MEMORANDUM
ON
FRIENDS' RECIPES

124   *DOMESTIC COOKERY.*

Omelet a la Mode.—Beat the yelks and whites of six eggs separately until light, then beat together and add one tablespoonful of cream. Have in the omelet pan a piece of butter; when the butter is boiling hot, pour in the omelet and shake until it begins to stiffen, and then let it brown, and season to taste. Fold double and serve hot.

If a larger omelet is desired, a tablespoonful of milk to each egg may be added, and one teaspoonful of corn-starch or flour to the whole.

Cheese Omelet.—Butter the sides of a deep dish and cover with thin slices of rich cheese; lay over the cheese thin slices of well-buttered bread, first covering the cheese with a little red pepper and mustard; then another layer of cheese; beat the yelk of an egg in a cup of cream or milk, and pour over the dish, and put at once into the oven; bake till nicely browned. Serve hot, or it will be tough and hard, but when properly cooked it will be tender and savory.

Meat or Fish Omelet.—Make the same as plain omelet. When it is done, scatter thickly over the surface cold, boiled ham, tongue, poultry, fish, or lobster, chopped fine, and season nicely to taste; slip the broad knife under one side of the omelet and double, inclosing the meat. Then upset the frying-pan upon a hot dish, so transferring the omelet without breaking. Or the minced meat may be stirred in after the ingredients are put together, and before cooking. Be careful not to scorch the egg.

Omelet with Oysters.—Allow one egg for each person, and beat yelks and whites separately, very light; season to taste, and just before cooking add the oysters, which have been previously scalded in their own liquor.

Egg Sandwiches.—Hard boil some fresh eggs, and, when cold, cut them into moderately thin slices, and lay them between slices of bread and butter cut thin, and season well with celery salt. For picnic parties or for traveling, these sandwiches are very nice.

Deviled Eggs.—Boil the eggs hard, remove the shell, and cut in two as preferred. Remove the yelks, and add to them salt, cayenne pepper, melted butter, and mixed mustard to taste; then stuff the cavities of the hard whites, and put the halves together again. Serve garnished with parsley. For picnics, etc., each egg can be wrapped in tissue paper to preserve its form.

Pickled Eggs.—Boil the eggs until very hard; when cold, shell them, and cut them in halves lengthways. Lay them carefully in large-mouthed jars, and pour over them scalding vinegar, well seasoned with whole pepper, allspice, a few pieces of ginger, and a few cloves of garlic. When cold, tie up closely, and let them stand a month. They are then fit for use. With cold meat, they are a most delicious and delicate pickle.

Egg Balls.—Rub the yelks of hard-boiled eggs with the raw yelk of an egg, well beaten, and season to taste. Roll this paste into balls the size of marbles, adding flour if necessary to thicken, and boil two minutes. A valuable embellishment and enrichment of soups.

MEMORANDUM
ON
FRIENDS' RECIPES

X.—BREAD, BISCUIT, HOT CAKES, ETC.

AN immense department is opened up by the title of this chapter; and it is a department of immense importance. Bread is confessedly the "staff of life," and, therefore, it should be good. And whatever takes the place of bread, be it biscuits, hot cakes, muffins, or what not, should also be good, or nothing is gained by the exchange. Many a housekeeper can make excellent pies, cakes, etc., but when bread is needed, she flies to the bakery, confessing her total inability to prepare this indispensable commodity.

But even bread may become distasteful as a steady diet. To vary it with the long line of splendid substitutes which are possible, and which are discussed in this chapter, is a most desirable ability. This department, therefore, is worthy of every housewife's devout study.

I.—BREAD.

ESSENTIALS TO MAKING GOOD BREAD; HOW TO KNOW GOOD FLOUR; YEAST; RAISING BREAD; BAKING BREAD. TWELVE RECIPES FOR BREAD.

THREE things are essential to the making of good bread, namely, good flour, good yeast, and judicious baking.

A fourth might be added, experience, without which none of the domestic arts can be successfully carried on.

In selecting flour, first look to the color. If it is white, with a yellowish straw-color tint, buy it. If it is white, with a bluish cast, or with black specks in it, refuse it. Next, examine its adhesiveness; wet and knead a little of it be-

MEMORANDUM ON FRIENDS' RECIPES

tween your fingers; if it works soft and sticky, it is poor. Then throw a little lump of dried flour against a smooth surface; if it falls like powder, it is bad. Lastly, squeeze some of the flour tightly in your hand; if it retains the shape given by the pressure, that too is a good sign. It is safe to buy flour that will stand all these tests.

Good yeast may easily be obtained in cities, in the form of fresh yeast cakes or at the baker shops. Where access cannot be had to these aids, home-made yeast must be depended on, which see under "Yeast," at the end of this chapter. After the yeast is properly added, the dough must stand several hours in an even temperature of moderate warmth, so that the process of "rising" may go on. This is simply a fermenting, or leavening, or lightening of the dough. If this process, by too much heat or other causes, goes too fast or too far, sour bread is the result; if it goes too slow, or not far enough, heavy bread is the result. It must go just far enough, and just at the right moment the process must be arrested by baking. The walls of dough which inclose the innumerable vesicles of gas formed in the fermenting are thus made firm around those open spaces, and what we know as "light bread" is secured.

The baking is the final test in the case. The oven must be just right at the outset, and must be kept so as the operation proceeds. Experience must decide the exact heat required, but an oven in which the bared arm may be held for about half a minute is regarded as approximately correct.

Hot bread, or hot cake, should always be cut with a hot knife. If so cut, it will not become clammy.

RECIPES.

Wheat Bread.—Put seven pounds of flour into a breadpan; hollow out the centre, and add a quart of lukewarm water, a teaspoonful of salt, and a wineglassful of yeast. Have

MEMORANDUM
ON
FRIENDS' RECIPES

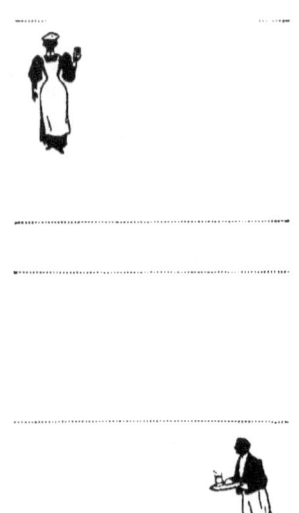

ready more warm water, and add gradually as much as will make a smooth, soft dough. Knead it well, dust a little flour over it, cover it with a cloth, and set it in a warm place four hours; then knead it again for fifteen minutes and let it rise again. Divide it into loaves, and prick them with a fork, and bake in a quick oven from forty minutes to an hour.

Potato Bread.—Three and one-half quarts of sifted flour, three boiled potatoes, one quart warm water, one teacupful of yeast, one even tablespoonful salt. Mix at night; put the flour in a large bowl; hollow a place in the centre for the mashed potatoes, water, and salt. Stir in flour enough to make a smooth batter; add yeast; stir in the rest of the flour. Put the dough on the floured board; knead fifteen minutes, using barely enough flour to prevent sticking. Flour the bowl, lay the dough in it, cover and leave it to rise. In the morning, divide in four parts; mold into loaves; when light, prick, and bake in a moderate oven.

Salt Rising Bread.—Pour a pint of hot water in a two-quart pail or pitcher on one-half tablespoonful of salt; when it has cooled a little, add one and one-third pints of flour; mix well, and leave the pitcher in a kettle of water, as warm as that used for mixing. Keep it at the same temperature until the batter is nearly twice its original bulk, which will be in from five to eight hours. It may be stirred once or twice during the rising. Add to this a sponge made of one quart of hot water, two and one-half quarts of flour—adding as much more as may be necessary to make a soft dough; mix well, and leave in a warm place to rise. When light, mold into loaves, keeping them as soft as possible; lay in buttered tins. When light again, prick and bake.

Milk Bread.—Let two quarts of milk come to a boil; stand it aside to cool, and when it becomes tepid, add flour to it gradually until it makes a batter just soft enough to beat up with a spoon. To this add one cake of compressed yeast thoroughly dissolved in lukewarm water. The batter should then be well beaten. Cover with a towel and set in a warm place to rise. When light, add two tablespoonfuls of salt, one of lard, one of light brown sugar, and flour enough to make a soft dough. Knead steadily for about half an hour. This quantity should make four or five medium-sized loaves. Put them in greased pans and let them rise again. When light, prick with a fork and bake in a quick oven.

Vienna Bread.—The Vienna bread that became so famous on the Centennial Exhibition grounds in 1876 was made on the following recipe: Sift in a tin pan four pounds of flour; bank up against the sides; pour in one quart of milk and water, and mix into it enough flour to form a thin batter, and then quickly and lightly add one pint of milk, in which is dissolved one ounce of salt and one and three-quarter ounces of yeast; leave the remainder of the flour against the sides of the pan; cover the pan with a cloth, and set in a place free from draught for three quarters of an hour; then mix in the rest of the flour until the dough will leave the bottom and sides of the pan, and let it stand two and a half hours; finally, divide the mass into one-pound pieces, to be cut in turn into twelve parts each; this gives square pieces about three and a half inches thick, each corner of which is taken up and folded over to the centre, and then the cases are turned over on a dough-board to rise for half an hour, when they are put in a hot oven that will bake them in ten minutes.

Rye Bread.—Scald two handfuls of corn-meal with a quart of boiling water, and add a quart of milk and a tablespoonful of salt. When cool, add a teacupful of yeast, and enough rye flour to make it as stiff as wheat-bread dough. After it has risen put it in pans and bake an hour and a half.

Brown Bread.—Take one cup of bread-crumbs, one pint of

MEMORANDUM
ON
FRIENDS' RECIPES

130   *DOMESTIC COOKERY.*

sweet milk, one cup of molasses, butter the size of an egg, one teaspoonful of soda, corn-meal enough to make a stiff batter, with salt to taste. Turn the whole into a buttered basin and steam for two hours; then bake in a quick oven half an hour.

Boston Brown Bread.—Take three and three-fourth cupfuls of Indian corn-meal, two and one-half cupfuls rye-meal, two-thirds cupful molasses, one quart milk, either sweet or sour; two even teaspoonfuls soda, dissolved in the milk; steam in a tin pudding boiler five hours; take off the cover and set in the oven to brown.

Corn Bread.—Two heaping cupfuls Indian meal, one cupful wheat flour, two heaping teaspoonfuls Durkee's baking-powder; mix well together while dry; one teaspoonful salt, two tablespoonfuls white sugar, two eggs, one tablespoonful lard, two and a half cupfuls cold milk; beat the eggs, melt the lard, and dissolve the salt and sugar in the milk before adding them to the flour; bake in buttered pans in a *quick* oven.

Graham Bread.—Three quarts of Graham flour; one quart of warm water; one gill of yeast; one gill of sirup; one tablespoonful of salt; one even teaspoonful of soda. Mix thoroughly and put in well-buttered pans to rise. Bake about an hour and a half.

This same mixture may be thinned and baked in gem pans for Graham gems.

Rice Bread.—After a pint of rice has been boiled soft, mix it with two quarts of rice flour or wheat flour. When cold, add half a teaspoonful of yeast, a teaspoonful of salt, and enough milk to make a soft dough. When it has risen, bake in small buttered pans.

Unleavened Bread.—Mix wheat flour into a stiff dough with warm water or milk; add a little lard, or suet, and bake in thin cakes. Bake as soon as mixed, and eat hot.

II.—TOAST.

WHAT TOAST IS GOOD FOR. SIX METHODS OF PREPARING TOAST.

AS a palatable method of disposing of stale bread, as well as to furnish a variety of agreeable dishes, toast is an important factor in the culinary economy of the home. As a dish for invalids it is indispensible.

RECIPES.

Dry Toast is produced by browning stale baker's bread over glowing coals. A toasting fork, or rack, of which there are various patterns, is a great convenience. Do not burn the toast, nor allow it to be so browned as to harden it. It should be eaten hot, as it becomes tough when allowed to cool.

Buttered Toast.—For buttered toast, the slices should be thicker than for dry toast. Butter the slices as toasted, and keep warm until served. Excessive buttering should be avoided.

Egg Toast.—On slices of buttered toast lay poached eggs. Serve with Worcestershire sauce for breakfast.

French Toast.—Beat three eggs light, add one cupful of milk, with pepper and salt to taste. Dip into this slices of bread, then fry them in hot butter to a delicate brown.

Milk Toast.—Toast the bread an even, delicate brown, and pile into a hot dish. Boil milk with a little salt, a teaspoonful of flour, and one of butter, rubbed together; pour it over the toast and serve hot.

Cream Toast.—Take slices of baker's bread from which the crust has been pared and toast it to a golden brown. Have on the range a shallow bowl or pudding-dish, more than half full of boiling water, in which a tablespoonful of butter has been melted. As each slice is toasted, dip in this

MEMORANDUM
ON
FRIENDS' RECIPES

MEMORANDUM
ON
FRIENDS' RECIPES

132   *DOMESTIC COOKERY.*

for a second, sprinkle lightly with salt, and lay in the deep heated dish in which it is to be served. Have ready, by the time all the bread is toasted, a quart of milk scalding hot, but not boiling. Thicken this with two tablespoonfuls of corn-starch or best flour; let it simmer until cooked; put in two tablespoonfuls of butter, and when this is melted, the beaten whites of three eggs. Boil up once, and pour over the toast, lifting the lower slices one by one, that the creamy mixture may run in between them. Cover closely, and set in the oven two or three minutes before serving.

III.—FANCY BREADS.

FANCY BREADS AND PLAIN CAKES; THEIR GENERAL USEFULNESS. EIGHT RECIPES FOR FANCY BREADS.

SOME special preparations come naturally between bread and cake. For convenient classification, they are grouped here under the title of Fancy Breads, though they might as well be classed as Plain Cakes. They serve a good purpose for variety, for luncheon, etc. See plainer forms of cakes.

RECIPES.

Sally Lunn.—One quart of flour, a piece of butter the size of an egg, three tablespoonfuls of sugar, two eggs, two teacupfuls of milk, two teaspoonfuls of cream tartar, one of soda, and a little salt. Scatter the cream of tartar, the sugar, and the salt into the flour; add the eggs, the butter (melted), and one cup of milk; dissolve the soda in the remaining cup, and stir all together steadily a few moments. Bake in two round pans.

Sally Lunn, No. 2.—Rub into a quart of flour two teaspoonfuls of baking-powder; beat together nearly half a cup of butter and two tablespoonfuls of sugar; put into the flour and mix with a pint of milk; then add two eggs, beaten light. Mix and bake as above.

Johnny Cake.—One quart of buttermilk or sour milk, one quart Indian meal, one quart of flour, one cup of molasses, a teaspoonful of soda, two scant teaspoonfuls if the milk is sour, a teaspoonful of salt. Bake in shallow pans in a quick oven.

Hoe Cake.—Scald one quart of Indian-meal in enough water to make a thick batter; add a teaspoonful of salt, one of molasses, and two of butter. Bake on a board before a hot fire or in a pan.

Scotch Short-cake.—Two pounds of fine flour, one pound of fresh, sweet butter, half a pound of finest sifted sugar, throughly knead together without water; roll out to half an inch in thickness, and place it on paper in a shallow pan; bake very slowly until of proper crispness. The cake, to be good, must be very brittle.

Pumpkin Bread.—Stew and strain a sufficient quantity of pumpkin; add enough Indian-meal to stiffen it, with yeast and a little salt; when sufficiently raised, bake as in ordinary bread.

Pone.—This is a dish prepared by the Indians, called also *panne*. Take two cupfuls of corn-meal, two of wheat flour, one of sugar, and half a cup of melted butter. Add one egg, one teaspoonful of salt, one of soda, and two of cream of tartar. Mix with enough milk to make a moderately stiff batter, and bake in a hot oven.

Barley Bread.—In Scotland, Norway, and other climates where wheat is not grown, barley bread is used extensively. It is both wholesome and palatable. Mix the barley meal with warm water and a little salt, but no yeast. Mix to a stiff dough, roll into flat cakes, and bake before the fire or in an oven. Eat hot, with butter.

MEMORANDUM ON FRIENDS' RECIPES

MEMORANDUM
ON
FRIENDS' RECIPES

IV.—ROLLS.

A FAVORITE BREAKFAST DISH. SEVEN VARIETIES OF ROLLS.

A FAVORITE departure from the ordinary forms of bread is furnished in rolls. They are exceedingly popular for breakfast, served warm. There are sufficient variations in rolls to make them suitable for use day after day, if this be desired.

RECIPES.

Plain Rolls.—Boil six potatoes in two quarts of water, and when done pour and press the whole through the colander; when cool, but not cold, add flour to make a thick batter; add half a cup of yeast, or one-half cake of compressed yeast, and set to rise; when light, add half a cup of lard and butter mixed, a tablespoonful of sugar, teaspoonful of salt, and flour to make a soft dough; knead well and set again to rise; when light, knead down again; repeat three or four times; an hour before they are to be used cut in small pieces, roll out, spread with melted butter, and fold over, laying them in a pan so that they will not touch each other; set them in a warm place, and when light bake quickly. Or, make into an oblong roll without spreading and rolling, and just before putting them into the oven, gash deeply across the top with a sharp knife.

English Rolls.—Two pounds of flour, two ounces of butter, three tablespoonfuls of yeast, one pint of warm milk; mix well together, and set in a warm place to rise; knead, and make into rolls; let them rise again and bake twenty minutes.

Breakfast Rolls.—One quart of sifted flour, three teaspoonfuls baking-powder, half teaspoonful salt; mix well together dry, then add three and half gills of cold milk, or enough to make it the consistency of batter, and drop with a spoon

BREAD, BISCUIT, HOT CAKES, ETC. 135

into gem baking-pans, which should have been previously heated very *hot* and buttered.

French Rolls.—One pint of milk, scalded; put into it while hot half a cupful of sugar, and one tablespoonful of butter; when the milk is cool, add a little salt and half a cupful of yeast, or one cake of compressed yeast; stir in flour enough to make a stiff sponge, and when light mix as for bread. Let it rise until light, punch it down with the hand, and let it rise again, and repeat this process two or three times; then turn the dough on to the molding board, and pound with rolling-pin until thin enough to cut. Cut out with a tumbler, brush the surface of each one with melted butter, and fold over. Let the rolls rise on the tins; bake, and while warm brush over the surface with melted butter to make the crust tender.

Vienna Rolls.—One quart sifted flour, two heaping teaspoonfuls of a good baking-powder; mix well while dry; then add a tablespoonful of butter or lard, made a little soft by warming and stirring, and about three-fourths of a pint, or enough cold, sweet milk for a dough of usual stiffness, with about half a teaspoonful of salt dissolved in it. Mix into a dough easily to be handled without sticking; turn on the board and roll out to the thickness of half an inch, cut it out with a large cake-cutter, spread very lightly with butter, fold one-half over the other, and lay them in a greased pan without touching. Wash them over with a little milk, and bake in a hot oven.

Parker House Rolls.—One teacupful of yeast, or one cake of compressed yeast, a little salt, one tablespoonful sugar, piece of lard size of an egg, one pint milk, flour sufficient to mix. Put the milk on the stove to scald with the lard in it. Prepare the flour with salt, sugar, and yeast. Then add the milk, not too hot. Knead thoroughly, and when mixed set to rise; when light, knead again slightly. Then roll out

MEMORANDUM
ON
FRIENDS' RECIPES

and cut with large biscuit-cutter. Spread a little butter on each roll and lap together. Let them rise again very light, and bake in a quick oven.

Geneva Rolls.—Into two pounds of flour break three ounces of butter, add a little salt, and make into a sponge with yeast, previously mixed with milk and water. Allow the batter to rise; then mix in two eggs, made lukewarm by the adding of hot milk, and work the sponge to a light dough. Let it stand for three-quarters of an hour longer; mold into small rolls; place them in buttered pans. When light, brush them with beaten yelks of eggs, and bake for twenty minutes or half an hour. Serve hot.

V.—BISCUIT, RUSK, AND BUNS.

SPECIAL CARE REQUISITE IN THIS DEPARTMENT; ATTENTION TO INGREDIENTS, OVEN, ETC.; HOW TO BAKE THEM; BAKING-POWDER BISCUITS, SODA BISCUITS, ETC.; CARE OF PANS. FIFTEEN RECIPES FOR BISCUITS, BUNS, ETC.

GREAT care is requisite in making biscuits that quantities be accurately observed and that the ingredients used are of proper quality. Flour should be a few months old. New flour will not make good biscuits. It should always be sifted.

The oven, too, needs careful attention. On its condition the success of biscuit baking will depend. Rolls and biscuit should bake quickly. To make them a nice color, rub them over with warm water just before putting them into the oven; to glaze them, brush lightly with milk and sugar.

Baking-powder biscuit and soda biscuit should be made as rapidly as possible, laid into hot pans, and put in a quick oven. Gem pans should always be heated and well greased.

MEMORANDUM
ON
FRIENDS' RECIPES

BREAD, BISCUIT, HOT CAKES, ETC. 137

RECIPES.

Potato Biscuit.—Pare ten potatoes, boil them thoroughly, and mash fine; add two cups of lukewarm milk, two tablespoonfuls of white sugar, half a cup of yeast, and flour enough to make a thin batter. Mix well and allow it to rise. Then add four tablespoonfuls of melted butter, a little salt, and enough flour to make a soft dough. Let this rise again; roll into a sheet about an inch thick, and cut into cakes. Set to rise again, and bake in a quick oven.

Light Biscuit.—When kneading bread, set aside a small loaf for biscuits. Into this, work a heaping tablespoonful of lard and butter mixed and a teaspoonful of sugar. The more it is worked the whiter it will be. As it rises, mold it down twice before making into biscuit. Roll out and cut with a biscuit-cutter. The dough should be quite soft.

Soda Biscuits.—One quart of flour, a tablespoonful of butter and two of lard, a teaspoonful of salt, and one teaspoon even full of cream of tartar, one teaspoonful of soda; sift the cream tartar with the flour dry; rub the butter and lard very thoroughly through it; dissolve the soda in a pint of milk and mix all together. Roll out, adding as little flour as possible; cut with a biscuit-cutter, and bake twenty minutes in a quick oven.

Tea Biscuit.—Take one quart sifted flour, one tablespoonful shortening, half teaspoonful salt, and two teaspoonfuls Durkee's baking-powder; mix well together dry, then add sufficient cold milk or water to form a very soft dough; bake immediately in a quick oven.

Cream Biscuits.—Dissolve one teaspoonful of soda in a quart of sour cream, add to it flour sufficient to make a soft dough and a little salt; or use sour *milk*, and rub a tablespoonful of butter into the flour.

MEMORANDUM
ON
FRIENDS' RECIPES

DOMESTIC COOKERY.

Graham Biscuits.—Take one quart of water or milk, butter the size of an egg, three tablespoonfuls sugar, two of baker's yeast, and a pinch of salt; take enough white flour to use up the water, making it the consistency of batter cakes; add the rest of the ingredients and as much Graham flour as can be stirred in with a spoon; set it away till morning; in the morning grease the pan, flour your hands; take a lump of dough the size of a large egg, roll it lightly between the palms, and let the biscuits rise twenty minutes, then bake in a tolerably hot oven.

Maryland Biscuits.—Take three pints of sifted flour, one tablespoonful of good lard, one pint of cold water, salt to the taste; make into a stiff dough; work it till it cracks or blisters, then break, but do not cut it, into suitable portions, and make into biscuits; stick the top of each with a fork and bake.

Yorkshire Biscuits.—Make a batter with flour sufficient and one quart of boiling hot milk. When the batter has cooled to lukewarmness, add a teacupful of yeast and a half teaspoonful of salt. Set to rise again and let it become very light; then stir in a half teaspoonful of soda, two eggs, and a tablespoonful of melted butter. Add flour enough to make the dough into small, round cakes; let them rise fifteen minutes, and bake in a slow oven.

Short Biscuits.—Mix one quart of flour with a quarter pound of butter melted in boiling water. Add enough cold milk to make a stiff dough. Work into small biscuits and bake in a quick oven.

Flavored Biscuits.—Biscuit dough made as for Light Biscuit may be flavored with any essence, or with lemon or orange peel, as desired.

Tea Rusk.—Three cups of flour, one cup of milk, three-

MEMORANDUM ON FRIENDS' RECIPES

fourths of a cup of sugar, two heaping tablespoonfuls of butter, melted; two eggs, three teaspoonfuls baking-powder. Let them rise, and bake in a moderate oven. Glaze while hot with white of egg, in which has been stirred, not beaten, a little powdered sugar, or sift the powdered sugar in while the egg is still moist on the top. Rusks should never be eaten hot.

Sweet Rusk.—One pint of warm milk—new is best—one-half cup of butter, one cup of sugar, two eggs, one teaspoonful of salt, two tablespoonfuls of yeast; make a sponge with the milk, yeast, and enough flour to make a thin batter, and let it rise over night. In the morning add the sugar, butter, eggs, and salt, well beaten up together, with enough flour to make a soft dough; let it rise again; then work out into round balls, and set to rise a third time. Bake in a moderate oven.

Buns.—One cupful of warm water, one cupful of sweet milk, yeast and sugar, with flour enough to make a stiff batter; let this rise over night; in the morning add a cupful of sugar, a cupful of raisins or currants, mold well; let it rise till light, then make into buns; rise again till very light, and bake. Use any spice desired.

Hot Cross Buns.—Three cupfuls sweet milk; one cupful of yeast; flour to make thick batter. Set this as a sponge over night. In the morning add one cupful of sugar; one-half cupful butter, melted; half a nutmeg; one saltspoonful salt, and flour enough to roll out like biscuit. Knead well, and set to rise five hours. Roll half an inch thick, cut into round cakes, and lay in rows in a buttered baking-pan. When they have stood half an hour, make a cross upon each with a knife, and put instantly into the oven. Bake to a light brown, and brush over with a feather or soft bit of rag. dipped in the white of an egg beaten up stiff with white sugar.

MEMORANDUM
ON
FRIENDS' RECIPES

Pop Overs.—Mix four cupfuls of flour, four cupfuls of milk, four eggs, and a little salt. This quantity will make about twenty puffs in gem-pans, which must be baked quick and done to a nice brown.

VI.—MUFFINS AND WAFFLES.

HOW MUFFINS AND WAFFLES DIFFER; THEIR RELATION TO OTHER KINDRED PREPARATIONS; MUFFIN-RINGS AND WAFFLE-IRONS; WHEN TO USE MUFFINS AND WAFFLES; HOW TO SERVE THEM. ELEVEN RECIPES FOR MUFFINS AND WAFFLES.

MUFFINS are baked in rings on a griddle, or in gem-pans, over a quick fire. Waffles are baked in waffle-irons, which inclose the batter and imprint both sides of the cake as it rises in the process of baking. Both muffins and waffles form a medium between bread and biscuits on the one side and griddle-cakes on the other. Muffin-rings were formerly about four inches in diameter, but now, with better taste, they are used much smaller. The approved waffle-irons of to-day are circular, baking four waffles at once, and suspended on a pivot that permits them to be turned with a touch of the fork. Both muffins and waffles are suitable for tea, and with stewed chicken and such delicacies they are really delicious. They should always be served hot and with the best of butter. Waffles and catfish are a famous dish at some eating-houses.

RECIPES.

Muffins.—Two eggs lightly beaten, one quart of flour, one teaspoonful of salt, three teaspoonfuls of Durkee's baking-powder, one tablespoonful of melted butter, one pint of milk, and two teaspoonfuls of vanilla extract, if liked. Beat up quickly to the consistency of a cake batter; bake in buttered gem-pans in a hot oven.

BREAD, BISCUIT, HOT CAKES, ETC.

Muffins, No. 2.—One cup of home-made yeast or half of a compressed yeast cake, one pint of sweet milk, two eggs, two tablespoonfuls of melted butter, two tablespoonfuls of sugar. Beat the butter, sugar, and eggs well together; then stir in the milk, slightly warmed, and thicken with flour to the consistency of griddle-cakes. When light, bake in muffin-rings or on a griddle. If wanted for tea, the batter should be mixed immediately after breakfast. Muffins should never be cut with a knife, but be pulled open with the fingers.

Rice Muffins.—Take one quart of sour milk, three well-beaten eggs, a little salt, a teaspoonful of soda, and enough of rice flour to thicken to a stiff batter. Bake in rings.

Hominy Muffins.—Substitute hominy, well cooked and mashed, for the rice, and proceed as above.

Bread Muffins.—Cut the crust off four thick slices of bread; put them in a pan and pour on them just enough boiling water to soak them thoroughly. Let them stand an hour, covered; then drain off the water and stir the bread to a smooth paste. Stir in two tablespoonfuls of flour, a half pint of milk, and three well-beaten eggs. Bake to a delicate brown in well-buttered muffin-rings.

Graham Muffins.—One quart of Graham flour, two teaspoonfuls of baking-powder, a piece of butter the size of a walnut, one egg, one tablespoonful of sugar, one-half teaspoonful of salt, milk enough to make a batter as thick as for griddle-cakes. Bake in gem-pans or muffin-rings in a hot oven.

Corn Muffins.—Mix two cupfuls of corn-meal, two cupfuls of flour, one cupful of sugar, half a cupful of melted butter, two eggs, and one teaspoonful of salt. Dissolve one teaspoonful of soda and two of cream tartar in a little milk, and beat it through. Add milk enough to make a moderately stiff batter, and bake in rings or gem-pans.

MEMORANDUM
ON
FRIENDS' RECIPES

MEMORANDUM
ON
FRIENDS' RECIPES

142 DOMESTIC COOKERY.

Crumpets.—Three cupfuls of warm milk, half a cupful of yeast, two tablespoonfuls of melted butter, one saltspoonful each of salt and soda dissolved in hot water, flour enough to make a good batter. Set these ingredients—leaving out the butter and soda—as a sponge. When very light, beat in the melted butter, with a *very* little flour; stir in the soda hard, fill patty-pans or muffin-rings with the mixture, and let them stand fifteen minutes before baking.

Raised Waffles.—One quart of warm milk, one tablespoonful of butter, three eggs, one gill of yeast, one tablespoonful of salt, and flour to make a stiff batter. Set to rise, and bake in waffle-irons, which must be well heated before used.

Quick Waffles.—One quart flour, two teaspoonfuls Durkee's baking-powder, one teaspoonful salt; mix dry; then stir in one tablespoonful melted butter, two well-beaten eggs, and enough cold, sweet milk for a batter thin enough to pour; bake at once in waffle-irons.

Rice Waffles.—Mix a teacupful and a half of boiling rice with a pint of milk, rubbing it smooth over the fire. Take from the fire and add a pint of cold milk and a teaspoonful of salt. Stir in four well-beaten eggs with enough flour to make a thin batter, and bake as above. Waffles should always be served hot. Powdered sugar with a flavor of powdered cinnamon makes a pleasing dressing for them.

VII.—GRIDDLE-CAKES.

WHAT GRIDDLE-CAKES ARE ; HINTS ABOUT GRIDDLES ; HOW TO COOK GRIDDLE-CAKES ; HOW TO SERVE THEM ; WHEN TO SERVE THEM ; WITH WHAT TO SERVE THEM. TEN RECIPES FOR GRIDDLE-CAKES.

CAKES made of a batter so thin that it flows easily upon a griddle, and that can, therefore, be quickly baked and be served hot, are griddle-cakes, and great favorites they are.

BREAD, BISCUIT, HOT CAKES, ETC. 143

MEMORANDUM
ON
FRIENDS' RECIPES

All new griddles are hard to manage, but as the only way to get old ones is to make them out of new ones, we are shut up to the necessity of using the new, though they do not work so well. Opinions divide between iron griddles and those of soapstone. The latter require no greasing. Hence trouble is saved, and the smoke of the fat used in the constant greasing of a hot iron griddle is entirely avoided. But still, many housekeepers prefer the old style.

A hot griddle is essential to good griddle-cakes. But it must not be hot enough to burn before it bakes. A cold griddle will make cakes tough, unpalatable, and decidedly unwholesome.

Hot cakes may be served with powdered sugar, molasses, maple sirup, or any other of the many excellent sirups in the market. Cold days are the gala days for hot cakes. Time immemorial, buckwheat cakes and sausage have gone to the table side by side. There is delightful harmony in this union; but to serve hot cakes and fish together would introduce discord into the best regulated family. There is an eminent fitness between hot cakes and certain other dishes, and it must never be disregarded.

RECIPES.

Buckwheat Cakes.—One quart of buckwheat-meal, one pint of wheat-flour or Indian-meal, half a teacupful of yeast, salt to taste; mix the flour, buckwheat, and salt with as much water moderately warm as will make it into a thin batter; beat it well, then add the yeast; when well mixed, set it in a warm place to rise; as soon as it is very light, grease the griddle and bake the cakes to a delicate brown. Butter them with good butter and serve hot.

Graham Griddle-cakes.—Scald a cupful of Indian-meal in a pint of boiling water, and strain it over night. Thin it with a quart of milk, and make into a sponge with a cupful of

MEMORANDUM
ON
FRIENDS' RECIPES

144   *DOMESTIC COOKERY.*

Graham flour, a large tablespoonful of molasses, and half a cupful of yeast. In the morning, add salt to taste, a cupful of white flour, half a teaspoonful of soda, dissolved in hot water, and a tablespoonful of butter or lard. Stir in enough water to make batter of the right consistency, and bake on a hot griddle.

Flannel Cakes.—Three eggs, one quart of sweet milk, about one quart of flour, a small teaspoonful of salt, two tablespoonfuls of prepared baking-powder; beat the yelks, and half of the milk, salt, and flour together; then the remainder of the milk; and last, the whites of the eggs well beaten. Bake in small cakes on a hot griddle.

Flannel Cakes, No. 2.—One quart of milk, three eggs, one cupful of yeast, one dessertspoonful of salt, flour enough for a thinnish batter, and a teaspoonful of butter; set to rise; bake like buckwheat cakes. Cakes half Indian and half wheat are very nice, and good cakes may be made even without the eggs.

Rice Cakes.—Soak a cupful of rice five or six hours in enough warm water to cover it. Then boil slowly till soft. While still warm, but not hot, stir in a tablespoonful of butter, a tablespoonful of sugar, a teaspoonful of salt, and a quart of milk. When cold, add three eggs, beaten very light. Sift a half teaspoonful of cream of tartar into a quarter cupful of rice flour, and add them to the batter, first beating into it a quarter teaspoonful of soda dissolved in hot water.

Rice Cakes, No. 2.—Boil a cupful of rice until quite soft, setting it aside until cool. Beat three eggs very light, and put them into the rice, with a pint of flour, into which you have sifted three teaspoonfuls of prepared baking-powder. Add a teaspoonful of butter and one of salt, making it into a batter with a quart of milk. Bake on a griddle.

Hominy Cakes.—Mix with cold boiled hominy an equal quantity of white flour until perfectly smooth; add a teaspoonful of salt and thin off with buttermilk, in part of which a teaspoonful of soda has been dissolved; when of the proper consistency for griddle cakes, add a dessertspoonful of melted butter, and bake as usual.

Sour Milk Cakes.—One pint sour milk, one teaspoonful of soda, a little salt, two eggs, and flour to make a thin batter; bake on a hot griddle.

Indian Griddle Cakes.—One large cupful Indian-meal, four tablespoonfuls of wheat flour, two tablespoonfuls of Durkee's baking-powder, one teaspoonful salt, mix together dry, then add sufficient cold water for a batter; bake at once on a hot griddle.

Slapjacks.—One pint of milk, three eggs, one teaspoonful of soda, and one of salt, flour enough to make a thin batter. Butter your griddle, and fry them the size of a tea-plate; when one is done, turn it on the dish, sprinkle with a little white sugar, and continue in this way till they are all fried. Always fry them with butter. A little nutmeg may be grated with the sugar on each cake.

VIII.—YEAST AND YEAST CAKES.

NATURE OF YEAST; ACTION OF YEAST IN DOUGH; CAUSES OF LIGHT BREAD AND HEAVY BREAD; CARE OF YEAST. SIX RECIPES FOR YEAST AND YEAST CAKES.

IN this chapter, yeast has been so often referred to that its special consideration seems important just here. Analytically considered, it consists of an innumerable quantity of infinitesimal fungi, called the *yeast-plant*. The remarkable characteristic of these minute plants is, that under favoring conditions they multiply to an incredible

MEMORANDUM
ON
FRIENDS' RECIPES

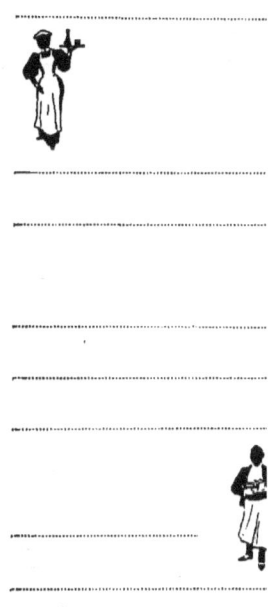

MEMORANDUM
ON
FRIENDS' RECIPES

146　　　　　*DOMESTIC COOKERY.*

extent in a very short time. Thus the production of yeast, in proper mixtures, is an easy matter.

When yeast is placed in dough, it immediately produces fermentation, in the process of which gases are generated, which permeate the dough, filling it with gas-vessels and so producing the spongy appearance so familiar in raised bread. If this process goes too far, it sours the dough and unfits it for food. If arrested by placing the dough in a hot oven, the gases will be driven off by the heat, and the thin dough walls will be set and baked. If the oven be slow, the gases will be driven off, the dough walls will collapse, and heavy bread will be the result. The proper use of yeast is most important, therefore. It must be watched as carefully as any other tender plant. Excessive heat or cold, or rough mechanical usage will quickly destroy it.

RECIPES.

Brewer's Yeast.—This yeast is produced during the process of fermenting malt liquors. It is the most effective yeast in use, being about eight times the strength of any other kind.

Hop Yeast.—Boil four pounds of pared potatoes in three quarts of water and stir through a colander. Boil a handful of hops in one quart of water for ten minutes, and strain this upon the potatoes. Add a half pint of salt, a half pint of sugar, and a tablespoonful of ginger. The quantity should now measure five quarts. If it be less, add enough tepid water to make the quantity correct. When lukewarm, add a half pint of home-brewed yeast, mix thoroughly, and stand in a warm place till bubbles form on the surface, which indicate that it has become light. Cover the vessel containing the yeast, and allow it to stand in a dry, cool place. It will keep well for months. A gill of this yeast will suffice for an ordinary baking, requiring a quart of water or milk.

BREAD, BISCUIT, HOT CAKES, ETC.

Patent Yeast.—Boil two ounces of hops in four quarts of water for a half hour. Strain and cool till lukewarm, then add a handful of salt, a half pound of sugar, and a pound of flour, all mixed well and beaten up together. After it has stood forty-eight hours, add three pounds of potatoes, boiled and well-mashed. Let it stand twenty-four hours, stirring it often; then strain and bottle. It is ready for immediate use, or will keep several months. Keep in a cool place.

Potato Yeast.—Pare and boil six potatoes; mash them through a colander and mix with them six tablespoonfuls of flour. Pour on a quart of boiling water from that in which the potatoes were boiled. Add half a teacupful of sugar, a tablespoonful of salt, and when cool, a teacupful of home-made yeast, or one-fourth the quantity of brewer's yeast.

Yeast Cakes.—Thicken good yeast with Indian-meal till it becomes a stiff batter. A little rye will make it adhere better. Make into cakes an inch thick and two by three inches in area. Dry them in the air, but not in the sun. Keep them in a bag in a cool, dry place. One of these cakes is enough for four quarts of flour. To use them, soak in milk or water several hours and use as other yeast.

Compressed Yeast.—There are many valuable preparations of this yeast, excellent in quality, and convenient to use. They must be fresh, however, or they will fail of their purpose.

MEMORANDUM
ON
FRIENDS' RECIPES

MEMORANDUM
ON
FRIENDS' RECIPES

XI.—PASTRY AND PUDDINGS.

CARE IN INGREDIENTS AND MANIPULATION ESSENTIAL; KEEP INGREDIENTS COOL; MIX QUICKLY; HOW TO SHORTEN; HOW TO ROLL; THE FILLING; THE BAKING. SEVENTY-NINE RECIPES FOR PASTRY AND PUDDINGS.

THAT pastry may be wholesome and appetizing, great care in the selection of ingredients and in their manipulation is absolutely essential. One fact must always be borne in mind—that inferior ingredients cannot be made into superior compounds—though the finest ingredients may be ruined by careless or unskillful handling. Some suggestions of general application are therefore desirable.

Be careful to have all the materials *cool*, and the butter and lard hard; use cold water (ice-water if convenient); use a cool knife, and work on a marble slab if it can be had.

Put the ingredients together quickly, handling as little as possible; slow mixing and much contact with the hands or fingers make tough crust. Always use well-sifted flour.

Except in puff-paste, lard and butter in about equal proportions make the best crust; if made of butter alone, it is almost sure to be tough. That of lard alone, though tender, is usually white and insipid. Beef drippings, or the drippings of fresh pork, make a very light and palatable crust, lighter and more tender indeed than that made with butter alone, much better tasted than that made with lard alone, and quite equal to that made with butter and lard combined. Never use mutton drippings in crust.

Use very little salt and very little water; pour the latter in gradually, only a few drops at a time, unless you want tough crust.

Use plenty of flour on your paste-board, to keep the paste from sticking. Work the crust of one pie at a time, and always roll from you—one way only.

The filling for the pie should be perfectly cool when put in, or it will make the bottom crust heavy.

In making juicy pies, cut a slit in the top to let the steam escape, else the pie will be puffed unduly.

The oven should be hot, but not sufficiently so to scorch or to set the paste before it has had time to rise; if too slack, the paste will not rise at all, but will be white and clammy. The best paste has a tinge of yellow. If permitted to scorch or brown, even the best paste becomes rancid.

RECIPES.

Pie Crust.—Take one-half cupful of lard, one-half cupful of butter, one quart of sifted flour, one cupful of cold water and a little salt. Rub the butter and lard *slightly* into the flour; wet it with the water, mixing it as little as possible. This quantity will make two large or three small pies.

Pie Crust Glaze.—To prevent juice from soaking the under crust, beat up the white of an egg, and before filling the pie, brush over the crust with the beaten egg. Brush over the top crust also, to give it a beautiful yellow brown.

Puff Paste.—Take one pound of sifted flour, on which sprinkle a very little sugar; take the yelks of one or two eggs, and beat into them a little ice-water, and pour gently into the centre of the flour, and work into a firm paste, adding water as is necessary; divide three-quarters of a pound or a pound of firm, solid butter, as you prefer, into three parts; roll out the paste, and spread one part of the butter on half of the paste; fold the other half over, and roll out again, repeating the process until the butter is all rolled in; then set the paste on the ice for fifteen or twenty

MEMORANDUM
ON
FRIENDS' RECIPES

MEMORANDUM ON FRIENDS' RECIPES

150   *DOMESTIC COOKERY.*

minutes, after which roll out again three times, each time rolling it the opposite direction; then put on the ice again until cold, when it is ready for use. Such paste will keep several days in a refrigerator, but should not be allowed to freeze.

Paste Shells.—Take sufficient rich puff-paste prepared as in the preceding recipe, roll very thin, cut to shape, and bake in a brisk oven in tin pans. Baked carefully, before filling with fruit, the paste rises better. When cool, the shells may be filled with stewed fruit, jelly, preserves, rich cream whipped to a stiff froth, raspberries, strawberries, or sliced peaches. These are delicious light desserts. Raspberries, strawberries, or sliced peaches, smothered with whipped cream on these shells, are really exquisite.

Apple Pie.—Line a pie plate with paste, and fill it heaping full with tart apples, sliced very thin. Sweeten and spice to taste, mixing well into the apples. Put in plenty of butter, and moisten well with cream. Bake until the apples are thoroughly done. Use no upper crust.

Apple Meringue Pie.—Stew and sweeten ripe, juicy apples. Mash smooth, and season with nutmeg. Fill the crust, and bake until just done. Spread over the apple a thick meringue, made by whipping to a stiff froth the whites of three eggs for each pie, sweetening with a tablespoonful of powdered sugar for each egg. Flavor this with vanilla; beat until it will stand alone, and cover the pie three-quarters of an inch thick. Set back in the oven until the meringue is well set. Eat cold.

Peach Meringue Pie.—Proceed as above in all respects, simply substituting peaches for apples. Whipped cream will make a delightful substitute for the whipped egg in either of these meringue pies.

Peach Pie.—Bake rich shells about two-thirds done; if your peaches are fully ripe, cut them into halves or quarters, put in the shell, sweeten and flavor to taste, cover or not as you choose, and finish baking in a *quick* oven; if the peaches are ripe, but not soft, it will improve the flavor to sugar them down some hours before you wish to use them; if not ripe, they should be stewed.

Gooseberry Pie.—Stew the gooseberries with plenty of white sugar, and use plain puff-paste for crust.

Cherry Pie.—Having removed the stones, put in sugar as may be needed, and stew the cherries slowly till they are quite done, if you use shells, or till nearly done if you use paste. A few of the pits added in stewing increase the richness of the flavor; but they should not go into the pies. If baked slowly the cherries need not be stewed at all.

Rhubarb Pie.—Remove the skin from the stalks; cut them in small pieces; pour boiling water over and let stand for ten minutes; drain thoroughly; then fill the pie-dish evenly full; put in plenty of sugar, a little butter, and dredge a trifle of flour evenly over the top; cover with a thin crust, and bake the same as apple pie. Equal quantities of apple and rhubarb used in the same manner make a very good pie.

Pumpkin Pie.—Stew the pumpkin until thoroughly done, and pass it through a colander. To one quart of stewed pumpkin, add three eggs, and one pint of milk. Sweeten, and spice with ground ginger and cinnamon to taste. Add butter, rose water, and a little brandy. The quantity of milk used will vary as the pumpkin may be moist or dry.

Sweet Potato Pie.—Scrape clean two good-sized sweet potatoes; boil; when tender, rub through the colander; beat the yelks of three eggs light; stir with a pint of sweet milk into the potato; add a small teacupful of sugar, a pinch of salt; flavor with a little fresh lemon, or lemon extract; bake to a nice brown; when done, make a meringue top with the whites of eggs and powdered sugar; brown this a moment in the oven.

MEMORANDUM
ON
FRIENDS' RECIPES

MEMORANDUM
ON
FRIENDS' RECIPES

DOMESTIC COOKERY.

Custard Pie.—Take one quart of milk, five eggs, four tablespoonfuls of sugar, a small piece of butter. Sift over the top Durkee's mixed spice.

Lemon Pie.—Let two cupfuls of water come to a boil; put in two tablespoonfuls of corn-starch dissolved. When it has boiled enough, take it from the stove, add the juice and rind of two lemons, two cupfuls of sugar, a piece of butter the size of a walnut, and the yelks of two eggs. Beat the whites of these eggs with pulverized sugar, and put on the top of the pies when done. Put into the oven to brown.

Orange Pie.—Beat the yelks of three eggs until light, and add to them the juice and grated rind of one orange, three-quarters of a cupful of sugar, and a tablespoonful of corn-starch mixed in half a cupful of water. Bake without upper crust, using the whites of the eggs for meringue.

Cream Pie.—One pint of milk, scalded; two tablespoonfuls of corn-starch, three tablespoonfuls of sugar, yelks of two eggs. Wet the starch with a little cold milk; beat the eggs and sugar until light, and stir the whole into the scalding milk. Flavor with lemon or vanilla, and set aside to cool. Line a plate with pie-crust and bake; fill it with the cream, and cover with frosting made of the whites of the eggs, beaten dry, with two tablespoonfuls of sugar. Bake to a delicate brown.

Cocoanut Pie.—One quart of milk, half a pound of grated cocoanut, three eggs, six tablespoonfuls of sugar, butter the size of an egg. Bake in open shells.

Cheese-cake Pie.—This may be made from the above recipe, substituting cottage-cheese for the cocoanut. Sprinkle the top with Durkee's mixed spices.

Mince Pie.—Seven pounds of beef, three and a half pounds of beef suet, five pounds of raisins, two pounds of currants, one-half peck of apples, four pounds of sugar, three-quarters of a pound of citron, one-quarter of a pound of preserved lemon, two large oranges, four nutmegs, half an ounce of cinnamon, half an ounce of cloves, and three pints of brandy. This quantity of mince-meat will make from twenty to twenty-five pies. When making the pies, moisten the meat with sweet cider.

Tarts.—Use the best of puff-paste; roll it out a little thicker than pie-crust, and cut with a large biscuit-cutter twice as many as you intend to have of tarts. Then cut out of half of these a small round in the centre, which will leave a circular rim of crust; lift this up carefully, and lay it on the other pieces. Bake in pans, so providing both the bottom and the top crusts. Fill with any kind of preserves, jam, or jelly.

Pineapple Tart.—Take a fine, large, ripe pineapple; remove the leaves and quarter it without paring, grate it down till you come to the rind; strew plenty of powdered sugar over the grated fruit; cover it, and let it rest for an hour; then put it into a porcelain kettle, and steam in its own sirup till perfectly soft; have ready some empty shells of puff-paste, or bake in patty-pans. When they are cool, fill them full with the grated pineapple; add more sugar, and lay round the rim a border of puff-paste.

Tea Baskets.—Make a short, sweetened pie-crust; roll thin, and partly bake in sheets; before it is quite done take from the oven, cut in squares of four inches or so, take up two diagonal corners and pinch together, which makes them basket-shaped; now fill with whipped cream, or white of egg or both, well sweetened and flavored, and return to the oven for a few minutes.

Strawberry Short-cake.—Make a good biscuit crust, and roll out about one-quarter of an inch thick, and cut into two cakes the same size and shape; spread one over lightly with melted butter, and lay the other over it, and bake in a

MEMORANDUM
ON
FRIENDS' RECIPES

MEMORANDUM
ON
FRIENDS' RECIPES

hot oven. When done, they will fall apart. Butter them well as usual. Mix the berries with plenty of sugar, and set in a warm place until needed. Spread the berries and cakes in alternate layers, berries on the top, and over all spread whipped cream or charlotte russe. The juice that has run from the fruit can be sent to the table in a tureen and served with the cake as it is cut.

Strawberry Short-cake, No. 2.—Take one quart of flour and sift into it two teaspoonfuls of sea-foam, a little salt, quarter of a pound of butter rubbed in, with milk enough to moisten properly. Handle as little as possible, divide into two parts, roll each flat, and place in two jelly pans. Bake quickly, then split apart the top and bottom of each crust; spread on plenty of butter, have the strawberries washed and drained in a sieve, crush them slightly, and sweeten well. Spread plenty of berries over each layer of the crust, and have some of the crushed and sweetened berries in a deep dish. When the cake is cut and served, cover each piece with the crushed berries, using this as sauce.

Batter Pudding.—Beat the yelks and whites of four eggs separately, and mix them with six or eight ounces of flour and a saltspoonful of salt. Make the batter of the proper consistency by adding a little more than a pint of milk; mix carefully; butter a baking-tin, pour the mixture into it, and bake three-quarters of an hour. Serve with vanilla sauce.

Apple Batter Pudding.—Core and peel eight apples, put in a dish, fill the places from which the cores have been taken with brown sugar, cover and bake. Beat the yelks of four eggs light, add two teacupfuls of flour, with three even teaspoonfuls of baking-powder sifted with it, one pint of milk, and teaspoonful of salt, then the whites well beaten; pour over the apples and bake. Use sauce with it.

Suet Pudding.—Take a pint of milk, two eggs well beaten, half a pound of finely chopped suet, and a teaspoonful of

PASTRY AND PUDDINGS.

salt. Add flour gradually till you have a pretty thick batter; boil two hours, and eat with molasses.

Suet Pudding, No. 2.—One cupful of suet or butter, one cupful of molasses, one bowlful of raisins and currants, one egg, one cupful of sweet milk, one teaspoonful of saleratus dissolved in milk; one-fourth teaspoonful of cloves, and one-half of nutmeg. Mix stiff with flour and steam three hours. A fine sauce for this pudding may be made thus: One cupful of butter and two cupfuls of sugar, beat into a cream; add three eggs beaten very light; stir in two tablespoonfuls of boiling water. Flavor with wine, brandy, or vanilla.

Hasty Pudding.—Wet a heaping cupful of Indian-meal and a half cupful of flour with a pint of milk; stir it into a quart of boiling water. Boil hard for half an hour, stirring from the bottom almost constantly. Put in a teaspoonful of salt and a tablespoonful of butter, and simmer ten minutes longer. Turn into a deep, uncovered dish, and eat with sugar and cream, or sugar and butter with nutmeg.

Baked Hasty Pudding.—Take from a pint of new milk sufficient to mix into a thin batter two ounces of flour, put the remainder, with a *small* pinch of salt, into a clean saucepan, and when it boils quickly, stir the flour briskly to it; keep it stirred over a gentle fire for ten minutes, pour it out, and when it has become a little cool, mix with it two ounces of fresh butter, three of powdered sugar, the grated rind of a small lemon, four large or five small eggs, and half a glass of brandy or as much orange-flower water. Bake the pudding half an hour in a gentle oven.

Minute Pudding.—Take six eggs, two tablespoonfuls of sugar, one cupful of flour, a lump of butter large as an egg, and half a nutmeg; you may add, if desired, a half pound of raisins; mix well and bake quick.

Corn Pudding.—Twelve ears of sweet corn grated to one

MEMORANDUM
ON
FRIENDS' RECIPES

MEMORANDUM
ON
FRIENDS' RECIPES

quart of sweet milk; add a quarter of a pound of good butter, quarter of a pound of sugar, and four eggs; bake from three to four hours.

Farina Pudding.—Boil one quart of milk, stir in slowly three tablespoonfuls of farina, let it boil a few minutes; beat two eggs and four tablespoonfuls of sugar with one pint of milk, and mix thoroughly with the farina; when it has cooled so as to be little more than lukewarm, put in pans, and bake in a *moderate* oven. Serve with cream sauce.

Plain Tapioca Pudding.—A cup not quite full of tapioca to a quart of milk; let it stand on the side of the range till it swells; add while hot a tablespoonful of butter and a cupful of white sugar, and let it cool; then add five eggs (three will do quite well), well beaten, and flavor to your taste. To be baked from three-quarters of an hour to an hour. It is very nice when dressed with wine sauce, but may be eaten with plainer dressing.

Tapioca and Apple Pudding.—One coffeecupful of Durkee's farina-tapioca, one dozen good-flavored, tart apples, pared and cored, one quart of water, a little salt. Cover the tapioca with the water, and set it in a tolerably warm place to soak five or six hours, stirring occasionally. Lay the apples in a deep dish, put a little sugar and spice in the centre, pour over the tapioca, and bake one hour.

Peaches may be substituted for apples, which will make a delightful dish. Serve with hard sauce.

Vermicelli Pudding.—Into a pint and a half of boiling milk drop four ounces of fresh vermicelli, and keep it simmering and stirred up gently ten minutes, when it will have become very thick; then mix with it three and one-half ounces of sugar, two ounces of butter, and a little salt. When the whole is well blended, pour it out, beat it for a few minutes to cool it, then add by degrees four well-beaten eggs, and the grated rind of a lemon; pour a little clarified butter over the top; bake it from one-half to three-fourths of an hour.

Sago Pudding.—Two large spoonfuls of sago boiled in one quart of water, the peel of one lemon, a little nutmeg; when cold add four eggs and a little salt. Bake about one hour and a half. Serve with sugar and cream.

Arrow-root Pudding.—Boil one quart of milk, and stir into it four heaping tablespoonfuls of arrow-root dissolved in a little milk, mixed with four well-beaten eggs and two tablespoonfuls of white sugar. Boil three minutes. Eat with cream and sugar. This pudding is improved by flavoring with lemon. It should be prepared for table by pouring into wet molds.

Cocoanut Pudding.—One cocoanut finely grated (use both the meat and milk), one quart of milk, one cupful of sugar, five eggs, half a cupful of butter, a little salt, and a teaspoonful of rose-water. Boil the milk, and pour upon the cocoanut, add the eggs well beaten, and the other ingredients, and bake in a deep dish, with or without an undercrust.

Cocoanut Pudding, No. 2.—Put a pint of milk to boil in a farina kettle. Take four tablespoonfuls of corn-starch and dissolve it in a little cold milk, then stir it into the boiling milk. Add half a cupful of sugar, the well-beaten whites of four eggs, half a grated cocoanut, and a teaspoonful of vanilla extract; turn into a mold to cool. For a suitable sauce put a pint of milk to boil, beat the yelks of four eggs with two tablespoonfuls of sugar till light, then add the boiling milk, with a tablespoonful of vanilla extract. Cook for two minutes in a farina kettle, then turn out to cool.

Rice Pudding.—One quart of milk, three eggs, half a cupful of rice, three-fourths of a cupful of sugar, half a cupful of butter, one cupful of raisins, seeded. Soak the rice in a

MEMORANDUM
ON
FRIENDS' RECIPES

158   DOMESTIC COOKERY.

pint of the milk an hour, then set the saucepan containing it where it will slowly heat to a boil. Boil five minutes; remove and let it cool. Beat the eggs, add the sugar and butter, the rice and the milk in which it was cooked, with the pint of unboiled milk, and finally the raisins. Grate nutmeg on the top, and bake three-quarters of an hour, or until the custard is well set and of a light brown. Serve with hard brandy sauce.

Rice Pudding, No. 2.—Three-quarters of a cupful of soaked rice, one cupful of sugar, three pints of milk, one tablespoonful of butter. Season with lemon rind or spice to taste. Bake three-quarters of an hour.

Cottage Pudding.—Three cupfuls flour, or sufficient to make the batter; one teaspoonful butter, one cupful sugar, two eggs, one cupful milk, half a teaspoonful soda, one teaspoonful each of cream of tartar and salt; mix the cream of tartar with the flour, beat the whites of the eggs; put the butter, sugar, and yelks of the eggs together; then work in the milk, soda, and salt, adding gradually the flour and whites of the eggs; there should be flour enough to make a fairly stiff batter; butter a mold or dish, and bake; it may be turned out or served from the dish; to be eaten with any liquid sauce.

Rennet Pudding.—Take one quart of milk, and warm it enough to remove the chill; in summer it does not need warming at all; stir into it three tablespoonfuls of granulated sugar, two of rose-water, and four of rennet wine; stir it gently, not more than a minute; let it stand, and do not move it till it is curdled, then place it gently in the ice chest and grate nutmeg on the top. Be careful not to shake it in moving, for if the curd is disturbed it will turn to whey.

Lemon Pudding.—Take the yellow part of the rind of one, and the juice of two large, juicy lemons. Beat to a cream half a pound of butter, and the same of powdered sugar. Beat

MEMORANDUM ON FRIENDS' RECIPES

six eggs very light, and stir them gradually into the mixture. Add a glass of wine or brandy. Put the whole into a dish with a broad edge; put round two or three layers of puff-paste. Bake half an hour, and when cold sprinkle white sugar over it. Oranges may be used in the same way. To be eaten cold.

Orange Pudding.—Two oranges—the juice of both and grated peel of one; juice of one lemon; one half-pound lady's-fingers—stale and crumbled; two cupfuls of milk; four eggs, one-half cupful sugar; one tablespoonful cornstarch, wet with water; one tablespoonful butter, melted. Soak the crumbs in the cold milk, whip up light, and add the eggs and sugar, already beaten to a cream with the batter. Next add the corn-starch, and when the mold is buttered and water boiling hard, stir in the juice and peel of the fruit. Do this quickly, and plunge the mold directly into the hot water. Boil one hour; turn out and eat with very sweet brandy sauce.

Apple Pudding.—Fill an earthen baking-dish with finely chopped apples; season with sugar and nutmeg, add a little water, set it on the back of the range until the apples are tender; then make a crust of one teacupful of sweet milk, one tablespoonful of butter, a little salt, one teaspoonful baking-powder, flour enough to roll out; lay the crust on top of the apples and bake. To be eaten hot with sweet sauce, flavored with lemon or vanilla. Other kinds of fruit may be used in the same manner.

Bread Pudding.—One pint bread-crumbs; one quart milk; rind of one lemon grated into milk; yelks four eggs, beaten and mixed with one-half cupful sugar. Bake one-half hour. Spread meringue on top.

Fruit Bread Pudding.—Soak three large cupfuls of very fine bread-crumbs, through which has been mixed two teaspoonfuls of cream tartar, in a quart of milk; next, beat in three

MEMORANDUM
ON
FRIENDS' RECIPES

eggs well whipped, and a cupful of sugar; add half a cupful of finely chopped suet, a little salt, nutmeg, and cinnamon. Whip the batter very light, and then add fruit as follows, it having been well dredged with flour: Half pound of raisins, seeded and cut in too; one tablespoonful of finely sliced citron; half a pound of Sultana raisins, washed well and dried. Add a teaspoonful of soda, dissolved in hot water; heat for three minutes; put into a buttered mold, and boil hard for two hours. Eat with brandy sauce.

Delmonico Pudding.—One quart of milk, four eggs, using the white of one only; three tablespoonfuls of sugar, two tablespoonfuls of corn-starch, one cupful of cocoanut, a little salt. Put the milk in a farina boiler to scald; wet the starch in cold milk; beat the eggs and sugar, and stir all into the scalding milk; add the cocoanut, and pour the whole into a pudding-dish; whip dry the three whites, reserved as above, with three tablespoonfuls of sugar; flavor with lemon or vanilla; spread over the pudding and bake a light brown. Eat hot or cold.

Almond Pudding.—Turn boiling water on to three-fourths of a pound of sweet almonds; let it remain until the skin comes off easily; rub with a dry cloth; when dry, pound fine with one large spoonful of rose-water; beat six eggs to a stiff froth with three spoonfuls of fine white sugar; mix with one quart of milk, three spoonfuls of pounded crackers, four ounces of melted butter, and the same of citron cut into bits; add almonds; stir all together, and bake in a small pudding-dish with a lining and rim of pastry. This pudding is best when cold. It will bake in half an hour in a quick oven.

Cup Custard.—One quart of milk, five eggs, teaspoonful of butter, sugar to taste. Pour into buttered cups, season with Durkee's mixed spices, and bake. This can be baked in a pudding-pan, if preferred.

PASTRY AND PUDDINGS.

Rice Custard.—Into a quart of boiling water stir two tablespoonfuls of rice flour, dissolved in a little cold milk; add two well-beaten eggs to the boiling mixture; sweeten and flavor to taste.

Chocolate Custard.—Three pints of sweet milk, four tablespoonfuls of grated chocolate, three tablespoonfuls of cornstarch, and two eggs. Put the chocolate and a little milk on to boil, stir it until smooth, then add a little cold milk. Beat up the eggs in the remainder of the milk, and pour all into the chocolate. Stir until it thickens; take off the fire, and add sugar and vanilla to taste. Place in a glass dish, and when cold, drop large spoonfuls of the whites of eggs, beaten very light with sugar, over the top, in the centre of each, a little currant jelly. This makes a very ornamental, as well as palatable dish.

Chocolate Pudding.—Make a corn-starch pudding with a quart of milk, three teaspoonfuls of corn-starch, and three tablespoonfuls of sugar. When done, remove about half and flavor to taste, and then to that remaining in the kettle add an egg beaten very light and two ounces of vanilla chocolate. Put in a mold, alternating the dark and light, and serve with whipped cream.

Baked Indian Pudding.—Boil one pint of milk; while boiling stir in one cupful of Indian-meal; let it cool a little, and add three eggs well-beaten, one pint of cold milk, one tablespoonful of flour, one-half cupful of sugar, one cupful of molasses, one teaspoonful of ginger, one of cinnamon, and a little salt. Bake an hour and a half.

Queen's Pudding.—One pint of bread-crumbs, one quart of milk, yelks of four eggs, rind of one lemon; sweeten to taste. Bake as a custard. After baking, spread the top with currant jelly. Beat the whites of the eggs, add to them one cupful of sugar dissolved in the juice of a lemon. Spread this over the pudding, and brown

MEMORANDUM
ON
FRIENDS' RECIPES

MEMORANDUM
ON
FRIENDS' RECIPES

DOMESTIC COOKERY.

Brown Betty.—One loaf of stale bread crumbled fine, one-half cupful of milk, and twelve apples. Alternate layers of bread and sliced apples, sugared, buttered, and spiced. Moisten with the milk. Bake in a tin pudding-pan for three hours.

Poor Man's Plum Pudding.—One cupful of molasses, one cupful of suet chopped very fine, beaten smoothly together; one teaspoonful of salt and one of soda mixed through a half-pound of flour, one pint of milk, one pound of raisins, seeded and chopped, and a half-pound of sliced citron. Boil three hours.

English Plum Pudding.—Two pounds of chopped suet, three pounds of seeded raisins, two pounds of currants, one-half pound of citron, two pounds of sugar, five eggs, one pint of milk, one-half pint of brandy, two nutmegs, a little salt, flour sufficient to make it very stiff. Put it into one or two bags, and boil in a large quantity of water seven or eight hours. Serve with sauce.

Spice Pudding.—One cupful of sour milk, one cupful of butter, four cupfuls of flour, two cupfuls of currants, one cupful of sugar, four eggs, four teaspoonfuls of cinnamon, one teaspoonful of cloves, and one teaspoonful of soda. Bake in a quick oven, and serve with brandy sauce.

Paradise Pudding.—Stew until tender three ounces of rice in a pint and a quarter of milk, add four ounces of raisins, three ounces of suet chopped fine, two and a half ounces of sugar, two eggs, a little nutmeg and lemon peel. Boil three hours. Serve with hard sauce.

Jelly Pudding.—Two cupfuls *very* fine stale biscuit or bread-crumbs; one cupful of rich milk—half cream, if you can get it; five eggs, beaten very light; one-half teaspoonful of soda, stirred in boiling water; one cupful of sweet jelly, jam, or marmalade. Scald the milk and pour over the crumbs. Beat until half cold, and stir in the beaten yelks, then whites, finally the soda. Fill large cups half full with the batter; set in a quick oven and bake half an hour. When done, turn out quickly and dexterously; with a sharp knife make an incision in the side of each; pull partly open, and put a liberal spoonful of the conserve within. Close the slit by pinching the edges with your fingers. Eat warm with sweetened cream.

Cabinet Pudding.—Take of the remains of any kind of cake broken up two cupfuls, half a cupful of raisins, half a can of peaches, four eggs, one and a half pints of milk. Butter a plain pudding mold and lay in some of the broken cake, one-third of the raisins, stoned, one-third of the peaches; make two layers of the remainder of the cake, raisins, and peaches. Cover with a very thin slice of bread, then pour over the milk beaten with the eggs and sugar. Set in a saucepan of boiling water to reach two-thirds up the side of the mold, and steam three-quarters of an hour.

Turn out carefully on a dish, and serve with peach sauce, made as follows: Place the peach juice from the can into a small saucepan; add an equal volume of water, a little more sugar, and eight or ten raisins; boil ten minutes, strain, and just before serving add six drops of bitter almond.

Delicious Pudding.—Bake a common sponge cake in a flat-bottomed pudding-dish; when ready for use, cut in six or eight pieces; split and spread with butter, and return them to the dish. Make a custard with four eggs to a quart of milk, flavor and sweeten to taste; pour over the cake and bake one-half hour. The cake will swell and fill the custard. Any stale cake will do about as well as sponge cake.

Bird's-nest Pudding.—Make the foundation of the nest of corn-starch or blanc-mange. Cut strips of lemon peel, boil in a sirup of water and sugar till tender, and arrange around the blanc-mange to represent straw. Extract the contents

MEMORANDUM
ON
FRIENDS' RECIPES

164   DOMESTIC COOKERY.

of four eggs through a small hole, and fill the shells with hot blanc-mange or corn-starch. When cold, break off the shells, and lay the molded eggs in the nest.

Snow Pudding.—Soak an ounce of gelatine in a pint of cold water for one hour; then place it over the fire, stir gently, and remove as soon as it is dissolved; when almost cold, beat to a stiff froth with an egg-beater. Beat the whites of three eggs to a stiff froth, and add it to the gelatine froth, together with the juice of three lemons, and pulverized sugar to the taste. Mix the whole well together, pour into a mold, and set aside to cool. Serve on a dish with soft custard made from the yelks of the eggs.

Cherry Pudding.—Two eggs, one cupful sweet milk, flour enough to make a stiff batter, two teaspoonfuls of baking-powder, and as many cherries as can be stirred in. Eat with sauce made of the cherries.

Blackberry Mush.—Put the berries into a preserving kettle and mash with sugar enough to make sweet; set over the fire, and when it begins to simmer, stir in very gradually one tablespoonful, or more if needed, of corn-starch to a quart of fruit; stir until well cooked, and eat either hot or cold with cream; raspberries also may be used this way.

Roley-poley.—Make a good biscuit dough, and roll about three-quarters of an inch thick, and spread with berries, preserves, or slices of apple; roll up and tie in a cloth; boil or steam an hour and a half.

Berry or Fruit Puddings.—One quart sifted flour, two tablespoonfuls shortening, half teaspoonful salt, and two teaspoonfuls baking-powder; mix well, then form a soft dough of milk or water, roll out thin, and spread with any kind of berries, fruit, or preserves; roll it up, tie in a cloth, and place in the steamer, or boil in a mold. This makes fine dumplings.

PASTRY AND PUDDINGS.

German Puffs.—Two cups of sweet milk, two cups of flour, three eggs, and a little salt. Bake in buttered cups.

Indian Puffs.—Into one quart of boiling milk stir eight tablespoonfuls of corn-meal and four tablespoonfuls of brown sugar; boil five minutes, stirring constantly; when cool, add six well-beaten eggs; bake in buttered cups half an hour. Eat with sauce.

White Puffs.—One pint rich milk; whites of four eggs whipped stiff; one heaping cupful prepared flour; one scant cupful powdered sugar; grated peel of half a lemon; a little salt. Whisk the eggs and sugar to a meringue, and add this alternately with the flour to the milk. Cream, or half cream half milk, is better. Beat until the mixture is very light, and bake in buttered cups or tins. Turn out, sift powdered sugar over them, and eat with lemon sauce.

Oak Balls.—Three cupfuls each of flour and milk, three eggs, whites and yelks beaten separately and very light, three tablespoonfuls of melted butter, a little salt. Pour in well-buttered muffin-rings, and bake to a nice brown.

Apple Dumplings.—Make a biscuit dough, and cover the apples (pared and cored), singly; tie in cloths and drop in boiling water. Let it boil half an hour. If preferred, mix flour and a little salt, and scald with boiling water. When cold enough to handle, roll it out and cover the apples. Or a pie-crust may be made for a cover and the dumplings may be baked in the oven.

Peach Dumplings.—These may be made according to the preceding recipe, substituting peaches for apples.

Lemon Dumplings.—Take suet, four ounces; moist sugar, four ounces; bread-crumbs, one-half pound; one lemon. Grate the rind of the lemon, squeeze out the juice, mix all the ingredients. Put in buttered teacups and bake three-quarters of an hour.

MEMORANDUM
ON
FRIENDS' RECIPES

MEMORANDUM
ON
FRIENDS' RECIPES

XII.—CREAMS, JELLIES, AND LIGHT DESSERTS.

LIGHT DESSERTS FOR HOME USE; FROZEN PREPARATIONS: FREEZERS; HOW TO FREEZE CREAMS, ETC.; HOW TO TURN OUT THE MOLDS; WHIPPED-CREAMS, JELLIES, ETC. FORTY-FIVE RECIPES FOR CREAMS, JELLIES, BLANC-MANGES, ETC.

THERE is a delightful range of light desserts which need to be introduced more generally into our homes. They have too long been allowed to rest in the confectioner's under the erroneous notion that they were beyond the capacity of the ordinary housekeeper.

Prominent among these desserts are ice-cream and water-ices with all their splendid possibilities of variety. For hints concerning freezers and other tools for the home manufacture of these preparations, see the last chapter of this department.

In making ice-cream, use only the best materials. Avoid milk thickened with arrow-root, corn-starch, or any farinaceous substance. Pure cream, ripe natural fruits, or good extracts of the same, and sugar of the purest quality, combine to make a perfect ice-cream. To freeze the cream, assuming it be already flavored, first pound up ice and mix with it a quantity of coarse salt, in the proportion of about one-third the quantity of salt to the amount of ice used. Put the freezing-can in the centre of the tub, taking care that the lid is securely fastened down, and pile the mixed ice and salt around it to within three inches of the top, or certainly as high as the cream reaches on the inside.

Begin to stir the cream at once, and stir rapidly and constantly. This is essential to make the cream smooth. If

CREAMS, JELLIES, AND LIGHT DESSERTS.

the cream is allowed to freeze to the sides of the can without being quickly removed, there will inevitably be lumps of ice through it. The freezing has progressed sufficiently far when the cream will stand heaped upon a spoon.

When a small can of cream has been made for table use, it is desirable to serve it in a cylindrical form as it comes solid from the can. To remove it in this form, take the can from the ice and wipe off all the salt and ice which adheres to it. Remove the lid and invert the can upon a plate. Wrap about the can a towel wet with warm water. This will sufficiently relax the freezing within the can to allow the cream to slide out in compact form. Molds of cream may be removed in the same manner, by dipping them in warm water for a moment. Water-ices and frozen fruits need the same general treatment.

For whipping cream, etc., some of the improved beaters, described at the end of this department, will be found to be superior to the old hand methods. In all delicate dishes the best ingredients must invariably be used.

RECIPES.

Vanilla Ice-cream.—Two quarts of pure cream, fourteen ounces of white sugar, flavored with vanilla bean or extract of vanilla to taste; mix well, and freeze as directed above. Pure cream needs no thickening or boiling. Milk may be boiled or thickened with arrow-root or corn-starch, but it will not produce ice *cream*.

Lemon Ice-cream.—For the same quantity of cream and sugar, as above, stir in the juice of from four to eight lemons, according to size and juiciness, and grate in a little of the rind. Then freeze as above.

Orange Ice-cream.—Proceed as in lemon cream, using oranges, and regulating the quantity of sugar as the fruit is more or less sweet.

MEMORANDUM
ON
FRIENDS' RECIPES

MEMORANDUM ON FRIENDS' RECIPES

168　　　　　　*DOMESTIC COOKERY.*

Chocolate Ice-cream.—For one gallon of ice-cream, grate fine about one-half cake of Baker's chocolate; make ice-cream as for the recipe above; flavor lightly with vanilla and stir in the chocolate.

Strawberry Ice-cream.—Mash one pint of fresh, ripe strawberries; sprinkle them with half a pound of fine sugar; let it stand about an hour; strain though a fine sieve, or a cloth; if the sugar is not dissolved, stir it well; add a little water; stir this juice into the cream prepared as above and freeze.

Raspberry Ice-cream.—Make the same as strawberry, substituting the raspberries merely.

Peach Ice-cream.—Take fine, ripe freestone peaches; pare, chop fine, mash, and work as for strawberry cream.

Pine-apple Ice-cream.—Pare the fruit, shred fine, and work as in strawberry cream.

Orange Water-ice.—Take one dozen oranges; grate the skin and squeeze out the juice; add six quarts of water and ten ounces of white sugar to each quart of water; mix well and put into the freezer. Be careful to stir steadily while freezing, or the mixture will cake into lumps. The amount of sugar and of orange-juice may be varied to suit taste.

Lemon Water-ice.—To one quart of water, add the juice of four lemons and one pound of sugar. Then proceed as above. Currants, raspberries, strawberries, and all the juicy fruits may be treated in the same way.

Tutti Frutti.—One quart of rich cream, one and one-half ounces of sweet almonds, chopped fine; one-half pound of sugar; freeze, and when sufficiently congealed, add one-

MEMORANDUM
ON
FRIENDS' RECIPES

CREAMS, JELLIES, AND LIGHT DESSERTS.

half pound of preserved fruits, with a few white raisins chopped, and finely sliced citron. Cut the fruit small, and mix well with the cream. Freeze like ice-cream, and keep on ice until required.

Frozen Fruits.—Take two quarts of rich cream and two teacupfuls of sugar, mix well together and put into a freezer with ice and salt packed around it. Have ready one quart of peaches, mashed and sweetened. When the cream is very cold, stir them in and freeze all together. Strawberries can be used in the same way, but will require more sugar. Cherries are specially delightful in this form.

Whipped Cream.—To one quart of cream whipped very thick, add powdered sugar to taste; then add one tumbler of wine. Make just before using.

Italian Cream.—Divide two pints of cream equally in two bowls; with one bowl mix six ounces of powdered sugar, the juice of two large lemons, and two glassfuls of white wine; then add the other pint of cream, and stir the whole very hard; boil two ounces of isinglass with four small teacupfuls of water till reduced one-half; then stir the isinglass, lukewarm, in the other ingredients; put them in a glass dish to harden.

Syllabub.—Whip a small cupful of powdered sugar into a quart of rich cream, and another cupful of sugar into the whites of four eggs. Mix these together, and add a glass of white wine and flavoring to taste.

Spanish Cream.—Three half-pints of milk, half a box of gelatine, five tablespoonfuls of white sugar, three eggs, and two teaspoonfuls of vanilla. Soak the gelatine in cold milk; put on to boil; when boiling, add the yelks of the eggs with the sugar and flavoring extract beaten together. When it thickens to the consistency of cream, or after about three

MEMORANDUM
ON
FRIENDS' RECIPES

minutes' boiling, take off the fire, and stir in the whites of the eggs well beaten. Pour into molds, and set aside to cool. To be eaten cold, with or without cream.

Tapioca Cream.—Soak half a cupful of tapioca in water over night. Let a quart of milk get steaming hot, and add to it the tapioca. Let it boil three minutes, then mix five tablespoonfuls of white sugar with the yelks of four eggs; stir them into the milk and tapioca, and let it come to a boil again. Beat the whites up stiff; stir them rapidly and thoroughly through the boiling tapioca; add two tablespoonfuls of wine and a pinch of salt. Let it stand till cold and garnish with macaroons.

Orange Cream.—Put half a box of gelatine to soak for half an hour in cold water enough to cover it. Take three half-pints of cream, whip half of it, and heat the other half; dissolve the gelatine in the heated cream; then strain it, and return to the boiler again. Take the yelks of five eggs and a cupful of sugar; beat them together till light, and add to the boiling cream; cook about two minutes, stirring constantly; take from the fire, and while it cooks, stir in the whipped cream and the juice of four oranges, and pour into a mold to stiffen. Stir the cream constantly before putting into the mold, to prevent it from thickening in lumps.

Pink Cream.—Three gills of strawberry or currant juice; mix with one-half pound of powdered sugar, one-half pint of thick cream; whisk until well mixed; serve in a glass dish.

Chocolate Bavarian Cream.—Whip one pint of cream to a stiff froth, laying it on a sieve; boil a pint of rich milk with a vanilla bean and two tablespoonfuls of sugar until it is well flavored; then take it off the fire and add half a box of gelatine, soaked for an hour in half a cupful of water in a warm place near the range; when slightly cooled, add two tablets of Baker's chocolate, soaked and smoothed. Stir in the eggs

CREAMS, JELLIES, AND LIGHT DESSERTS.

well-beaten. When it has become quite cold and begins to thicken, stir it without ceasing a few minutes, until it is very smooth; then stir in the whipped cream lightly until it is well mixed. Put it into a mold or molds, and set it on ice or in a cool place.

Turret Cream.—Soak one box of gelatine in a cupful of milk four hours. Scald three cupfuls of milk; add one cupful of the sugar; when this is dissolved, add the soaked gelatine. Stir over the fire until almost boiling hot; strain and divide into two equal portions. Return one to the fire and heat quickly. When it nears the boiling-point, stir in the beaten yelks of three eggs. Let all cook together two minutes, and turn out into a bowl to cool. When it has cooled, churn one pint of cream very stiff, and beat the whites of the eggs until they will stand alone. Divide the latter into two heaps. As the yellow gelatine begins to "form," whip one-half of the whites into it, a little at a time. To the white gelatine add the rest of the whites in the same manner, alternately with the whipped cream. Season the yellow with vanilla, the white with lemon juice beaten in at the last. Wet the inside of a tall, fluted mold with water, and arrange in the bottom, close to the outside of the mold, a row of crystallized cherries. Then put in a layer of the white mixture; on this crystallized apricots or peaches cut into strips; a layer of the yellow, another border of cherries, and so on until your mold is full. When firm, which will be in a few hours if set on ice, wrap a cloth wrung out in hot water about the mold, and invert upon a flat dish. Eat with sweet cream, or, if you like, with brandied fruit. Not only is this a very palatable dish, but it is also very beautiful, well repaying the trouble of its preparation.

Velvet Cream.—Half an ounce of isinglass dissolved in one and a half cupfuls of white wine; then add the juice and grated peel of a lemon, three-quarters of a pound of loaf

MEMORANDUM
ON
FRIENDS' RECIPES

MEMORANDUM
ON
FRIENDS' RECIPES

172　　　*DOMESTIC COOKERY.*

sugar; simmer all together until mixed well; strain and add one and a half pints of rich cream, and stir until cool; pour into molds, and let it stand till stiff enough to turn out.

Calf's Foot Jelly.—Take one pair of calf's feet, and put them into a gallon of water; let it boil half away and skim constantly; strain it when cold; take the fat from the top and bottom; then warm it; add sugar, the juice of three lemons, a pint of Madeira wine, and the whites of seven eggs; boil it half an hour, strain through a flannel bag, and cool in molds.

Wine Jelly.—One box of Coxe's gelatine dissolved in one pint of cold water, one pint of wine, one quart of boiling water, two cupfuls of granulated sugar, and three lemons. Cool in molds.

Wine Jelly, No. 2.—Soak one package of sparkling gelatine in a large cupful of cold water. Add to this all the juice and half the rind of a lemon, two cupfuls of white sugar, and a half teaspoonful of bitter almond or two peach leaves, and cover for half an hour; then pour on boiling water, stir, and strain. After adding two cupfuls of pale sherry or white wine, strain again through a flannel bag. Wet a mold and set it in a cold place until the next day.

Jelly Oranges.—Soak a package of Coxe's gelatine about three hours in a cup of cold water. Cut from the top of each of a dozen fine oranges a round piece, leaving a hole just large enough to admit the bowl of a small spoon or the handle of a larger. The smaller the orifice, the better your dish will look. Clean out every bit of the pulp very carefully, so as not to tear the edges of the hole. Scrape the inner skin from the sides with your fore-finger, and when the oranges are emptied lay them in cold water while you make the jelly. Strain the juice of all and grated peel of three of the oranges through coarse, thin muslin over three cupfuls of sugar, squeezing rather hard to get the coloring matter.

CREAMS, JELLIES, AND LIGHT DESSERTS. 173

Stir this until it is a thick sirup, and add a quarter teaspoonful of cinnamon. Pour two cupfuls of boiling water upon the soaked gelatine, and stir over the fire until well dissolved; add the juice and sugar, stir all together, and strain through a flannel bag into a pitcher, not shaking or squeezing it, lest it should become cloudy. Wipe off the outside of the oranges, set them close together in a dish, the open ends uppermost, and fill *very* full with the warm jelly, as it will shrink in cooling. Set it away in a cold place where there is no dust. Next day cut each in half with a sharp knife, taking care to sever the skin all around before cutting into the jelly. If neatly divided, the rich amber jelly will be a fair counterfeit of the orange pulp. Pile in a glass dish, with green leaves around, as you would the real fruit. This is a delicious dish, and it is highly ornamental on the table.

Apple Jelly.—Soak half a package Coxe's gelatine in one cupful of cold water. Pare, core, and slice a dozen well-flavored pippins, throwing each piece into cold water as it is cut to preserve the color. Pack them in a glass or stoneware jar with just cold water enough to cover them; cover the jar loosely that the steam may escape; set in a pot of warm water and bring to a boil. Cook until the apples are broken into pieces. Have ready in a bowl the soaked gelatine, two cupfuls of powdered sugar, the juice of two lemons, and the grated peel of one. Strain the apple pulp scalding hot over them; stir until the gelatine is dissolved; strain again through a flannel bag, without shaking or squeezing it; wet a mold with cold water, fill it, and set in a cold place until firm. This preparation is greatly improved if formed in a mold with a cylinder in the centre, the cavity being filled and heaped with whipped cream or syllabub.

Peach Jelly.—Proceed as in apple jelly, using peaches, with a few peach-kernels broken up and boiled with the fruit.

MEMORANDUM
ON
FRIENDS' RECIPES

MEMORANDUM
ON
FRIENDS' RECIPES

174   *DOMESTIC COOKERY.*

Lemon Jelly.—Stir together two large cupfuls of sugar, the juice of six lemons and grated peel of two, and a package of well-soaked gelatine. Cover for an hour. Pour three pints of boiling water over them; stir until the gelatine is quite melted; strain through a close flannel bag, and pour into a wet mold.

Orange Jelly.—Soak a package of gelatine in two cupfuls of water; add two cupfuls of sugar, the juice of six large oranges, and grated peel of one, the juice of two lemons, and peel of one, and cover for an hour. Pour three pints of boiling water over them; stir until the gelatine is quite melted; strain through a flannel bag; add a little good brandy if desired and strain again; pour into a wet mold.

Orange Trifle.—Stir half a package of soaked gelatine into a cupful of boiling water. Mix the juice of two oranges and rind of one with a cupful of powdered sugar, and pour the hot liquid over them. Should the gelatine not dissolve readily, set all over the fire and stir until clear. Strain, and stir in the beaten yelks of three eggs. Heat quickly within a vessel of boiling water, stirring constantly lest the yelks curdle. If they do curdle, strain again through coarse flannel. Set aside until perfectly cold and slightly stiff, then whip in a pint of frothed cream. Wet a mold, fill, and set it on ice.

Orange Dessert.—Pare five or six oranges; cut into thin slices; pour over them a coffeecupful of sugar. Boil one pint of milk; add, while boiling, the yelks of three eggs, one tablespoonful of corn-starch (made smooth with a little cold milk); stir all the time; as soon as thickened, pour over the fruit. Beat the whites of the eggs to a froth; add two tablespoonfuls of powdered sugar; pour over the custard, and brown slightly in the oven. Serve cold.

CREAMS, JELLIES, AND LIGHT DESSERTS.

MEMORANDUM ON FRIENDS' RECIPES

Apple Snow.—Grate half a dozen apples to a pulp; press them through a sieve; add half a cupful of powdered sugar and a teaspoonful of extract of lemon; take the whites of six eggs, whip them for several minutes, and sprinkle two tablespoonfuls of powdered sugar over them; beat the apple pulp to a froth, and add the beaten egg; whip the mixture until it looks like stiff snow; then pile it high in rough portions on a glass dish; garnish with small spoonfuls of currant jelly.

Floating Island.—Beat the yelks of six eggs until very light; sweeten and flavor to taste; stir into a quart of boiling milk; cook till it thickens; when cool, pour into a low glass dish; whip the whites of the eggs to a stiff froth; sweeten, and place over a dish of boiling water to cook. Take a tablespoon and drop on the whites of the cream, far enough apart so that the "little white islands" will not touch each other. By dropping little specks of bright jelly on each island a pleasing effect will be produced.

Blanc-mange.—Take one quart of milk, one ounce gelatine, and sugar to sweeten to taste; put it on the fire, and keep stirring until it is all melted, then pour it into a bowl and stir until cold; season with vanilla; pour it into a mold, and set in a cool place to stiffen.

Tapioca Blanc-mange.—Take one pint of new milk, half a pound of the best farina-tapioca soaked in water four hours, three-fourths of a cupful of sugar, two teaspoonfuls of almond or vanilla extract, a little salt. Heat the milk, and stir the soaked tapioca. When it has dissolved, add the sugar. Boil slowly fifteen minutes, stirring all the time; take from the fire, and beat until nearly cold. Flavor and pour into a mold dipped in cold water. Sago blanc-mange may be made in the same manner.

MEMORANDUM
ON
FRIENDS' RECIPES

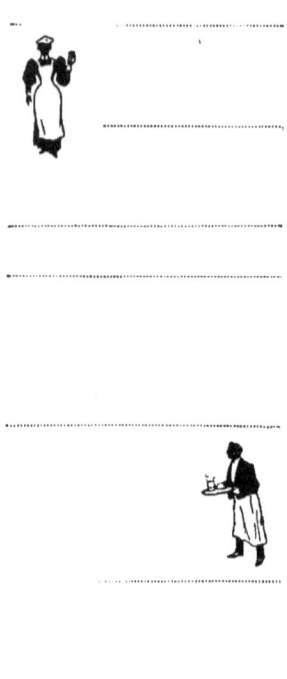

176   *DOMESTIC COOKERY.*

Corn-starch Blanc-mange.—One quart of milk, four table spoonfuls of corn-starch, wet with a little water, three eggs, whites and yelks beaten separately, one cupful of sugar, a little salt, flavor with lemon extract. Heat the milk to boiling; stir in the corn-starch and salt, and boil together five minutes; then add the yelks, beaten light, with the sugar; boil two minutes longer, stirring all the while; remove the mixture from the fire, and beat in the whipped whites while it is boiling hot. Pour into a mold wet with cold water, and set in a cold place. Eat with sugar and cream.

Chocolate Blanc-mange.—Heat a quart of milk; stir in a cupful of sugar and half a package of soaked gelatine; strain through flannel; add three large spoonfuls of grated chocolate; boil ten minutes, stirring all the time. When nearly cold, beat until it begins to stiffen. Flavor with vanilla; whip up once, and put into a wet mold. It will be firm in six or eight hours.

Neapolitan Blanc-mange.—Dissolve one-third of a box of gelatine, and stir into one quart of milk. Add three-fourths of a cupful of sugar. As soon as the gelatine is thoroughly dissolved, remove from the fire, and divide into three parts. Flavor one with vanilla; color another with the beaten yelk of one egg; color the third with grated chocolate. Set away, and when quite cold and a little stiff, pour into a mold—first the white, then the yellow, and last the brown.

Peach Meringue.—Put on to boil a scant quart of new milk, omitting half a teacupful, with which moisten two tablespoonfuls of corn-starch. When the milk boils, add corn-starch, stir constantly, and when it commences to thicken, remove from the fire; add one tablespoonful of perfectly sweet butter; let cool; then beat in the yelks of three eggs until the custard seems light and creamy; add one-half teacupful of fine sugar; cover the bottom of a well-buttered baking-dish with ripe, juicy peaches, that have been pared, stoned, and halved; sprinkle two tablespoonfuls of sugar over the fruit, pour the custard over gently, and bake in a quick oven twenty minutes; draw it out, and cover with the well-beaten whites of the three eggs; sprinkle a little fine sugar over the top, and set in the oven until brown. Eat warm with sauce, or cold with cream.

Charlotte Russe.—Dissolve half a box of gelatine in cold water. Beat the yelks of four eggs with two cupfuls of white sugar. Whip one quart of sweet cream very stiff, add flavoring, then the yelks and sugar, and blend all the ingredients. Add the whites, turn into a bowl lined with sponge cake or lady-fingers, and set away to cool.

Charlotte Russe, No. 2.—Two tablespoonfuls gelatine soaked in a little cold milk two hours; two coffeecupfuls rich cream; one teacupful milk. Whip the cream stiff in a large bowl or dish; set on ice. Boil the milk and pour gradually over the gelatine until dissolved, then strain; when nearly cold add the whipped cream, a spoonful at a time. Sweeten with pulverized sugar and flavor with vanilla. Line a dish with lady-fingers or sponge cake; pour in the cream and set in a cool place to harden.

Chocolate Charlotte Russe.—Soak in cold water one ounce of isinglass or of gelatine; shave down three ounces of the best chocolate, without spice or sugar, and mix it gradually into one pint of cream, adding the soaked isinglass; set the cream, chocolate, and isinglass over the fire in a porcelain kettle, and boil slowly till the isinglass is dissolved, and the whole well mixed; take it off the fire and let it cool; have ready eight yelks of eggs and four whites beaten together until very light; stir them gradually into the mixture with half a pound of powdered sugar; simmer the whole, but do not let it boil; then take it off, and whip to a strong froth; line the molds with sponge cake, fill with the paste, and set them on ice.

MEMORANDUM
ON
FRIENDS' RECIPES

DOMESTIC COOKERY.

Figs a la Genevieve.—Dissolve two ounces of best sugar in half a pint of cold water in an enameled stewpan, with half the very thin rind of a large lemon; when this is done, put into it half a pound of Turkey figs, and put the stewpan over a moderate fire, so that the figs may stew very slowly; when quite soft, add one glassful of common port or any other wine, and the strained juice of half a lemon; serve them cold for dessert. About two hours or two hours and a half is the average time for stewing the figs, and the flavor may be varied by using orange peel and juice instead of lemon, and by boiling two or three bitter almonds in the sirup.

Biscuit Glace.—Make a quart of rich boiled custard, flavor it with vanilla, and let it cool. Then mix with it a quart of grated pineapple or mashed peaches. Stir them well together, and add enough sugar to allow for the loss in freezing. Freeze in the usual way, stirring in a pint of cream, whipped, when it is beginning to set in the freezer. Partly fill little paper cases with the mixture, and smooth the tops nicely. Place them carefully in the cleaned and dried freezer, and let them remain embedded in ice for several hours. Sometimes the cases are filled with pistachio or chocolate ice-cream, in which case blanched almonds are laid over the top, when they are served. Or they may be filled with frozen whipped cream, and served with a spoonful of some bright sherbet upon the top of each.

XIII.—CAKES AND CAKE-BAKING.

BEST MATERIALS REQUISITE FOR CAKE-MAKING; WHAT THEY SHOULD BE; WEIGHING AND MEASURING INGREDIENTS; HOW TO MIX CAKE; FRUITS AND FLAVORS FOR CAKE; HOW TO BAKE CAKE; HOW TO TEST IT; HOW TO KEEP IT; HOW TO ICE IT. NINETY-SEVEN RECIPES FOR CAKES.

IN cake-making it is absolutely essential that the best materials be employed. Stale eggs, strong butter, musty flour, or common sugar are not so much as to be thought of in this connection. The idea that such refuse "will do for cooking" is most unworthy. When a luxury, such as cake, is attempted, the maker should certainly be willing to luxuriate in acceptable ingredients.

Flour for cake should be white and dry. It should always be carefully sifted. Sugar should be white, dry, and free from lumps. Eggs and butter should be sweet and fresh; the milk rich and pure. Fruit and extracts must be of the best. The weighing and measuring of ingredients must be accurately done. Guessing at quantities has spoiled many a cake.

For mixing cake, an earthen or wooden dish and a wooden spoon are requisite. Butter and sugar should be beaten together to a cream before using. Butter may be softened for this purpose, if too hard to manage readily, but it must not be melted. Whites and yelks of eggs must be beaten separately, until there is no stringiness visible, and the froth can be taken up on a spoon. Beat eggs in a broad, shallow dish, and in a cool place. It is well to lay the eggs in cold water for an hour before beating them, as they will beat the lighter for such treatment. Sweet milk is best for

MEMORANDUM ON
FRIENDS' RECIPES

MEMORANDUM ON FRIENDS' RECIPES

DOMESTIC COOKERY.

solid cake; sour milk, for light cake. The two should never be mixed.

Baking-powder should be mixed dry through the flour. Soda and cream of tartar should be dissolved in milk. Flavoring extracts, fruit, and spices must be added the last thing, and fruit should always be well sprinkled with flour before it is put in the dough. Currants and such fruit should be washed, picked over, and dried before using. Almonds should be blanched by pouring boiling water over them till they pop from their skins. Cake should be beaten as little as possible after the flour has been added. When it requires long baking, the bottom and sides of the pan should be lined with paper well buttered. This will insure the easy turning out of the cake when done.

Much of the success in cake-baking depends on the heating of the oven. If the oven is very hot when the cake goes in, it will bake on top before it becomes light. If the oven is too cool, it will rise and fall again before done. If the top of the cake browns too fast, cover it with thick paper. Try it by inserting a broom-splinter or knitting-needle in the thickest part of the cake, and if nothing adheres when it is drawn out, it is done. Turn out of the tins at once, taking care not to expose the cake to draft.

Cake should be kept in earthen pans or crocks, or tin boxes, but never in wooden boxes or drawers. It will keep better for being wrapped in a cloth, and more than is needed should not be cut.

Cake that is to be frosted should be baked in pans with perpendicular sides. The icing should be put on as soon as the cake is removed from the oven. This will insure its drying smooth and hard.

RECIPES.

Loaf Dutch Cake.—Take one cupful of light bread dough, one egg, sugar and salt to taste, half a teaspoonful of soda,

CAKES AND CAKE-BAKING.

half a pound of raisins, and, if desired, a little butter and nutmeg; work all together very smooth; let the dough rise about half an hour, and bake as bread.

Bread Cake.—Two coffeecupfuls of bread dough, two teacupfuls of sugar, two eggs, one teacupful of butter, two teaspoonfuls essence of lemon, one nutmeg, a teaspoonful each of cloves, cinnamon, and allspice, a wineglass of brandy, and a coffeecupful of raisins. Let it rise before baking

Cinnamon Bun.—Put one pint of milk on to boil and mix a cupful of butter in a little lukewarm water; add a teaspoonful of salt, and half an yeast cake dissolved in lukewarm water; add two quarts of sifted flour; mix all together, and let it stand over night till morning. Now beat two eggs and half a cupful of sugar until light, and mix it with the dough; use just flour enough on the board to keep the dough from sticking; roll the dough out into a sheet one-fourth of an inch in thickness; spread a little butter, and sprinkle a little sugar on it, then some pulverized cinnamon, a few currants or chopped raisins. Now roll the sheet up into one long roll and cut in pieces about one inch thick; a sharp knife must be used for this purpose; put the pieces in a baking-pan, the cut side or end downward, and let them stand in a warm place for an hour, when they will be ready for the oven, which must be moderately heated.

Soft Molasses Cake.—Into one pint of molasses, put one tablespoonful of ginger, one teaspoonful of cinnamon, one tablespoonful of butter; add one teaspoonful of soda and two teaspoonfuls cream of tartar in one-half cupful of milk, one egg, and two and a half cupfuls of flour. Bake half an hour.

Gingerbread.—One cupful of molasses, one cupful of butter, two cupfuls of sugar, one cupful of sour milk, four eggs, three cupfuls of flour, one tablespoonful of ginger, and one teaspoonful of soda. Mix well and bake quickly.

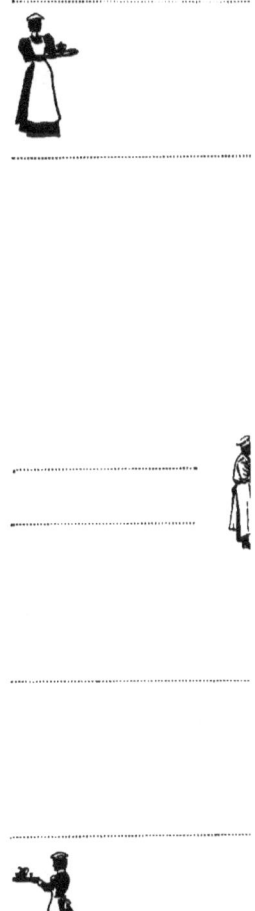

MEMORANDUM
ON
FRIENDS' RECIPES

MEMORANDUM
ON
FRIENDS' RECIPES

Ginger Snaps.—Mix one pint of flour, one cupful of sugar, a piece of butter the size of two eggs; three heaping table spoonfuls of ginger, and a little salt. Pour into this two cupfuls of heated molasses. Add flour enough to make it roll out thin. Bake three or four minutes.

Cookies.—Six cupfuls of flour, two of sugar, one of butter, one of milk, teaspoonful of soda, flavored with cinnamon or nutmeg, as you like. Roll thin, cut with biscuit-cutter, and bake quick.

Small Sugar Cakes.—One heaping teacupful of sugar; three-quarters teacupful of butter; one-quarter teacupful sweet milk; two eggs, well beaten; two teaspoonfuls cream tartar; one teaspoonful soda, dissolved in hot water; use flour sufficient to enable you to roll out the dough; one saltspoonful salt, nutmeg and cinnamon to taste. Cut into round cakes and bake quickly.

Knickerbocker Cakes.—Beat half a pound of fresh butter to a cream; add half a pound of powdered sugar, three-quarters of a pound of sifted flour, a tablespoonful of orange-flower water, and one of brandy, and four ounces of washed currants; add five well-beaten eggs, and beat the mixture until very light. Line some shallow cake-tins with buttered paper, pour in the mixture until they are half full, and bake in a quick oven.

Scotch Wafers.—Take one pound of sugar, half a pound of butter, one pound of flour, two eggs, two teaspoonfuls of cinnamon. Roll thin and bake quickly.

Shrewsbury Cakes.—Mix a pound of flour and a half pound of butter; stir in a pound of brown sugar and two tablespoonfuls of cinnamon. Mix all thoroughly into a paste with three eggs, roll very thin, using as little flour as possible, and bake in a quick oven.

Soft Cookies.—One egg, two cupfuls of sugar, two cupfuls of cream, one even teaspoonful of soda, salt and flavor to taste. Flour to stiffen so they will drop from the spoon; leave a space between them, as they spread in baking.

Apees.—One cupful of butter, one large cupful of sugar, three eggs, half a teaspoonful of soda, one teaspoonful of cream tartar, and flour enough to roll out thin. Bake quickly.

Cinnamon Cakes.—Take six ounces of butter, a pound of fine, dry flour, three-quarters of a pound of sifted sugar, and a dessertspoonful of pounded cinnamon. Make these ingredients into a firm paste with three eggs, or four, if needed. Roll it, not very thin, and cut out the cakes with a tin shape. Bake them in a very gentle oven from fifteen to twenty minutes, or longer, should they not be done quite through.

Lemon Cakes.—Lemon cakes can be made on the above recipe by substituting for the cinnamon the rasped or grated rinds of two lemons, and the strained juice of one, when its acidity is not objected to.

Seed Cakes.—Two pounds of flour, one pound of sugar, fourteen ounces of butter, one tablespoonful of caraway seed, half a pint of milk, two tablespoonfuls of saleratus. Rub the butter, sugar, and flour together, then add all the other ingredients; knead all well together into a smooth dough; roll it out quite thin, cut with a round cutter, place the cakes on tins, and bake in a *moderate* oven.

Walnut Cakes.—One pound of sugar, six eggs, three teaspoonfuls of yeast-powder, half a pound of butter, flour to make a dough, and one cupful of walnut kernels; bake in a moderate oven.

Jumbles.—Three-fourths of a cupful of butter, one and a half cupfuls of sugar, three eggs, three tablespoonfuls of

MEMORANDUM
ON
FRIENDS' RECIPES

MEMORANDUM
ON
FRIENDS' RECIPES

milk, flour enough to make it roll, and a teaspoonful of baking-powder; roll; sprinkle with granulated sugar and gently roll it in; cut out, with a hole in centre, and bake.

Currant Jumbles.—One pound each of flour and powdered loaf sugar, half a pound each of butter and currants, eight eggs, brandy to taste; cut out as in plain jumbles and bake on tins.

Cocoanut Cookies.—One cupful of butter, two cupfuls of sugar, two cupfuls of prepared or grated cocoanut, two eggs, flour enough to make a stiff batter, and one teaspoonful of soda; drop on buttered paper in pans.

Doughnuts.—Two teacupfuls of sugar, three eggs, one and a half teacupfuls of buttermilk or sour milk, two teaspoonfuls of saleratus, one teaspoonful of salt, six tablespoonfuls of melted lard, flour enough to roll out nicely; boil or fry in lard enough to cover them. If not well covered in the cooking they will be tough.

Raised Doughnuts.—One pint of sweet milk, one half pint of lard, one pint of sugar, three eggs. Mix soft at night, using the milk, one-half the sugar and lard, and one-half pint of yeast. In the morning, add the rest with the eggs, one nutmeg, two tablespoonfuls of whisky, and a little soda. Knead well, and allow to rise. When light, roll out thin, and after cutting, let rise again before frying. One-half beef suet and one-half lard is better to fry them in than all lard.

Crullers.—Two cupfuls of sugar, one-half cupful of butter, one-half cupful of milk, two eggs, one teaspoonful of soda, two of cream tartar. Roll out, and cut according to fancy, and boil in fat.

French Straws.—Mix well eight eggs, ten ounces of sugar, and half a teaspoonful of cinnamon and nutmeg with flour enough to form a dough; beat the eggs very thick and add the sugar, spices, and flour; knead well, and roll to about half an inch thick; cut in strips, give each a twist, and boil them in plenty of lard to a rich yellow; sift sugar on when cool.

Love Knots.—Five cupfuls of flour, two of sugar, one of butter, a piece of lard the size of an egg, two eggs, three tablespoonfuls of sweet milk, half a teaspoonful of soda; rub the butter, sugar, and flour together fine, add the other ingredients, roll thin, cut in strips one inch wide and five inches long, lap across in true-love knots, and bake in a quick oven.

One, Two, Three, Four Cake.—One cupful of butter, two cupfuls of sugar, three cupfuls of flour, four eggs; rub well together, and add some milk or cream, with one teaspoonful of soda and two teaspoonfuls of cream of tartar; flavor with grated lemon rind and juice; bake carefully in a quick oven.

Tea Cake.—Three and a half cupfuls of flour, two of sugar, one of butter, four eggs, a teaspoonful of soda in a tablespoonful of milk or wine, and a half grated nutmeg. Bake carefully in quick oven.

Tumbler Cake.—Five tumblerfuls of flour, three of sugar, two of butter, four eggs, one of milk, one pint and a half of raisins, stoned, one nutmeg, one teaspoonful of allspice, a teaspoonful of soda dissolved in the milk. Bake in deep pan with a hot oven.

Cider Cake.—Two cupfuls of sugar, one cupful of butter, five eggs, one and one-half cupfuls of cider, with one teaspoonful of soda dissolved in it; spices or nutmeg to taste; four and one-half cupfuls of flour, two cupfuls of fruit. Bake quickly.

Puff Cake.—Two cupfuls of sugar, one of butter, one of sweet milk, three of flour, three eggs, one and one-half teaspoonfuls of yeast powder, extract of lemon. Bake quickly.

MEMORANDUM
ON
FRIENDS' RECIPES

MEMORANDUM
ON
FRIENDS' RECIPES

DOMESTIC COOKERY.

Pinafore Cake.—One cupful of butter, three half cupfuls of sugar, three half cupfuls of flour, one-half cupful of cornstarch, one-half cupful of milk, four eggs, one teaspoonful o. cream of tartar, one-half teaspoonful of soda, and a pinch of salt. Flavor to taste.

Cork Cake.—Two cupfuls of sugar, two-thirds of a cupful of butter, three eggs, one cupful of warm milk, three cupfuls of flour, a teaspoonful of baking-powder, and a half pound of currants. Use the whites of two of the eggs for icing and put the yelks into the cake

Poor Man's Cake.—One cupful of cream, one of sugar, two of flour, one egg, one teaspoonful of soda, and two of cream tartar.

Cup Cake.—One cupful of butter, two cupfuls of sugar, half a cupful of molasses, one teaspoonful of soda, two of cream tartar in half a cup of milk, two eggs, and two and a half cups of flour.

Moravian Cake.—Two cupfuls of sugar, one cupful of butter, five eggs, two cupfuls of flour, half a cupful of sour milk, one teaspoonful of cream tartar, and half a teaspoonful of soda. Flavor with a little grated nutmeg and a teaspoonful of vanilla.

Silver Cake.—Whites of twelve eggs, five cupfuls of flour, three cupfuls of sugar, one cupful of butter, one and one-half cupfuls of sweet milk, one teaspoonful of soda, two teaspoonfuls of cream tartar, one teaspoonful of almond extract.

Gold Cake.—Substitute the yelks for whites of eggs, and flavor with vanilla, then make it same as preceding recipe.

Lincoln Cake.—Two cupfuls of sugar, half a cupful of butter, two eggs, one cupful of cream or sour milk, three cupfuls of flour, one teaspoonful of cream tartar, half a teaspoonful of soda, and one teaspoonful of essence of lemon

CAKES AND CAKE-BAKING.

Washington Cake.—One pound of flour, one pound of sugar, half a pound of butter, five eggs, one pound of raisins, one cupful of brandy and water, one teaspoonful of soda, two of cream tartar.

Pound Cake.—One pound of butter, one pound of sugar, one pound of flour, and eight eggs. Bake one hour.

White Pound Cake.—Beat to a cream one pound of sugar and one-half pound of butter; two teaspoonfuls of baking-powder in one pound of flour; whites of sixteen eggs beaten very stiff and added last. Cover with frosting before it cools.

Sponge Cake.—Five eggs, half a pound of sugar, quarter pound of flour, juice and rind of half a lemon. Beat yelks of eggs, sugar, and lemon together till light; add half the beaten whites, then half the flour, the balance of the whites and balance of flour. Avoid beating after the ingredients are all together.

Almond Sponge Cake.—Take half a pound of loaf sugar; rub the rind of a lemon on a few of the lumps, and crush the whole to a powder; separate the whites from the yelks of five eggs, beat the yelks, and add the sugar gradually; then beat the whites to a stiff froth; add it to the dish, and sift in flour enough to make a batter; add a tablespoonful of essence of almonds; butter and paper a tin, pour in the mixture until the tin is two-thirds full, and bake one hour in a moderate oven. The bottom of the tin may be studded with small pieces of almonds.

Cream Sponge Cake.—Beat together a cupful of sugar and the yelks of three eggs. Add a half teaspoonful of soda, a teaspoonful of cream tartar, a cupful of flour, and the whites of the eggs. Bake in three layers, and put between them the following filling: One egg, a half cupful of cream, a cupful of sugar, and a piece of butter the size of a walnut. Boil till like a cream, and when cold flavor to taste.

MEMORANDUM
ON
FRIENDS' RECIPES

MEMORANDUM
ON
FRIENDS' RECIPES

DOMESTIC COOKERY.

Snow Cake.—Take one pound of arrowroot, quarter of a pound of powdered white sugar, half a pound of butter, the whites of six eggs, flavoring to taste. Beat the butter to a cream; stir in the sugar and arrowroot gradually, at the same time beating the mixture; whisk the whites of the eggs to a stiff froth; add them to the other ingredients, and beat well for twenty minutes; flavor with essence of almond, vanilla, or lemon, as may be preferred; pour into a buttered mold or tin, and bake in a *moderate* oven.

Spice Cake.—One cupful each of butter and cold water, three cupfuls of flour, two cupfuls of sugar, three eggs, one teaspoonful of soda, two teaspoonfuls of ground cinnamon, one-fourth pound each of currants and raisins.

Spice Cake, No. 2.—One cupful of butter, two cupfuls of sugar, four eggs, a teaspoonful of cream tartar, half a teaspoonful of soda, half a cupful of sour milk, one cupful of molasses, three cupfuls of flour, a teaspoonful of ground cloves, two teaspoonfuls of cinnamon, two teaspoonfuls of ginger, one nutmeg, and a small pinch of Cayenne pepper.

Coffee Cake.—One cupful of brown sugar, one cupful of butter, one cupful of strained coffee, one cupful of molasses, three eggs well beaten, one pound of raisins, two cupfuls of flour, two teaspoonfuls of baking-powder.

Wine Cake.—Beat to a cream half a cupful of butter with two full cups of powdered sugar; add the yelks of four eggs, and half a glass of sherry wine; beat till very light; add half a cupful of cream with a pinch of soda in it; beat two minutes, and stir in very quickly the whites of the eggs, three and a half cupfuls of prepared flour, and a little grated nutmeg.

Fig Cake.—One cupful butter, two and a half cupfuls sugar, one cupful of milk, six cupfuls of flour, three teaspoonfuls baking-powder, whites of sixteen eggs, and, at the last, one and a quarter pounds of figs, cut and floured. Bake well but do not burn.

Walnut Cake.—One coffeecupful of sugar, two of raisins (stoned and chopped), one cupful and a half of flour, half a cupful of butter, half a cupful of sweet milk, three eggs, two teaspoonfuls of baking-powder, half a nutmeg grated, one teaspoonful of lemon or vanilla, one cup heaping full of nuts, which must be cracked and picked, before anything else is done to the cake. Bake slowly, with a buttered paper in the bottom of the tin.

Hickorynut Cake.—One pound of flour, three-quarters of a pound of sugar, half a pound of butter, half a pint of milk, five eggs, two quarts of hickorynuts, one teaspoonful of soda, and two of cream tartar.

Cocoanut Cake.—One pound of grated cocoanut, one pound of sugar, one-half pound of butter, six eggs, three-quarters of a pound of flour. Flavor to taste.

New Year's Cake.—One and a quarter pound of raisins, seeded, one and a quarter pounds of currants, half a pound of sliced citron, half a pound of butter, half a pound of brown sugar, half a pound of flour, five eggs, half a tumblerful of brandy, half a bottle of rose-water, one teaspoonful of cinnamon, two of cloves, two of mace, and a grated nutmeg.

Currant Cake.—One cupful of butter, two cupfuls of powdered sugar, four eggs, half a cupful of sweet milk, three cupfuls of prepared flour, half a nutmeg grated, and half a pound of currants washed, dried, and dredged with flour.

Citron Cake.—Six eggs, beaten light and the yelks strained; two cupfuls of sugar, three-quarters of a cupful of butter, two and one-half cupfuls of prepared flour, or enough to make good pound cake batter. With some brands you may need three cupfuls; one-half pound of citron cut in thin

MEMORANDUM
ON
FRIENDS' RECIPES

MEMORANDUM ON FRIENDS' RECIPES

DOMESTIC COOKERY.

shreds; juice of an orange, and one teaspoonful of grated peel. Cream the butter and sugar; add the yelks, the whites, and flour by turns, then the orange, and lastly, the citron, dredged with flour. Beat all up hard, and bake in two loaves.

Plum Cake.—Two and a half pounds of raisins, two and a half pounds of currants, one pound of citron, one pound of butter, one pound of sugar, ten eggs, one pound of flour, one-half pint of brandy, and a little molasses.

Fruit Cake.—Take of butter two cupfuls; sugar, four cupfuls; molasses, one cupful; sour milk, two cupfuls; flour, eight cupfuls; eggs, eight; soda, one tablespoonful; cloves, two tablespoonfuls; cinnamon, two tablespoonfuls; raisins, two pounds; currants, two pounds; almonds, one pound; citron, half a pound; two nutmegs; two lemons cut fine; bake four hours.

Wedding Cake.—One pound of powdered sugar, one pound of butter, one pound of flour, twelve eggs, one pound of currants well washed and dredged, one pound of raisins, seeded and chopped, one-half pound of citron cut in slips, one tablespoonful of cinnamon, two teaspoonfuls of nutmeg, one teaspoonful of cloves, one wineglass of brandy. Cream the butter and sugar, add the beaten yelks of the eggs, and stir all *well* together before putting in half of the flour. The spice should come next, then the whipped whites stirred in alternately with the rest of the flour, lastly the brandy. The above quantity is for two large cakes. Bake at least two hours in deep tins lined with well-buttered paper. The icing should be laid on stiff and thickly. Bake this well, and, if kept in a cool, dry place, it will not spoil in two months. Test the cakes well, and be sure they are quite done before taking them from the oven.

Black Cake.—One pound of browned flour, one pound of brown sugar, one pound of citron, two pounds of currants, three pounds of stoned raisins, three-quarters of a pound of butter, one teacupful of molasses, two teaspoonfuls of mace, two teaspoonfuls of cinnamon, one teaspoonful of cloves, one teaspoonful of soda, twelve eggs.

Farmers' Fruit Cake.—Three cupfuls of dried apples, two cupfuls of molasses, one cupful of butter, one cupful of brown sugar, one pound of raisins, one quarter pound of citron, two eggs, one lemon (both juice and rind), two teaspoonfuls of soda, one pound and small cup of flour. Soak the apples over night, chop fine, and boil till done in the molasses and one cupful of the water they were soaked in. Flavor with nutmeg, cinnamon, and a very little cloves. Bake three hours.

Chocolate Cake.—One cupful butter, two cupfuls sugar, two and one-half cupfuls flour, five eggs, one cupful sour milk, one teaspoonful soda, dissolved in a little boiling water; one-half cake Baker's chocolate, grated and put in the cake before stirring in the flour, with one teaspoonful of vanilla. Bake in jelly tins in four layers.

Chocolate Cake, No. 2.—One cupful of butter, two cupfuls of sugar, three cupfuls of flour, half cupful sweet milk, half teaspoonful soda, one teaspoonful of cream tartar, seven eggs. Bake in layers, and put between the layers the following filling: Quarter of a pound of Baker's best vanilla chocolate, one gill of sweet milk, one egg, sugar to taste. Scald the gill of milk and the chocolate together; beat one egg thoroughly, and stir it in; add sugar and vanilla to taste.

Chocolate Cake, No. 3.—Two cupfuls of sugar, one of butter, five eggs, half a teaspoonful of soda, a teaspoonful of cream tartar, half a cupful of sour milk. Grated nutmeg and vanilla. Bake in layers, and put between the layers the following filling: One cupful of Baker's chocolate, grated, and a small cupful of sugar. Put in a dry bowl, and stand

MEMORANDUM
ON
FRIENDS' RECIPES

MEMORANDUM ON FRIENDS' RECIPES

DOMESTIC COOKERY.

the bowl in a pan of boiling water. Stir until the heat of the bowl dissolves the chocolate and sugar into a thick paste. Add a tablespoonful of clear table sirup and two eggs well beaten. Let this cook in the boiling water about ten minutes, then add two teaspoonfuls of vanilla.

Jelly Cake.—Beat three eggs well, the whites and yelks separately; take a cupful of fine white sugar, and beat that in well with the yelks, and a cupful of sifted flour, stirred in gently; then stir in the whites, a little at a time, and a teaspoonful of baking-powder and one tablespoonful of milk; pour it in three jelly-cake plates, and bake from five to ten minutes in a well-heated oven, and when cold spread with currant jelly, and place each layer on top of the other and sift powdered sugar on the top.

Jelly Roll.—Add one cupful of powdered sugar and one cupful of flour to three well-beaten eggs; stir well, and add one teaspoonful of cream of tartar, half a teaspoonful of saleratus dissolved in three teaspoonfuls of water; bake in two pie-pans; spread as evenly as possible; as soon as done, turn the cake, bottom side up, on to a dry towel; spread it evenly with jelly, roll up quickly, and wrap closely in the towel.

Peach Cake.—Bake sponge cake in layers; cut peaches in very thin slices, and spread upon the cake; sweeten, flavor, and whip some sweet cream, and spread over each layer and over the top.

Pineapple Cake.—One cupful of butter, two cupfuls of sugar, one cupful milk, three cupfuls of flour, whites of six eggs and yelks of four, three teaspoonfuls of baking-powder well mixed through flour; bake in jelly-cake pans; grate a pineapple; sprinkle with sugar, spread between the layers; pineapple jam may be substituted; frost the outside; beat two tablespoonfuls of the pineapple into the frosting.

CAKES AND CAKE-BAKING.

Cocoanut Cake.—Two eggs, one cupful white sugar, one-half a cupful sweet milk, one-quarter cupful of butter, one and one-half cupfuls of flour, one and one-half teaspoonfuls baking-powder. Bake in a moderate oven in pans one inch deep. To prepare the desiccated cocoanut, beat the whites of two eggs to a stiff froth, add one cupful of pulverized sugar and the cocoanut, after soaking it in boiling milk. Spread the mixture between the layers of cake and over the top.

White Mountain Cake.—Make the cake with one pound of flour, one pound of sugar, half a pound of butter, six eggs, one cupful of milk, one small teaspoonful of saleratus dissolved in the milk. Bake four thin cakes in flat pie plates; frost each of these cakes, laying one on another. When all are done, even the edges with a knife and frost the sides. Use the following frosting preparation: Beat to a standing froth the whites of four eggs made thick with sifted, refined sugar, and add the sugar and juice of one lemon.

Delicate Cake.—Two cupfuls of pulverized sugar, half a cupful of butter, three cupfuls of flour, nearly three-fourths of a cupful of milk, whites of eight eggs, half a teaspoonful of cream tartar, one-fourth teaspoonful soda. This may be baked in jelly cake tins and put together with icing.

Cream Cake.—Take two cupfuls of sugar, two-thirds of a cupful of butter, one cupful milk, one teaspoonful of soda, one and a half teaspoonfuls of cream of tartar, two and a half cupfuls of flour, three eggs. Make the custard for the cake with one cupful of milk, and one teaspoonful of cornstarch dissolved in it, and brought to a boiling heat, with the yelk of one egg dropped in to color it. Flavor with lemon or vanilla; let it cool. Bake your cake in round pie-tins; use just enough batter in the tin so that when they are baked two of them put together will make one proper sized cake. Make the custard first, and let it cool; put the

MEMORANDUM
ON
FRIENDS' RECIPES

MEMORANDUM ON FRIENDS' RECIPES

cakes together when they are warm, with plenty of custard between them.

Orange Cake.—Two cupfuls of sugar, one of butter, five eggs, half a cupful of sour milk, one teaspoonful of cream tartar, half a teaspoonful of soda, and two cupfuls of flour. Bake in four layers, and put between the layers the following filling: Beat two eggs, add to them a small cupful of sugar, heaping tablespoonful of butter. Simmer gently until it thickens. Remove from the fire, add the juice, grated pulp, and part of the rind of one large orange.

Ice-Cream Cake.—Two cupfuls of sugar, half a cupful of butter, three eggs, a cupful of milk, three cupfuls of flour, two teaspoonfuls of baking-powder. Bake in layers. Boil two small cupfuls of sugar and two-thirds of a cupful of water for ten minutes. Beat the white of an egg, and pour it over the mixture when it cooks a little. Beat till cold and stiff, and put between the layers.

Union Cake.—Two-thirds of a cupful of butter, two cupfuls of sugar, one cupful of milk, three cupfuls of flour, four eggs, two-thirds of a teaspoonful of cream tartar, and one-third of a teaspoonful of soda. Divide into three equal parts, and into one part put a cupful of seeded raisins, two-thirds of a cupful of currants, and one-quarter pound of citron. Bake in three pans of the same size. Put icing, flavored with extract of lemon, between the layers and on the top and sides.

Marble Cake.—Two cupfuls of white sugar, one cupful of butter, the whites of seven eggs, two teaspoonfuls of cream tartar, one of soda, three and a half cupfuls of flour, and half a cupful of milk. In another bowl three cupfuls of brown sugar, one of butter, one of molasses, the yelks of seven eggs, two tablespoonfuls of cinnamon, two of allspice, one teaspoonful of cloves, half a nutmeg, half a cupful of milk, three cupfuls of flour, one teaspoonful of soda, and two of

cream tartar. Arrange by dropping in first a tablespoonful of dark batter, then of the light, to imitate marble.

Watermelon Cake.—White part: One-half cupful of butter, one cupful of powdered sugar, whites of three eggs, one-third of a cupful of sweet milk, half a tablespoonful of baking-powder, and three half cupfuls of flour.—Red part: One-half cupful of butter, one cupful of red sugar, yelks of five eggs, one-third of a cupful of sweet milk, one tablespoonful of baking-powder, two cupfuls of flour, and half a pound of seeded raisins. Put the red part in the centre of the pan, with the white on the outside. Raisins may be introduced in the red part to represent seeds. Red sugar can be had of the confectioners.

Neapolitan Cake.—Mix a *yellow* portion thus: Two cupfuls of powdered sugar, one cupful of butter stirred to light cream with sugar; five eggs beaten well, with yelks and whites separately; half a cupful of sweet milk, three cupfuls of prepared flour, a little nutmeg.

Mix a *pink and white* portion thus: One pound of powdered sugar, one pound of prepared flour, half a pound of butter creamed with sugar, the whites of ten eggs whisked stiff. Divide this batter into two equal portions. Leave one white, and color the other with a very little prepared cochineal or with red sugar.

Mix a *brown* portion thus: Three eggs beaten light, one cupful of powdered sugar, quarter cupful of butter creamed with sugar, two tablespoonfuls of cream, one *heaping* cupful of prepared flour, two tablespoonfuls of vanilla chocolate grated and rubbed smooth in the cream, before it is beaten into the cake.

Bake each of these parts in jelly-cake tins. The above quantities should make three cakes of each color.

Mix a filling for the cake thus: Two cupfuls of sweet milk, two tablespoonfuls of corn-starch, wet with milk, two

MEMORANDUM
OF
FRIENDS' RECIPES

MEMORANDUM
ON
FRIENDS' RECIPES

eggs, two small cupfuls of fine sugar. Heat the milk, stir in the sugar and corn-starch, boil five minutes, and put in the eggs. Stir steadily until it becomes quite thick. Divide this custard into two parts. Stir into one two tablespoonfuls of grated chocolate and a teaspoonful of vanilla; into the other, bitter almond.

Prepare another filling thus: Whites of three eggs, whisked stiff, one heaping cup of powdered sugar, juice and half the grated peel of one lemon. Whip all together well. Lay the brown cake as the foundation of the pile; spread with the yellow custard; add the pink, coated with chocolate; then add the white and yellow with the frosting between them. Vary the order as fancy dictates. Cover the top with powdered sugar or with icing.

Angel's Food.—Use the whites of eleven eggs, a scant pint of granulated sugar, a large half pint of flour, one teaspoonful of cream tartar (even full), and a teaspoonful of vanilla. Sift the flour four times, then measure; add cream of tartar, and then sift again. Sift the sugar four times, then measure it. Beat the eggs to a stiff froth on a large dish, and on same dish add the sugar quickly and lightly; add the flour in the same way, and last of all the vanilla. Put at once into a moderate oven, and bake forty minutes or more. Do not grease the pans. Turn upside down to cool, putting small blocks of wood under the edges that air may reach the cake.

Macaroons.—Blanch half a pound of almonds with boiling water, and pound them to a smooth paste. Add a tablespoonful of essence of lemon, half a pound of powdered sugar, and the whites of two eggs. Work the paste well together with the back of a spoon. Wet your hands, and roll them in balls the size of a nutmeg, and lay them an inch apart on a sheet of paper. Wet your finger, and press gently over the surface to make them shiny. Bake three-quarters of an hour in a very moderate oven.

MEMORANDUM
ON
FRIENDS' RECIPES

Chocolate Macaroons.—Put three ounces of plain chocolate in a pan, and melt on a slow fire; then work it to a thick paste with one pound of powdered sugar and the whites of three eggs; roll the mixture down to the thickness of about one-quarter of an inch; cut it in small, round pieces with a paste-cutter, either plain or scalloped; butter a pan slightly, and dust it with flour and sugar in equal quantities; place in it the pieces of paste or mixture, and bake in a hot but not quick oven.

Cream Puffs.—Stir one-half pound of butter into a pint of warm water, set it on the fire in a saucepan, and slowly bring it to a boil,stirring often. When it boils, put in three-quarters of a pound of flour, and let it boil one minute, stirring constantly. Take from the fire, and turn into a deep dish to cool. Beat eight eggs light, and whip into this cool paste, first the yelks, then the whites. Drop in great spoonfuls on buttered paper so as not to touch or run into each other, and bake ten minutes. Split them, and fill with the following cream: One quart of milk, four tablespoonfuls of corn-starch, two eggs, two cupfuls of sugar. Stir while boiling, and when thick, add a teaspoonful of butter. When cold, flavor.

Kisses.—Beat the whites of four eggs very stiff, add one-half pound of pulverized sugar, and flavor to taste. Beat until very light, then lay in heaps the size of an egg on paper. Place the paper on a piece of wood half an inch thick, and put in a hot oven. Make the surface shiny by passing over it a wet knife. Bake until they look yellowish, when they are done.

Chocolate Kisses.—Beat stiff the whites of two eggs; beat in gradually one-half pound of powdered sugar. Scrape fine one and a half ounces of chocolate; dredge with flour, mixing the flour well; add this gradually to the eggs and sugar, stirring the whole very hard. Cover the bottom of a pan with

MEMORANDUM

ON

FRIENDS' RECIPES

white paper, and place on it spots of powdered sugar the size of half-dollars. Heap the mixture on these spots, smooth with a broad knife, sift with powdered sugar, and bake quickly.

Cocoanut Steeples.—One pound of powdered sugar; one-half pound of grated cocoanut; whites of five eggs. Whip the eggs as for icing, adding the sugar as you go on until it will stand alone, then beat in the cocoanut. Mold the mixture with your hands into small cones, and set these far enough apart not to touch one another upon buttered paper in a baking-pan. Bake in a very moderate oven.

Meringues.—Mix the whites of four eggs, beaten to a stiff froth, with one pound of pulverized sugar, and flavored to the taste. Beat stiff, bake the same as macaroons, when light brown, slip them from the papers, and put the smooth sides together, with jelly between.

Lady-fingers.—One-half pound pulverized sugar and six yelks of eggs, well stirred; add one-fourth pound flour, whites of six eggs, well beaten. Bake in lady-finger tins, or squeeze through a bag of paper in strips two or three inches long.

Lady-fingers, No. 2.—Rub half a pound of butter into a pound of flour; to this add half a pound of sugar, the juice and grated rind of one large lemon, and, lastly, three eggs, the whites and yelks beaten separately, and the whites stirred in after all the other ingredients are well mixed together. This dough, if properly made, will be stiff enough to make rolls about the size of a lady's finger; it will spread when in the oven, so that it will be of the right size and shape. If you wish them to be especially inviting, dip them in chocolate icing after they are baked, and put two together. See that the icing is so hard that it will not run, and set the cakes on a platter in a cool room until the icing is firm.

Felairs a la Creme.—Three-fourths pound flour, one pint water, ten eggs, one-half cupful butter. Put the water on the fire in a stewpan with the butter; as soon as it boils stir in the sifted flour; stir well until it leaves the bottom and sides of the pan, when taken from the fire; then add the eggs, one at a time. Put the batter in a bag of paper, and press out in the shape of fingers on a greased tin. When cold, fill with cream, prepared as follows: One and one-half pints of milk, two cupfuls sugar, yelks of five eggs, one tablespoonful butter, three large tablespoonfuls corn-starch, two teaspoonfuls extract vanilla. Frosted with chocolate, they are much improved in appearance and flavor.

Icing for Cakes.—In making icing, use at least a quarter of a pound of pulverized sugar to the white of each egg; if not stiff enough, add more sugar. Break the whites into a broad, cool dish, and throw in a small handful of sugar. Begin whipping it in with long, even strokes of the beater, adding the sugar gradually. Beat until the icing is smooth and firm, then add the flavoring. Spread it on the cake with a broad-bladed knife, dipped in cold water. If ornamentation of the icing is desired, it may be done by affixing prepared leaves, flowers, etc., which can be had at the confectioners' stores or at their supply stores. To make letters, tracery, etc., for cakes, roll into a funnel shape a piece of thick, white paper; fill this with icing in the soft state, allowing it to drip out slowly from the small end of the paper cone. Apply this carefully, and allow it to harden.

Orange Icing.—Whites of two eggs, one-half pound of pulverized sugar, and the juice of a large orange, treated as above.

Lemon Icing.—Whites of two eggs, one-half pound of pulverized sugar, juice and part of the rind of one lemon.

Chocolate Icing.—Whites of two eggs, one-half pound of

MEMORANDUM
ON
FRIENDS' RECIPES

MEMORANDUM ON FRIENDS' RECIPES

pulverized sugar, and three tablespoonfuls of grated chocolate.

Almond Icing.—The whites of three eggs, one cupful of pounded blanched almonds, three-quarters of a pound of pulverized sugar, and a little almond extract.

Banana Icing.—Whites of two eggs, one-half pound of pulverized sugar, and one banana finely crushed through it. This cake should be eaten the same day it is made, as the banana discolors over night.

Cocoanut Frosting.—Whites of two eggs, one-half pound of pulverized sugar. Spread on the cake, then sprinkle thickly with grated cocoanut. This will make a whiter frosting than results from stirring in the cocoanut.

Cooked Frosting.—One cupful of granulated sugar, wet with a little water. Let it boil without stirring until it begins to thicken. Beat the whites of two eggs very light. Strain the boiled sugar into them slowly, beating all the time. Flavor to taste.

XIV.—FRESH FRUITS AND NUTS.

VALUE OF FRESH FRUITS ON THE TABLE; ABUNDANCE OF FRUITS; NUTRITIVE VALUE OF FRUITS; WHERE TO GATHER AND HOW TO STORE FRUITS. TWENTY-TWO RECIPES FOR SERVING FRESH FRUITS AND NUTS.

FRESH fruits are a most delightful accessory to the table supply of both rich and poor. They are so great in variety, so rich in flavor, so beautiful in appearance, so healthful, and of so long continuance in most parts of the country, that it behooves every housekeeper to familiarize herself with the best methods of using fresh fruits to advantage.

A few years ago each locality depended upon its own local crop of fruits. Now the railroads bring early fruits from the far South and late fruits from the far North, so that at the centres of population the several fruit seasons are delightfully prolonged. Nor are we restricted to our own country's production. Such are the facilities for rapid and safe communication from distant points, that the world lays her tribute of fruits, sweet and sound, at the door of the enlightened nations.

Fruits do not take an important place as nutrients. They belong rather among the luxuries, and yet, as an agreeable stimulant to digestion, they occupy a front rank. In many conditions of health, some of the fruits are the only articles the invalid can enjoy, and their genial influences contribute greatly to the general improvement of a patient's appetite.

Fruits intended for immediate use should be gathered early in the morning, while the coolness of the night dews

MEMORANDUM
ON
FRIENDS' RECIPES

MEMORANDUM ON FRIENDS' RECIPES

is upon them. They should be just ripe, neither overdone nor underdone, in nature's great process of preparing them for human food. Fruit for storage is best gathered at the middle of a dry day. It should be *nearly* ripe. If unripe, or overripe it will not keep well. A moist atmosphere, but not one positively damp, is best for the storing of fruit. An ordinary cellar does better than a dry storeroom. Fruit keeps better in the dark than in the light.

All varieties of nuts belong to the albuminous fruits and are very nutritious, though the richer nuts are not easy of digestion owing to their oily properties.

The supply of peanuts once came wholly from Africa, but our Southern States have so successfully cultivated this popular nut that we are now independent. The bulk of the supply is from Virginia, North Carolina, and Tennessee. During a single season the crop of Virginia rose to one million one hundred thousand bushels, of Tennessee, five hundred and fifty thousand bushels, and of North Carolina, one hundred and twenty thousand bushels.

The Texas pecan is especially in demand. While a few years ago several barrels of pecans abundantly supplied the demand, carloads and invoices of one or two hundred barrels are not now uncommon.

In the Eastern States hickory nuts are sufficiently plentiful to ship to New York half a dozen carloads a week when demanded.

The chestnut is becoming scarcer every year, but their great popularity will probably prevent their total disappearance, as they are already being successfully cultivated, and it is expected that in a few years the cultivated nut will equal in quality the high-priced Italian chestnuts.

RECIPES.

Watermelons.—Wipe watermelons clean when they are taken from the ice. They should lie on ice for at least four

FRESH FRUITS AND NUTS. 203

hours before they are eaten. Cut off a slice at each end of the watermelon, then cut through the centre; stand on end on platter, and slice down, allowing each slice a part of the centre, or heart.

Nutmegs, etc.—Wash nutmegs and muskmelons; wipe dry; cut in two; shake out the seeds lightly, and put a lump of ice in each half. Eat with pepper and salt. A silver spoon is a neat and pleasant article with which to eat small, ripe melons.

Pineapples.—Slice on a slaw-cutter, or very thin with a knife; mix with finely powdered sugar. Set on ice till ready to serve.

Oranges are nice served whole, the skins quartered and turned down. Form in a pyramid with bananas and white grapes.

Orange and Cocoanut.—A layer of oranges sliced, then sugar, then a layer of cocoanut, grated; then another of oranges, and so on until the dish is full. This is by many known as *Ambrosia*.

Sliced Peaches.—Peel and slice ripe peaches. Lay them in a dish with plenty of sugar for an hour or two, till tea time. Eat with cream.

Stewed Peaches.—Make a sirup of sugar and water; halve the peaches, leaving the stone in one half, and drop into sirup. Allow the whole to simmer slowly until fruit is tender; then remove fruit, and let sirup boil till thick; then pour over fruit and serve at once.

Frosted Peaches.—Put half a cupful of water and the beaten whites of three eggs together; dip in each peach, using fine, large freestones, after you have rubbed off the fur with a clean cloth; and then roll in powdered sugar. Set them on the stem end, upon a sheet of white paper, in a sunny window. When half dry, roll again in the sugar.

MEMORANDUM
ON
FRIENDS' RECIPES

MEMORANDUM
ON
FRIENDS' RECIPES

204   *DOMESTIC COOKERY.*

Expose to the sun and breeze until perfectly dry. Until ready to arrange them in the glass dish for table, keep in a cool, dry place. Decorate with green leaves.

Fried Peaches.—Cut the peaches in two, and remove the stones. Dust a little flour on the side from which the stone is taken, and fry, only on that side, in a little butter. When done, add sugar and a little butter.

Baked Apples.—Pare and core good, sound, tart apples. Fill them with sugar, butter, and a flavor of spice. Put a little water in the pan, and bake until the apples are thoroughly tender.

Apple Sauce.—Pare, core, and slice nice, juicy apples that are not very sweet; put them in a stewpan with a little grated lemon peel, and water enough to keep them from burning. Stew till soft and tender; mash to a paste, and sweeten well with brown sugar, adding a little butter and nutmeg.

Apples with Lemon.—Make a sirup of sugar and water. Slice a lemon into it, and let boil until clear. Pare and core sound, tart apples, cut into quarters, and lay them carefully into the sirup; let them cook gently until a straw can be run through them, taking care not to break them. Lay the pieces of apple in a glass dish, boil down the sirup, and when slightly cool, pour over the apples.

Apple Float.—Pare, slice, and stew six large apples in as much water as will cover them; when well done, press them through a sieve and sweeten highly with crushed sugar; while cooling, beat the whites of four eggs to a stiff froth, and stir into the apples; flavor with lemon or vanilla; serve with plenty of sweet cream.

Transparent Apple.—Boil tart, ripe, and juicy apples in a little water; then strain through a fine cloth, and add a pound of white sugar to a pint of juice. Boil till it jellies,

and then put into molds. It is very nice served with blanc-mange in saucers.

Baked Pears.—Place in a stone jar, first a layer of pears, with their skins on, then a layer of sugar, then pears, and so on until the jar is full. Then put in as much water as it will hold. Bake three hours.

Quinces.—Bake ripe quinces thoroughly; when cold, strip off the skins, place the quinces in a glass dish, and sprinkle them with white sugar; serve with rich cream.

Bananas and Cream.—Peel, slice, and heap up in a glass dessert-dish, and serve raw, with fine sugar and cream.

Fried Bananas.—Cut the bananas into slices, and fry in a little butter. This makes a very rich dish.

Stewed Rhubarb.—Carefully remove the outer stringy skin; then cut in pieces an inch long, and simmer gently till tender in water and sugar, and the rind and juice of a lemon. When done add a bit of butter and nutmeg.

Crystallized Fruit.—Pick out the finest of any kind of fruit; leave in the stones; beat the whites of three eggs to a stiff froth; lay the fruit in the beaten egg, with the stems upward; drain them, and beat the part that drips off again; select them out, one by one, and dip them into finely powdered sugar; cover a pan with a sheet of fine paper, place the fruit on it, and set it in a cool place; when the icing on the fruit becomes firm, pile them on a dish, and set them in a cold place.

Candied Fruits.—Make a very rich sirup with one pound of granulated sugar to a gill of water. Heat over boiling water till the sugar is dissolved. Pare and halve fine, ripe, but solid peaches. Put a single layer of them in the sirup, in a shallow vessel; cook slowly until clear; drain from the sirup, and put to dry in a moderately heated oven. When fairly dry they may be eaten at once; or, after drying

MEMORANDUM
ON
FRIENDS' RECIPES

MEMORANDUM ON FRIENDS' RECIPES

DOMESTIC COOKERY.

twenty-four hours, they may be packed for future use. Plums, cherries, and pears may be candied in the same manner.

Nuts.—Almonds are inseparably joined with raisins in table service; so for evening uses, hickory nuts and apples form a pleasant combination. All the harder-shelled nuts should be well cracked before they are served. With the softer-shelled, nut crackers should be furnished. Nut picks should always be at hand.

Sweet almonds, which are used for dessert, are of several varieties. Those known as the Syrian, or Jordan almonds, are regarded as the best. Those with hard shells are generally richer in flavor than those with the soft. Certainly the harder shell offers the more effective protection. The skin of almonds is not easily digested. For use in cooking they should be *blanched*, but for table use this is not desirable. Walnuts keep well and improve with age. Of the hickory-nut family, the *shell-bark* is considered best. These, too, are the better for age.

MEMORANDUM
ON
FRIENDS' RECIPES

XV.—JELLIES, JAMS, AND PRESERVES.

FRUIT FOR JELLIES, JAMS, AND PRESERVES; HOW PREPARED; PROPER SUGAR TO USE; QUANTITY OF SUGAR NEEDED; SUITABLE PRESERVING-KETTLES; WHAT NOT TO USE; THE FIRE; CANS AND JARS; WHERE STORED; MOLDING THE JELLY; THE JELLY-BAG; STRAINING JELLY; COVERING JELLY. FORTY-FOUR RECIPES FOR JELLIES, JAMS, AND PRESERVES.

TO insure success in preserving fruits, the first thing to be looked after is the fruit itself. This should be fully ripe, fresh, sound, and scrupulously clean and dry. It should be gathered in the morning of a sunny day, as it will then possess its finest flavor. Care should be taken to remove all bruised or decayed parts. Allowing them to remain will darken the sirup, and consequently impair the beauty of the preserves. Fruit requiring to be pared should be laid in water to preserve the color after the paring. The best sugar is the cheapest; indeed, there is no economy in stinting the sugar, either as to quality or proper quantity, for inferior sugar is wasted in scum, and the preserves will not keep unless a sufficient proportion of sugar is boiled with the fruit. At the same time, too large a proportion of sugar will destroy the natural flavor of the fruit, and in all probability make fruit candy, instead of the result sought.

The usual proportion in making preserves, is a pound of sugar to a pound of fruit. There are a few fruits which require more sugar. In making the sirup, use a small cupful of water to a pound of fruit. The sirup should always be boiled and strained before putting the fruit in.

Fruit should be cooked in brass kettles, or those of bell-metal. Modern kettles, lined with porcelain, are much used

MEMORANDUM ON
FRIENDS' RECIPES

DOMESTIC COOKERY.

for this purpose. The kettle should be broad and shallow, so that there will be no necessity for heaping the fruit. Never use tin, iron, or pewter spoons, or skimmers, for preserves, as they will convert the color of red fruit into a dingy purple, and impart, besides, a very unpleasant flavor.

Great care should be taken not to place the kettle flat upon the fire, as this will be likely to burn at the bottom.

Glass jars are much the best for preserves, as the condition of the fruit can be observed more readily. Whatever jars are used, however, the contents should be examined every three weeks for the first two months, and if there are any signs of either mold or fermentation it should be boiled over again. Preserves should be stored in a cool, dry place, but not in one into which fresh air never enters. Damp has a tendency to make the fruit mold, and heat to make it ferment.

A jelly-bag should be in every kitchen. It should be made of flannel, pointed at the bottom, so that the jelly will run out chiefly at one point. It is a good plan to sew a strong loop to the top of the bag, so that it may be hung upon a nail near the fire, that the juice of the fruit may run through gradually into a vessel below. The bag should not be squeezed with the hands, if you wish a very clear jelly. After the clear juice has been obtained, the remainder may be pressed, to make a very excellent, but inferior article of jelly or marmalade.

Rinse the tumblers or bowls to be used in cold water just before filling with jelly or marmalade. When the jelly is cold, fit a circle of tissue-paper, dip it in brandy, and place it directly on the surface of the fruit. This simple precaution will save the housekeeper much annoyance by protecting the conserve from mold. Should the fungus form inside the upper cover of the glass, the inner will effectually shield the contents. Paste thick paper over the top of the glass to exclude the air.

RECIPES.

Currant Jelly.—Never gather currants or other soft or small seed fruit immediately after a rain for preserving purposes, as they are greatly impoverished by the moisture absorbed. In this climate, the first week in July is usually considered the time to make currant jelly. Weigh the currants without removing the stems; do not wash them, but remove leaves and whatever may adhere to them; to each pound of fruit allow half the weight of granulated or pure loaf sugar; put a few currants into a porcelain-lined kettle, and press them with a potato-masher, or anything convenient, in order to secure sufficient liquid to prevent burning; then add the remainder of the fruit and boil freely for twenty minutes, stirring occasionally to prevent burning; take out and strain through a jelly-bag, putting the liquid into earthen or wooden vessels. When strained, return the liquid to the kettle, without the trouble of measuring, and let it boil thoroughly for a moment or so; then add the sugar; the moment the sugar is entirely dissolved, the jelly is done, and must be dished, or placed in glasses; it will jelly upon the side of the cup as it is taken up, leaving no doubt as to the result.

Currant Jelly, No. 2.—Take three quarts of fine, ripe, red currants, and four of white; put them into a jar, tie paper over the top, and put them into a cool oven for three or four hours, or else into a pan of boiling water, or set them on the side of the range; when they are thoroughly heated, strain through a jelly-bag. To every pint of juice, add one pound of granulated sugar, and boil from five to fifteen minutes; turn while hot into wet tumblers.

Currant Jelly without Cooking.—Press the juice from the currants and strain it; to every pint put a pound of fine white sugar; mix them together until the sugar is dissolved; then

---

MEMORANDUM
ON
FRIENDS' RECIPES

MEMORANDUM
ON
FRIENDS' RECIPES

DOMESTIC COOKERY.

put it in jars; seal them and expose them to a hot sun for two or three days.

Black Currant Jelly.—Boil the currants till the juice flows, then strain through a jelly-bag, and set it over the fire for twenty minutes, after which add half a pound of sugar to a pound of juice, and boil for about ten minutes.

White Currant Jelly.—Strip the fruit off the stems, and pound it in a clean wooden bowl. Drip the juice gently through a jelly-bag. Prepare a very pure, clear sirup of the best white sugar; allow a pint of juice to a pound of sugar; boil it ten minutes only. Put it in glass preserve-tumblers, cover with paper to fit exactly, and keep it dry and cool.

Apple Jelly.—Take twenty large, juicy apples; pare and chop; put into a jar with the rind of four large lemons, pared thin and cut in bits; cover the jar closely, and set in a pot of boiling water; keep water boiling all around it until the apples are dissolved; strain through a jelly-bag, and mix with the liquid the juice of four lemons; to one pint of mixed juice use one pound of sugar; put in kettle, and when the sugar is melted set it on the fire, and boil and skim about twenty minutes, or until it is a thick, fine jelly.

Apple Jelly, No. 2.—Peel and core sour apples; boil them in a very little water, and strain them through a jelly-bag Measure, and allow a pound of granulated sugar to a pint of juice. Mix the sugar and juice well together, and let it boil from five to ten minutes. Put it warm into glasses; cut some white paper to fit the top, dip it in brandy, and lay on when the jelly is cool; paste or tie thick paper over the glasses, and when cold put away in a dark, dry place.

Crab-apple Jelly.—Wash and quarter Siberian crab-apples. Cover with cold water and let cook until thoroughly tender. Strain through a jelly-bag, and to every pint of juice add one pound of sugar. Let cook until it will jelly A slight flavoring of essence of cinnamon is an improvement.

JELLIES, JAMS, AND PRESERVES.

Quince Jelly.—Take very ripe quinces; peel and core, and boil in a little water till very soft; drain off the juice through a coarse towel, add an equal measure of sugar, and boil twenty minutes.

Grape Jelly.—Mash the grapes thoroughly and strain out the juice. Add an equal measure of sugar, and boil twenty minutes.

Barberry Jelly.—Pick the berries from the stalks, mash them, and boil fifteen minutes. Squeeze through a jelly-bag; allow a pound of white sugar to a pound of juice; melt the sugar in the juice, and boil half an hour.

Raspberry Jelly.—Crush the raspberries and strain through a wet cloth. Add an equal measure of sugar, and boil from ten to twenty minutes.

Apple Marmalade.—Pare, core, and slice two or three dozen tart, juicy apples; three-quarters of a pound of sugar to every pint of juice. Stew until tender in just enough cold water to cover them. Drain off the juice through a colander, and put into a preserving-kettle, stirring into it three-quarters of a pound of sugar for every pint of the liquid. Boil until it begins to jelly; strain the juice of two lemons into it; put in the apples, and stew pretty fast, stirring almost constantly, until it becomes thick and smooth. If the apples are not entirely soft, rub them through the colander before adding them to the boiling sirup.

Quince Marmalade.—Take very ripe quinces; wash, pare and core them; to each pound of fruit allow one pound of loaf sugar. Boil the parings and cores together, with water enough to cover them, till quite soft; strain the liquid into the preserving-kettle with the fruit and sugar. Boil the whole over a slow fire, stirring frequently until the mass becomes thick.

Pear and Quince Marmalade.—Pare and core two dozen juicy pears and ten fine, ripe quinces. Add three-quarters

MEMORANDUM
ON
FRIENDS' RECIPES

MEMORANDUM
ON
FRIENDS' RECIPES

of a pound of sugar to every pound of fruit and the juice of three lemons. Throw them into cold water, and stew the parings and cores in a little water to make the sirup. When they have boiled to pieces, strain off the liquid; when cold, put in the sliced fruit and bring to a fast boil. When the mass is thick and smooth, cook steadily for an hour or more, working with a wooden spoon to a rich jelly.

Pineapple Marmalade.—Take ripe, juicy pineapples; pare, cut out the specks very carefully, and grate on a coarse grater all but the core. Weigh, and allow a pound of sugar to a pound of fruit. Cook from twenty minutes to half an hour.

Orange Marmalade.—Take eighteen sweet, ripe oranges, six pounds best white sugar. Grate the peel from four of these and reserve it for the marmalade. The rinds of the others will not be needed. Pare the fruit carefully, removing the inner white skin as well as the yellow. Slice the orange; remove the seeds; put the fruit and grated peel in a porcelain kettle, and boil steadily until the pulp is reduced to a smooth mass. Take from the fire, and put through a colander. Stir in six pounds of the best white sugar; return to the fire, and boil fast, stirring constantly half an hour or until thick.

Grape Marmalade.—Put green grapes into a preserving-pan with sufficient water to cover them. Put them on the fire, and boil until reduced to a mash; put the pulp through a sieve which will strain out the seeds; to each pound of pulp add two pounds of the best loaf sugar, and boil to the consistence of a jelly.

Peach Marmalade.—Select peaches which are quite ripe; pare and cut them in small pieces; to every pound of fruit add one pound of sugar; put the fruit and sugar into a preserving-kettle, and mash well together; place it over the fire, and when it begins to boil, stir until it becomes quite thick.

JELLIES, JAMS, AND PRESERVES.

Cherry Jam.—First stone and then weigh some freshly gathered preserving cherries; boil them over a brisk fire for an hour, keeping them almost constantly stirred from the bottom of the pan, to which they will otherwise be liable to stick and burn. Add for each pound of the fruit half a pound of good sugar roughly powdered, and boil quickly for twenty minutes, taking off the scum as it rises.

Blackberry Jam.—To four bowls of blackberries add four bowls of sugar; boil until it jellies.

Raspberry Jam.—Mash the raspberries, and allow a pound of sugar to a pound of fruit. Boil twenty minutes. A few currants added to raspberry jam is considered by many a great improvement.

Barberry Jam.—The barberries should be quite ripe, though they should not be allowed to hang until they begin to decay. Strip them from the stalks, throw aside such as are spotted, and for each pound of fruit allow eighteen ounces of well-refined sugar; boil this, with one pint of water to every four pounds, until it becomes white and falls in thick masses from the spoon; then throw in the fruit, and keep it stirred over a brisk fire for six minutes only; take off the scum, and pour it into jars or glasses.

Strawberry Jam.—Use fine, scarlet berries; weigh and boil them for thirty-five minutes, keeping them constantly stirred; add eight ounces of good sugar to the pound of fruit; mix them well off the fire, then boil again quickly for twenty-five minutes. One pound of white currant juice added at the outset to four of the strawberries will greatly improve this preserve.

White Currant Jam.—Boil together quickly for seven minutes equal quantities of fine white currants, picked very carefully, and of the best white sugar pounded and passed through a sieve. Stir the preserve gently the whole time,

MEMORANDUM
ON
FRIENDS' RECIPES

MEMORANDUM
ON
FRIENDS' RECIPES

and skim it thoroughly. Just before it is taken from the fire, throw in the strained juice of one good lemon to four pounds of the fruit.

Damson Jam.—The fruit for this jam should be freshly gathered and quite ripe. Split, stone, weigh, and boil it quickly for forty minutes; then stir in half its weight of good sugar roughly powdered, and when it is dissolved, give the preserve fifteen minutes additional boiling, keeping it stirred and thoroughly skimmed.

Green Gage Jam.—Rub ripe green gages through a sieve; put all the pulp into a pan with an equal weight of loaf sugar pounded and sifted. Boil the whole until sufficiently thick, and put into glasses.

Preserved Peaches.—Weigh the peaches, and allow three-quarters of a pound of sugar to every pound of fruit. Throw about half the sugar over the fruit, and let it stand over night. In the morning drain the sirup off the fruit, add the rest of the sugar, and let that come to a boil. Put the peaches in, and let them boil until you can stick a straw through them. In cooking the peaches, put a few at a time only in the sirup to cook.

Preserved Peaches, No. 2.—Weigh the fruit after it is pared and the stones extracted and allow a pound of sugar to every pound of peaches. Put the sugar in a preserving-kettle, and make the sirup; let it just boil; lay the peaches in, and let them boil steadily until they are tender and clear. Take them out with a perforated skimmer and lay upon flat dishes, crowding as little as possible. Boil the sirup almost to a jelly, until it is clear and thick, skimming off all the scum. Fill the jars two-thirds full of the peaches, pour on the boiling sirup, and, when cold, cover with brandied tissue-paper, then with thick paper tied tightly over them. Or put them in air-tight jars.

Preserved Quinces.—Use a pound of sugar to each pound of quince after paring, coring, and quartering; take half of the sugar and make a thin sirup; stew in this a few of the quinces at a time till all are finished. Make a rich sirup of the remaining sugar, and pour over them.

Pineapple Preserves.—Use pineapples as ripe as can be had. Pare and cut them into thin slices, weigh them, and allow one pound of the best granulated sugar to each pound of fruit. Take a deep china bowl or dish, and in it put a layer of fruit and sugar alternately, a coating of sugar on the top; let it stand all night. In the morning, take out the fruit and put the sirup into a preserving-kettle. Boil and skim it until it is perfectly clear; then, while it is boiling hot, pour it over the fruit, and let it stand uncovered until it becomes entirely cold. If it stands covered, the steam will fall into the sirup and thin it.

Preserved Pears.—Preserved pears are put up precisely as are peaches, but are only pared, not cored or divided. Leave the stems on.

Watermelon Rind Preserves.—Select rind which is firm, green, and thick; cut in any fanciful shape, such as leaves, stars, diamonds, etc. Then weigh, and to each pound of rind allow one and a half pounds of loaf sugar. To green them, take a brass or copper kettle, and to a layer of grapevine leaves, which should be well washed, add a layer of the rind, and so on until the last, which should be a thick layer of the leaves, and well covered with a coarse linen cloth. To each pound of the rind, add a piece of alum the size of a pea; then fill up with warm water sufficient to cover the whole, and let it stand upon the stove, where it will steam, but not boil, until the greening is completed, which will be in two or three hours. When green, lay them in clear, cold water, and make your sirup. To each pound of sugar add one and a half pints of water; clarify, put in

MEMORANDUM
ON
FRIENDS' RECIPES

216 DOMESTIC COOKERY.

your rind; slice lemons, two to each pound of rind, and when about half done add the lemons. Boil until the rind is perfectly transparent. A few pieces of ginger-root may be added, which will impart a high flavor, and will blend very delightfully with the lemons.

Preserved Citron.—Proceed the same as above, substituting citron for the watermelon rind.

Preserved Strawberries.—Procure fresh, large strawberries when in their prime, but not so ripe as to be very soft; hull and weigh them; take an equal weight of sugar, make a sirup, and when boiling hot, put in the berries. A small quantity only should be done at once. If crowded, they will become mashed. Let them boil about twenty minutes, or a half an hour; turn into tumblers or small jars, and seal with egg papers while hot.

Preserved Cherries.—Wash, stem, and stone the cherries; save every drop of the juice, and use it in place of water in making the sirup. Make a sirup, allowing a pound of sugar to every pound of fruit; add the fruit, and let it simmer gently for half an hour, skimming as is necessary.

Damson Preserves.—To four pounds of damsons use three pounds of sugar; prick each damson with a needle; dissolve the sugar with one-half pint of water, and put it on the fire; when it simmers, put in as many damsons as will lie on the top; when they open, take them out and lay them on a dish, and put others in, and so on until all have been in; then put them all in the kettle together and let them stew until done; put them in jars and seal them.

Green Gage Preserves.—When the fruit is ripe, wipe them clean, and to one pound of fruit put one-quarter pound of sugar, which will make a fine sirup; boil the fruit in this sirup until it is perfectly done; then use a fresh sirup of one pound of fruit to one pound of sugar; moistening the sugar

MEMORANDUM ON FRIENDS' RECIPES

JELLIES, JAMS, AND PRESERVES.

with water. When the sirup boils put in the fruit, and leave for fifteen minutes; then put the fruit in jars; boil the sirup until thick; when cooled to milkwarm, pour it over the fruit; tie the jars tightly and keep in a warm place.

Strawberries in Wine.—Put a quantity of the finest large strawberries in a bottle, strew in a few spoonfuls of powdered sugar, and fill the bottle up with Madeira or Sherry wine.

Grapes in Brandy.—Take some close bunches of grapes, white or black, not overripe, and lay them in a jar. Put a good quantity of pounded white candy upon them, and fill up the jar with brandy. Tie them close down, and keep in a dry place. Prick each grape with a needle three times.

Brandy Peaches.—Take large, juicy freestone peaches, not so ripe as to burst or mash on being handled. Rub the down from them with a clean thick flannel. Prick every peach down to the stone with a large silver fork, and score them all along the seam or cleft. To each pound of peaches allow a pound of granulated sugar and half a pint of water mixed with half a white of egg, slightly beaten. Put the sugar into a porcelain kettle and pour the water upon it. When it is quite melted, give it a stirring, set it over the fire, and boil and skim it till no more scum rises. Then put in the peaches, and let them cook (uncovered) in the sirup till a straw will penetrate them. Then take the kettle off the fire, and take out the fruit with a wooden spoon, draining it over the kettle. Let the sirup remain in the kettle a little longer. Mix a pint of the very best white brandy for each pound of peaches, with the sirup, and boil them together ten minutes or more. Transfer the peaches to large glass jars, making each about two-thirds full, and pour the brandy and sirup over them, filling the jars full. When cool, cover closely.

Spiced Peaches.—Seven pounds of fruit, one pint vinegar,

MEMORANDUM
ON
FRIENDS' RECIPES

DOMESTIC COOKERY.

three pounds sugar, two ounces cinnamon, one-half ounce cloves. Scald together the sugar, vinegar, and spices; pour over the fruit. Let it stand twenty-four hours; drain off, scald again, and pour over fruit, letting it stand another twenty-four hours. Boil all together until the fruit is tender. Skim it out, and boil the liquor until thickened. Pour over the fruit and set away in a jar.

Apple Butter.—Boil down a kettleful of cider to two-thirds the original quantity. Pare, core, and slice juicy apples, and put as many into the cider as it will cover. Boil slowly, stirring often with a flat stick, and when the apples are tender to breaking, take them out with a perforated skimmer, draining well against the sides of the kettle. Put in a second supply of apples and stew them soft, as many as the cider will hold. Take from the fire, pour all together into a tub or large crock; cover and let it stand twelve hours. Then return to the kettle and boil down, stirring all the while until it is the consistency of thick custard and brown in color. Spice well with Durkee's ground mixed spices.

Peach Butter.—To one bushel of peaches allow from eight to ten pounds of granulated sugar; pare and halve the peaches, put into the kettle, and stir constantly, to prevent sticking to the kettle, until perfectly smooth and rather thick; a part of the peach-stones thrown in and cooked with the peaches give it a nice flavor, and they can be afterward skimmed out; add the sugar a short time before taking from the fire; put in jars and cover tight; peaches for butter should be neither too mealy nor too juicy.

MEMORANDUM
ON
FRIENDS' RECIPES

XVI.—CANNED FRUITS AND VEGETABLES.

WIDESPREAD USE OF CANNED GOODS; PHILOSOPHY OF CANNING FRUITS; HOW TO FILL THE JARS; WHAT JARS ARE BEST; SELECTION OF THE FRUIT; WHERE TO STORE THE CANS; NEED OF WATCHING THE CANS. TWELVE RECIPES OF CANNING FRUIT AND VEGETABLES.

CANNED fruits and vegetables of all kinds may now be found abundantly in the stores. Their prices are so low that they present a strong inducement to the housekeeper to omit the labor incident to home canning, and simply to purchase what is needed.

What is aimed at in all these processes is the entire exclusion of air from the fruit. Its expulsion from them is effected by using heat enough to cook them, after which the hermetical sealing does the remaining service. Solder, wax, and rubber bands do this sealing work.

If it is desired to preserve the fruit whole, it may be put into the jars before heating. Fill the jars with water, and set them into a wash-boiler of cold water, the water reaching three-fourths of the way to the tops of the jars. Do not set them directly on the bottom, but on a little hay, lest the heat cause them to crack. Bring the water slowly to a boil, and let it boil about five minutes. The cans may then be taken out, stirred lightly, or shaken, to expel any remaining air bubbles; then fill to the brim with boiling water and close the jars. No air bubbles should remain in the can. If the fruit can be cooked before canning, the process is much simpler, as the boiling material itself expels the air. The cans in this case need simply to be filled and then sealed.

MEMORANDUM ON
FRIENDS' RECIPES

220 DOMESTIC COOKERY.

While filling jars, be careful that no current of cold air strike them, as this would suffice to crack a glass jar. When a jar has cracked, it is hardly safe to use its contents, as fragments of glass may be contained in the fruit, which would be fatal if swallowed.

Cans should be of glass or stoneware, as the acids of fruit act chemically on tin or other metals, often destroying the flavor of the fruit, and sometimes rendering it absolutely unwholesome. Do not use a metal spoon even. Either self-sealing cans, or those which require wax, may be used successfully, but probably the former are best for those of little experience, and they are unquestionably more convenient. There are several varieties of self-sealing cans, all of them highly recommended, and doubtless all of them sufficiently good. The "Valve Jar," the "Mason," and the "Hero" are among the best known and most reliable.

Fruit should be selected with the greatest care. Some varieties cannot be preserved at all, unless canned when perfectly fresh, and success is more certain with all kinds in proportion to freshness and soundness. The fruit should be nearly or quite ripe, but not over-ripe, and all which bears signs of decay should be rejected.

In canning, as in preserving, granulated sugar should always be used, and also a porcelain-lined kettle. Peaches, pears, or other large fruit may, by the aid of a fork, be tastily arranged in the jars, piece by piece. The boiling juice may be added afterward to cover them. Thus arranged they appear prettier in the jars, though, of course, the flavor is not improved.

All canning work should be done expeditiously, and the cans be set away to cool. They should be kept in a cool, dark place and closely watched for a few days, to see that the sealing is perfect. If the fruit shows signs of not being perfectly sealed, it should be at once taken out, scalded, and sealed again.

RECIPES.

Canned Strawberries.—Fill glass jars with fresh strawberries sprinkled with sugar, allowing a little over one-quarter of a pound of sugar to each pound of berries; set the jars in a boiler, with a little hay laid in the bottom to prevent the jars from breaking; fill with cold water to within an inch or two of the tops of the jars; let them *boil* fifteen minutes, then move back to the boiler, wrap the hand in a towel, and take out the jars; fill the jars to the top before sealing, using one or more of the filled jars for that purpose if necessary.

Canned Gooseberries.—Fill very clean, dry, wide-necked bottles with gooseberries gathered the same day and before they have attained their full growth. Cork them tightly, wrap a little hay round each of them, and set them up to their necks in a kettle of cold water, which should be brought very gradually to boil. Let the fruit be gently simmered until it appears shrunken and perfectly scalded; then take out the bottles, and with the contents of one or two fill up the remainder. Use great care not to break the fruit in doing this. When all are ready, pour *scalding* water into the bottles and cover the gooseberries entirely with it, or they will become moldy at the top. Cork the bottles well immediately, and cover the necks with melted resin; keep them in a cool place; and when they are used pour off the greater part of the water and add sugar as for the fresh fruit.

Canned Peaches.—Peel and quarter choice peaches. To peel, place them in a wire basket, dip into boiling water a moment and then into cold water, and strip off the skins. Have a porcelain-kettle with boiling water and another with sirup made with granulated sugar; drop the peaches into boiling water (some previously boil the pits in the water for their flavor) and let them cook until tender; then lift them out carefully into a can, pouring over them all the sirup the

MEMORANDUM
ON
FRIENDS' RECIPES

MEMORANDUM
ON
FRIENDS' RECIPES

222   *DOMESTIC COOKERY.*

can will hold, and seal immediately. Cook only peaches enough to fill one can at a time.

Canned Peaches, No. 2.—Pare and stone peaches enough for two jars at a time. If many are pared, they will become dark colored by standing. Rinse in cold water; then cook in a rich sirup of sugar and water about fifteen or twenty minutes, or until they are clear. Put into jars all that are not broken; fill up with the hot sirup, about as thick as ordinary molasses, and seal. The same sirup will do to cook several jars. After the sirup becomes dark, it, with the broken peaches, can be used for marmalade or peach butter. The same method can be used for pears, plums, and all light fruits.

Canned Pineapple.—Use three-fourths of a pound of sugar to one pound of fruit. Pick the pineapple to pieces with a silver fork. Scald and can while hot.

Canned Grapes.—Squeeze the pulp from the skin; boil the pulp until the seeds begin to loosen, having the skins boiling hard and separately in a little water. When the pulp seems tender, put it through the sieve; then add the skins, if tender, with the water they boil in, if not too much. Use a large coffeecupful of sugar for a quart can; boil until thick, and can in the usual way.

Canned Plums.—Prick each plum with a needle to prevent bursting; prepare a sirup, allowing a gill of pure water and a quarter of a pound of sugar to every three quarts of fruit. When the sugar is dissolved and the water blood-warm, put in the plums. Heat slowly to a boil. Let them boil five minutes—not fast or they will break badly—fill up the jars with plums, pour in the scalding sirup until it runs down the sides, and seal. Green gages are very fine put up in this way, also damsons for pies.

Canned Pears.—Select finely flavored fruit; either halve and core them or core whole; make a sirup of sugar and water,

MEMORANDUM
ON
FRIENDS' RECIPES

using as little water as will dissolve the sugar. Add a quarter of a pound of sugar to a pound of fruit. Place the fruit in the kettle carefully, and let it come to a boil or until the fruit is well scalded. Turn into the jars hot, and seal at once.

Canned Tomatoes.—Pour boiling water over the tomatoes to loosen the skins. Remove these; drain off all the juice that will come away without pressing hard; put them into a kettle and heat slowly to a boil. The tomatoes will look much nicer if all the hard parts be removed before putting them on the fire. Rub the pulp soft with your hands. Boil half an hour; dip out the surplus liquid, pour the tomatoes, boiling hot, into the cans, and seal. Keep in a cool, dark place.

Canned Beans.—Remove the strings at the sides, and cut into pieces about an inch long; put them into boiling water and scald, then can them.

Canned Asparagus.—Cut away all the hard part of the stem and boil the top portion until nearly done, just as if about to serve at once. Flat cans are best, into which the stems can be laid regularly, the water in which they were boiled being poured over them boiling hot, and the can sealed. If jars or high cans are used, pack the asparagus into them until they are full. Fill the cans with water; set them on hay in a boiler of cold water reaching to within an inch of their tops; then bring to a boil and nearly finish cooking the stems. Wrap the hand in a towel; take out the cans and seal or solder them as in other vegetables.

Canned Corn.—Boil sweet corn till nearly done; cut close from the cobs and fill the jars; pour on water in which the corn was boiled; place in a boiler and just bring to a boil, as above; then take out and seal.

MEMORANDUM
ON
FRIENDS' RECIPES

XVII.—PICKLES AND CATSUPS.

PICKLES MORE POPULAR THAN WHOLESOME; GREENING PICKLES; WHAT KETTLES AND JARS SHOULD NOT BE USED IN PICKLING; CHOOSING THE FRUIT, SPICES, ETC.; HOW TO KEEP PICKLES; CATSUPS, HOW MADE, ETC. THIRTY-THREE RECIPES FOR PICKLES AND CATSUPS.

PICKLES are very popular as a relish, but it must be confessed that they are not the most wholesome diet This is due chiefly to the fact that they are made of hard, crude, and often of unripe fruit. Then, too, the excess of acid and the high seasoning disagree with many constitutions.

It is deemed important that pickles for the market be well greened. To accomplish this end, copperas and other chemicals are employed or copper kettles are used. All this is poisonous, and should be shunned. No metal kettles or spoons should be tolerated in pickling. Glazed jars are not desirable either, as salt and vinegar decompose the glazing and set free the lead which it contains. An ordinary stone jar is the vessel to use, or a porcelain-lined kettle.

Be careful to select perfectly sound fruit or vegetables for pickling, and use none but the very best cider vinegar. Good white wine vinegar does well for some sorts of pickles, but be ever watchful against chemical preparations called vinegar, that destroy instead of preserving the articles put away in them. In the selection of spices there is so much diversity of taste that no general directions will be of practical value. But get the purest articles you can find.

Pickles must be kept from the air. It is a good plan to

PICKLES AND CATSUPS.

put them up in large jars, and for use to empty the large jar at once into smaller ones, using these one at a time. Keep them wholly covered with the vinegar. Water will soon cause the jar of pickles to spoil.

The same hints given above apply to the making of catsup, which is really but a pickle cooked to a more advanced point. It needs to be tightly corked and sealed, that it may keep well.

RECIPES.

Cucumber Pickles.—Make a weak brine, hot or cold; if hot, let the cucumbers stand in it twenty-four hours; if cold, forty-eight hours; rinse and dry the cucumbers with a cloth, take vinegar enough to cover them, allow one ounce of alum to every gallon of vinegar, put it in a brass kettle (or porcelain-lined, if the *greening* is not desired) with the cucumbers, and heat slowly, turning the cucumbers from the bottom frequently; as soon as they are heated through, skim them out into a crock, let the vinegar boil up, turn it over the pickles, and let them stand at least twenty-four hours; drain off the vinegar. Take fresh vinegar, and to every gallon allow two tablespoonfuls of white mustard-seed, one of cloves, one of celery-seed, one of stick cinnamon, one large, green pepper, a very little horse-radish, and, if you like, one-half pint of sugar. Divide the spices equally into several small bags of coarse muslin, scald with the vinegar, and pour over the pickles. If you like your pickles hard, let the vinegar cool before pouring over them.

Cucumber Pickles, No. 2.—To a gallon of water add a quart of salt, put in the cucumbers, and let them stand over night. In the morning, wash them out of the brine, and put them carefully into a stone jar. Boil a gallon of vinegar, put in, while cold, quarter of a pound of cloves, and a tablespoonful of alum; when it boils hard, skim it well and turn over the cucumbers. In a week they will be fit for use.

MEMORANDUM
ON
FRIENDS' RECIPES

MEMORANDUM
ON
FRIENDS' RECIPES

DOMESTIC COOKERY.

Pickled Onions.—Select small white onions, put them over the fire in cold water with a handful of salt. When the water becomes scalding hot, take them out and peel off the skins, lay them in a cloth to dry; then put them in a jar. Boil half an ounce of allspice and half an ounce of cloves in a quart of vinegar. Take out the spice and pour the vinegar over the onions while it is hot. Tie up the jar when the vinegar is cold, and keep it in a dry place.

Pickled Onions, No. 2.—Take small, white onions and peel them; lay them in salt water for two days; change the water once; then drain and put them in bottles. Take vinegar enough to cover them, spice with whole mixed spices, scald it, and pour over the onions.

Pickled Garlic and Eschalots.—Garlic and eschalots may be pickled in the same way as onions.

Pickled Nasturtiums.—Nasturtiums should be gathered quite young, and a portion of the buds, when very small, should be mixed with them. Prepare a pickle by dissolving an ounce and a half of salt in a quart of pale vinegar, and throw in the berries as they become fit, from day to day. They are used instead of capers for sauce, and by some persons are preferred to them. When purchased for pickling, put them at once into a jar and cover them well with the vinegar.

Pickled Watermelon.—Take the outer part of the rind of the melon, pare and cut in small pieces. To one quart of vinegar add two pounds of sugar, one ounce of cassia buds. In this boil the rind until clear and tender.

Pickled Walnuts.—Walnuts for this pickle must be gathered while a pin can pierce them easily. When once the shell can be felt, they have ceased to be in a proper state for it. Make sufficient brine to cover them well, with six ounces of salt to the gallon of water; take off the scum, which will rise to the surface as the salt dissolves, throw in the walnuts, and stir them night and morning; change the brine every three days, and if they are wanted for immediate eating, leave them in it for twelve days; otherwise, drain them from it in nine, spread them on dishes, and let them remain exposed to the air until they become black; this will be in twelve hours, or less. Make a pickle for them with something more than half a gallon of vinegar to the hundred, a teaspoonful of salt, two ounces of black pepper, three of bruised ginger, a drachm of mace, and from a quarter to half an ounce of cloves (of which some may be stuck into three or four small onions), and four ounces of mustard-seed. Boil the whole of these together for about five minutes; have the walnuts ready in a stone jar, or jars, and pour the vinegar on them as soon as it is taken from the fire. When the pickle is quite cold, cover the jar securely and store it in a dry place. Keep the walnuts always well covered with vinegar, and boil that which is added to them.

Pickled Red Cabbage.—Slice the red cabbage into a colander, and sprinkle each layer with salt; let it drain two days, then put it into a jar and pour boiling vinegar enough to cover, and put in a few slices of red beet-root. Use the purple red cabbage. Cauliflower cut in bunches, and thrown in after being salted, will take on the color of a beautiful red.

Pickled Mushrooms.—Rub the mushroom heads with flannel and salt, throw them in a stewpan with a little salt over them; sprinkle with pepper and a small quantity of mace; as the liquor comes out, shake them well, and keep them over a gentle fire until all the liquor is dried into them again; then put as much vinegar into the pan as will cover them; give it a scald, and pour the whole into bottles.

Pickled Beets.—Wash the beet perfectly, not cutting any of the fibrous roots, lest the juice escape; put in sufficient

MEMORANDUM
ON
FRIENDS' RECIPES

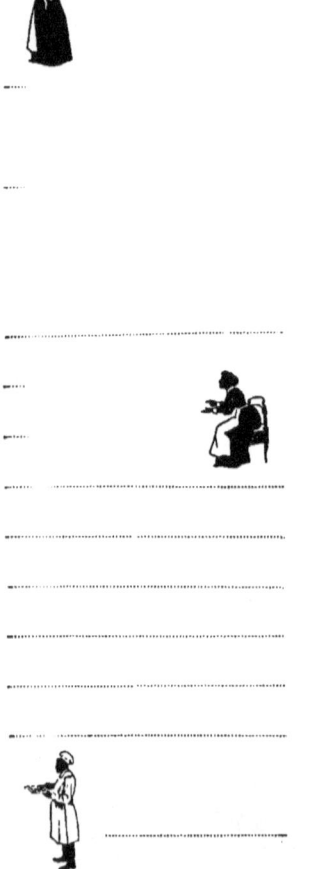

228 *DOMESTIC COOKERY.*

water to boil it, and when the skin will come off easily it is sufficiently cooked, and may be taken out and laid upon a cloth to cool. Having rubbed off the peel, cut the beet into thick slices, pour over it cold vinegar prepared as follows: Boil a quart of vinegar with an ounce of whole black pepper and an equal weight of dry ginger, and let it stand until quite cold. Keep closely corked.

Pickled Peppers.—Do not pick them till just as they begin to turn red; then soak them for ten or twelve days in strong salt and water; take them from the brine and soak them in clear water for a day. Wipe them dry, and put them away in cold vinegar; or if you wish them milder, remove the seeds and scald the vinegar, but do not boil.

Pickled Bell Peppers.—Cut a slit in the side of each pepper and take out all the seeds. Let them soak in brine (strong enough to float an egg) two days. Then, washing them in cold water, put them into a stone jar. Pour over them vinegar boiled with cinnamon, mace, and nutmeg. Whenever they are wanted to be served, stuff each one with a boiled tongue cut into dice and mixed with a *mayonnaise* dressing. Or little mangoes may be made, stuffing each one with pickled nasturtiums, grapes, minced onions, red cabbage, or cucumbers, seasoned with mustard-seed, root ginger, and mace.

Pepper-hash.—Take four dozen peppers, two very large cabbages, one ounce of *light* mustard-seed. Chop the peppers fine, cut the cabbage on a cabbage-knife, mix together, salt well, and let it stand over night, putting the dish or tub so the juice will run down; pour off in the morning. Add one ounce of cloves, one ounce of allspice; mix all through, and put the vinegar on cold.

Flint Pickles.—Make a brine of a gallon of water and a cupful of salt. This must be poured boiling hot on the cucumbers six days in succession. Rinse them in cold water;

put them in a kettle with a teaspoonful of allspice and a teaspoonful of cloves, a handful of cinnamon sticks, a little sliced horse-radish, and cider vinegar to cover them. Let them come to a boil, then take out and put in jars.

East India Pickle.—One hundred cucumbers (large and small), one peck of green tomatoes, one-half peck of onions, four cauliflowers, four red peppers (without the seeds), four heads of celery, one pint of bottled horse-radish. Slice all, and stand in salt twenty-four hours, then drain; pour on weak vinegar; stand on stove until it comes to a boil; then drain again. Take one ounce of ground cinnamon, one ounce of ground tumeric, one-half pound of mustard, one-quarter pound of brown sugar; wet these with cold vinegar; add to this sufficient vinegar to moisten all the pickles. Cook all together ten minutes. Seal in bottles while hot.

French Pickle.—Take one peck of green tomatoes, sliced; six large onions. Throw on them a teacupful of salt over night. Drain thoroughly, then boil in two quarts of water and one quart of vinegar fifteen or twenty minutes; drain in colander; then take four quarts of vinegar, two pounds of brown sugar, one-half pound of white mustard-seed, two tablespoonfuls of cloves, two tablespoonfuls of cinnamon, two tablespoonfuls of ginger, two tablespoonfuls of ground mustard, one teaspoonful of cayenne pepper; put all together and cook fifteen minutes.

Piccallily.—One peck of green tomatoes sliced, one-half peck of onions sliced, one cauliflower, one peck of small cucumbers. Leave in salt and water twenty-four hours; then put in a kettle with a handful of scraped horse-radish, one ounce of tumeric, one ounce of whole cloves, one-quarter pound of whole pepper, one ounce of cassia buds or cinnamon, one pound of white mustard-seed, one pound of English mustard. Put in kettle in layers, and cover with cold vinegar. Boil fifteen minutes, constantly stirring.

MEMORANDUM ON FRIENDS' RECIPES

MEMORANDUM
ON
FRIENDS' RECIPES

Chow-chow.—One quart of large cucumbers, one quart of small ones; two quarts of onions, four heads of cauliflower, six green peppers, one quart of green tomatoes, one gallon of vinegar, one pound of mustard, two cupfuls of sugar, two cupfuls of flour, one ounce of tumeric. Put all in salt and water one night; cook all the vegetables in brine until tender except the large cucumbers. Pour vinegar and spices over all.

Sweet Pickles.—Such fruit as peaches, plums, cherries, grapes, etc., are very palatable when sweet pickled. The process is the same as for other light pickles, except that the vinegar is sweetened to taste.

Sweet Tomato Pickles.—Eight pounds of peeled tomatoes, four of powdered sugar. Of cinnamon, cloves, and allspice, each one ounce. Boil one hour, and add a quart of boiling vinegar.

Tomato Catsup.—Take one bushel of tomatoes; boil soft, and pass through a sieve. Add half a gallon of cider vinegar, one pint of salt, two ounces of cloves, a quarter pound of allspice, a half ounce of cayenne pepper. Boil until reduced to half the quantity. When cool, bottle and cork tightly.

Tomato Catsup, No. 2.—Take one peck of ripe tomatoes, cut up, boil tender, and strain through a wire sieve; add one large tablespoonful of ground cloves, one large tablespoonful of allspice, one large tablespoonful of cinnamon, one teaspoonful of cayenne pepper, one-quarter pound of salt, one-quarter pound of mustard, one pint of vinegar. Boil gently three hours. Bottle and seal while warm.

Green Tomato Catsup.—One peck of green tomatoes, one dozen large onions, one-half pint of salt; slice the tomatoes and onions. To a layer of these add a layer of salt; let stand twenty-four hours, then drain. Add one-quarter pound

PICKLES AND CATSUPS.

of mustard-seed, three dessertspoonfuls of sweet oil, one ounce of allspice, one ounce of cloves, one ounce of ground mustard, one ounce of ground ginger, two tablespoonfuls of black pepper, two teaspoonfuls of celery-seed, one-quarter pound of brown sugar. Put all into a preserving-pan, cover with vinegar, and boil two hours.

Chili Sauce.—Thirty tomatoes, three large onions, three peppers, one tablespoonful each of allspice, cloves, and cinnamon, two nutmegs, two tablespoonfuls of salt, one quart of vinegar, one cupful of sugar. Chop the onions and peppers very fine. Cook the tomatoes somewhat first. Mix thoroughly.

Tomato Soy.—One-half bushel of green tomatoes, three onions, three green peppers, one-quarter pound of mustard-seed, three cupfuls of sugar, three cabbages. Chop the tomatoes and onions together fine; add to one gallon of the tomatoes one cupful of salt; let stand twenty-four hours, drain, and add the peppers (chopped fine), mustard-seed, sugar, and other spices to taste. Moisten all with vinegar and cook until tender. Before bottling, add the cabbages (chopped), and one cupful of chopped horse-radish.

Grape Catsup.—Take five pints of grapes; simmer until soft, then put through a colander; add to them two pints of brown sugar, one pint of vinegar, two tablespoonfuls of allspice, two tablespoonfuls of cinnamon, two tablespoonfuls of cloves, one and one-half teaspoonfuls of mace, one teaspoonful of salt, one and one-half teaspoonfuls of red pepper. Boil till thick; then bottle and seal tightly.

Walnut Catsup.—The vinegar in which walnuts have been pickled, when they have remained in it a year, will generally answer all the purposes for which this catsup is required, particularly if it be drained from them and boiled for a few minutes, with a little additional spice and a few eschalots, but where the vinegar is objected to, it may be made by

MEMORANDUM
ON
FRIENDS' RECIPES

MEMORANDUM ON FRIENDS' RECIPES

DOMESTIC COOKERY.

boiling either the expressed juice of young walnuts for an hour, with six ounces of fine anchovies, four ounces of eschalots, half an ounce of black pepper, a quarter ounce of cloves, and a drachm of mace to every quart.

Walnut Catsup, No. 2.—Pound in a mortar a hundred young walnuts, strewing among them as they are done half a pound of salt; then pour to them a quart of strong vinegar and let them stand until they have become quite black, keeping them stirred three or four times a day; next add a quart of strong, old beer, and boil the whole together for ten minutes; strain it, and let it remain until the next day; then pour it off clear from the sediment, add to :* one large head of garlic bruised, half an ounce of nutmegs bruised, the same quantity of cloves and black pepper, and two drachms of mace; boil these together for half an hour, and the following day bottle and cork the catsup well.

A bottle of port wine may be added before bottling, if desired, and a large bunch of sweet herbs.

Oyster Catsup.—Take fine, large fresh oysters, opened carefully, and wash them in their own liquor. To take any particle of shell that may remain, strain the liquor after. Pound the oysters in a mortar, add the liquor, and to every pint put a pint of sherry; boil it up and skim; then add two anchovies, pounded, an ounce of common salt, two drachms of pounded mace, and one of cayenne. Let it boil up, then skim, and rub it through a sieve. Bottle when cold and seal it. What remains in the sieve will do for oyster sauce.

Oyster Catsup, No. 2.—One quart oysters, one tablespoonful salt, one tablespoonful cayenne pepper, one tablespoonful mace, one teacupful cider vinegar, one teacupful sherry. Chop the oysters, and boil in their own liquor with the teacupful of vinegar, skimming the skum as it rises. Boil three minutes, strain through a hair cloth, return the liquor to the

PICKLES AND CATSUPS. 233

fire; add the wine, pepper, salt, and mace. Boil fifteen minutes, and when cold, bottle for use.

Mushroom Catsup with Spice.—Take full-grown and fresh-gathered mushrooms; put a layer of these at the bottom of a deep earthen pan and sprinkle them with salt; then another layer of mushrooms; sprinkle more salt on them, and so on alternately. Let them stand for two or three hours, by which time the salt will have penetrated the mushrooms and have made them easy to break; then pound them in a mortar, or break them well with your hands; let them remain in this state for two days, not more, washing them well once or twice a day; then pour them into a stone jar, and to each quart add an ounce and a half of whole black pepper and half an ounce of allspice; stop the jar very close, and set it in a saucepan of boiling water and keep it boiling for two hours at least. Take out the jar and pour the juice clear from the settlings through a hair sieve into a clean stewpan, and boil it very gently on a slow fire for half an hour.

Mushroom Catsup without Spice.—Sprinkle a little salt over your mushrooms. Three hours after, mash them; next day, strain off the liquor and boil it till it is reduced to half. It will not keep long, but an artificial mushroom bed will supply this, the very best mushroom catsup, all the year round.

MEMORANDUM
ON
FRIENDS' RECIPES

MEMORANDUM ON
FRIENDS' RECIPES

XVIII.—BEVERAGES.

HINTS ON HOME BEVERAGES; USE GOOD MATERIALS; WHAT TEA IS; KINDS OF TEA; ITS VALUE AS A BEVERAGE; KINDS OF COFFEE; ADULTERATIONS OF COFFEE; HOW TO GET IT PURE; HOW TO RETAIN ITS FLAVOR; THE COFFEEPOT; CHOCOLATE AND ITS PREPARATION; OTHER BEVERAGES. THIRTY-THREE RECIPES FOR BEVERAGES.

ASIDE from the spirituous and malt liquors, the composition of which is not attempted in the household, there is a long line of beverages concerning which some hints are of value. In general, it may be said, employ good materials, and do not stint them in quantity, if you want good results. What is worth doing at all in culinary lines is worth doing well, and beverages, being in the line of luxuries, should be good, if not positively luxuriant.

Tea is the leaf of the tea-tree cured in various ways, and so appearing in the various forms known to commerce. Black teas are subjected to the action of heat far beyond the green teas. The green teas go through a *greening* process also, the healthfulness of which may well be questioned.

Of the black teas, the *Pekoe* is the earliest gathered and mildest, while the *Souchong*, the *Congou*, and the *Bohea* are respectively older in growth and stronger in flavor.

Of the green teas, the *Young Hyson* is from the tenderest and mildest leaf, the *Gunpowder*, *Hyson*, and *Twankay* being of older growth respectively and of stronger flavor. The treatment of all these leaves, as well as their age, are important factors in their final quality.

234

BEVERAGES.

The nutritive value of tea is not appreciable, but as an excitant of respiratory action and a promoter of digestion it is very valuable. Tea should be kept closely covered in airtight canisters, in order that the flavor may be retained.

Coffee will grow in any climate where the temperature does not fall below fifty-five degrees. The best brands are the *Mocha* and the *Java*, but South America supplies the largest amount used in this country, which is sold under the general name of *Rio*. Coffee is often wretchedly adulterated, especially when sold in the roasted and ground form. It is safer to buy it green and to roast and grind it at home.

Roasted coffee should be kept in tight canisters or boxes, and it should be ground only as it is wanted for use. The coffeepot must be scalded clean and occasionally with soda, so that the inside may be absolutely pure.

Chocolate should never be made except it is intended to be used immediately. By allowing it to become cold or by boiling it again, the flavor is injured, the oily particles of the cocoa are separated and rise to the surface also, and they will never blend pleasantly again.

Other beverages are in occasional use, but those already mentioned are the standards in this land.

RECIPES.

Tea.—People must consult their own tastes as to the kind of tea. A mixed tea is generally preferred, combining the flavors of both green and black. Allow one teaspoonful for each person. Use boiling water, but do not boil the tea, and use while fresh. Tea is best made in an earthen teapot. It should never be made in tin.

Iced Tea.—Iced tea should be made several hours before it is needed and then set upon ice. When ready to use it, sweeten and drink without milk or cream. Use cracked ice

---

MEMORANDUM
ON
FRIENDS' RECIPES

MEMORANDUM
ON
FRIENDS' RECIPES

236 *DOMESTIC COOKERY.*

to put into the glass. The tea must be extra strong, and do not stint the ice.

Tea a la Russe.—Slice fresh, juicy lemons; pare them carefully, lay a piece in the bottom of each cup; sprinkle with white sugar and pour the tea, very hot and strong, over them.

Iced Tea a la Russe.—To each goblet of cold tea (without cream) add the juice of half a lemon. Fill up with pounded ice and sweeten well. A glass of champagne added to this makes what is called Russian punch.

Coffee.—To make choicest coffee, take equal quantities of Java and Mocha; grind finely together, allowing about two teaspoonfuls of ground coffee to each person; add an egg with its shell and a very little cold water; stir this thoroughly together and turn on boiling water. Set the pot on the back of the range for five minutes; then draw forward and allow it to boil up just an instant; clear the spout by pouring from it and returning it in the top of the pot. Then serve at once with plenty of cream and sugar.

Iced Coffee.—Make the coffee extra strong. When it is cold, mix with an equal quantity of fresh cream; sweeten to taste, and freeze as in ice-cream, or serve with abundance of broken ice.

Cafe Noir.—This is the strongest preparation of coffee, its very essence, indeed. It is used after dessert at course dinners. Make the coffee strong and clear as possible, but use only one-third the ordinary quantity of water. Serve with lump sugar, with which it should be highly sweetened, and use very small cups. Cream may be added if desired.

Meringued Coffee.—For six cupfuls of coffee take about one cupful of sweet cream, whipped light, with a little sugar. Put into each cup the desired amount of sugar and about a tablespoonful of boiling milk. Pour the coffee over these, and lay upon the surface of the hot liquid a large spoonful of the frothed cream. Give a gentle stir to each cup before sending it from the tray.

Frothed Cafe au Lait.—Pour into the table urn one quart of strong, clear coffee, strained through muslin, and one quart of boiling milk, alternating them, and stirring gently. Cover and wrap a thick cloth about the urn for five minutes before it goes to table. Have ready in a cream-pitcher the whites of three eggs, beaten stiff, and one tablespoonful of powdered sugar, whipped with them. Put a large spoonful of this froth upon each cupful of coffee as you pour it out, heaping it slightly in the centre.

Chocolate.—Scrape fine one square of a cake, which is one ounce; add to it an equal weight of sugar; put these into a pint of boiling milk and water, each one-half, and stir well for two or three minutes until the sugar and chocolate are well dissolved. This preparation may be improved by adding a well-beaten egg or two and stirring briskly through the mixture with a Dover egg-beater. A teaspoonful of vanilla extract added just before sending to table is a valuable addition.

Frothed Chocolate.—One cupful of boiling water; three pints of fresh milk; three tablespoonfuls of Baker's chocolate, grated; five eggs, the whites only, beaten light, and two tablespoonfuls of powdered sugar for froth. Sweeten the chocolate to taste; heat the milk to scalding; wet up the chocolate with the boiling water, and when the milk is hot, stir this into it; simmer gently ten minutes, stirring frequently; boil up briskly once; take from the fire; sweeten to taste, taking care not to make it too sweet, and stir in the whites of two eggs, whipped stiff, without sugar; pour into the chocolate pot or pitcher, which should be well heated. Have ready in a cream-pitcher the remaining whites,

MEMORANDUM
ON
FRIENDS' RECIPES

MEMORANDUM
ON
FRIENDS' RECIPES

238 DOMESTIC COOKERY.

whipped up with the powdered sugar; cover the surface of each cup with the sweetened *meringue* before distributing to the guests.

Choca.—This beverage, a favorite with many, is made by mixing coffee and chocolate, as prepared for the table, in equal quantities, and serving hot for breakfast.

Broma.—Dissolve a large tablespoonful of Baker's broma in as much warm water; then pour upon it a pint of boiling milk and water, in equal proportions, and boil it two minutes longer, stirring it frequently; add sugar at pleasure.

Breakfast Cocoa.—Into a breakfast cup put a teaspoonful of the powder, add a tablespoonful of boiling water, and mix thoroughly. Then add equal parts of boiling water and boiled milk, and sugar to the taste. Boiling two or three minutes will improve it.

Cocoa Shells.—Take a small quantity of cocoa shells (say two ounces), pour upon them three pints of boiling water, boil rapidly thirty or forty minutes; allow it to settle or strain, and add cream or boiling milk and sugar at pleasure.

Lemonade.—Squeeze the juice of lemons, and add sugar and ice-water to taste.

Concentrated Lemonade.—Make a rich sirup of two and a half pounds of sugar and one pint of cold water and boil gradually. Pour it hot on one and a half ounces of citric acid. Bottle tight while hot. One tablespoonful will make a tumblerful of lemonade.

Portable Lemonade.—Mix a quarter pound of white sugar with the grated rind of a large, juicy lemon. Pour upon this the strained juice of the lemon and pack in a jar. One tablespoonful will suffice for a glass of water.

Egg Nog.—To the yelks of six eggs, add six tablespoonfuls of powdered sugar, one quart of new milk, a half pint

BEVERAGES.

of French brandy, and one pint of Madeira wine. Beat the whites up separately, and stir them through the mixture just before pouring into glasses for use.

Roman Punch.—Beat stiff the whites of three eggs, with a half pound of powdered sugar. Add three teacupfuls of strong, sweet lemonade, one wineglassful each of rum and champagne, and the juice of two oranges. Ice abundantly, or freeze.

Milk Punch.—Boil one quart of milk, warm from the cow. Beat up the yelks of four eggs and four tablespoonfuls of powdered sugar together; add two glasses of the best sherry wine; pour into a pitcher, and mix with it the boiling milk, stirring all the time. Pour from one vessel to another six times; add cinnamon and nutmeg to taste, and serve as soon as it can be swallowed without scalding the throat.

Currant and Raspberry Shrub.—Pound four quarts of ripe currants and three quarts of red raspberries in a stone jar or wide-mouthed crock with a wooden beetle. Squeeze out every drop of the juice; put this into a porcelain, enamel, or very clean bell-metal kettle, and boil hard ten minutes. Put in four pounds of loaf sugar at the end of the ten minutes, and boil up once to throw the scum to the top; skim and let it get perfectly cold; then skim off all remaining impurities; add one quart of the best brandy and shake hard for five minutes. Bottle, seal the corks, and lay the bottles on their sides in dry sawdust.

Currant Wine.—One quart of currant juice, three pounds of brown sugar, and one gallon of water; dissolve the sugar in the water, then add the juice; when it ferments, add a little fresh water each day till it is done fermenting, which will be in from a month and a half to two months; turn it off, scald the keg, put it in again, and cork tightly.

MEMORANDUM
ON
FRIENDS' RECIPES

MEMORANDUM
ON
FRIENDS' RECIPES

240 *DOMESTIC COOKERY.*

Raspberry Wine.—Bruise the raspberries with the back of a spoon; strain them through a flannel bag; add one pound of loaf sugar to one quart of juice; stir well and cover closely, letting it stand for three days, stirring well each day. Pour off the clear juice and add one quart of juice to two quarts of sherry wine; bottle it and use in two weeks.

Raspberry Brandy.—Using brandy instead of wine, as above, will produce a very valuable medicinal drink, Raspberry Brandy.

Raspberry Vinegar.—Take three pints of red berries; pour over them one pint of cider vinegar and let stand twenty-four hours. Strain, and to one pint of juice add one pound of sugar; boil one-half hour, and when cold, bottle for use.

Cherry Brandy.—Use either morello cherries or small black cherries; pick them from the stalks; fill the bottles nearly up to the necks, then fill up with brandy (some use whisky, gin, or spirit distilled from the lees of wine). In three weeks or a month strain off the spirit; to each quart add one pound of loaf sugar clarified, and flavor with tincture of cinnamon or cloves.

Sherbet.—In a quart of water boil six or eight sticks of rhubarb ten minutes; strain the boiling liquor on the thin shaved rind of a lemon. Two ounces of clarified sugar, with a wineglassful of brandy, stir to the above, and let it stand five or six hours before using.

Ginger Beer.—Two ounces of ginger to a pint of molasses; add a gallon of warm water; stir it well, and add half a pint of lively yeast. If you wish it sweeter or hotter, add ginger or molasses before putting in the yeast, to suit your taste.

BEVERAGES.

Spruce Beer.—To three gallons of boiling water, add two pounds of molasses and two ounces of essence of spruce. Let the mixture cool, and when lukewarm, add a scant gill of yeast and set aside to ferment. While the fermentation goes on, skim frequently. When it becomes inactive, put in stone bottles and tie the corks down. White sugar may be used instead of molasses, and will give a better color.

Quick Beer.—To fourteen quarts of water add one quart of molasses, one quart of hop yeast, and four tablespoonfuls of ginger. Mix well; strain through a fine sieve; bottle immediately. Ready for use in twenty-four hours.

Imperial.—Mix in a jug one-half ounce of cream tartar and one quart of boiling water; flavor with lemon peel or essence of lemon, and sweeten to taste. This is a refreshing and pleasantly stimulating summer drink.

Mead.—Mix six gallons of water with six quarts of strained honey; add the yellow rind of two large lemons, pared thin, and the whites of three eggs beaten to a stiff froth. Mix well and boil three-quarters of an hour, skimming thoroughly. Pour into a tub, add three tablespoonfuls of good yeast, and leave it ferment. When it is well worked, pour into a barrel with some lemon peel, and let it stand six months. Then bottle and tie down the corks. It is ready for immediate use, or will keep for months in a cool place.

MEMORANDUM ON FRIENDS' RECIPES

MEMORANDUM
ON
FRIENDS' RECIPES

XIX.—CANDIES.

CARE NEEDED TO COOK CANDY; WHEN COOKED ENOUGH; FLAVORING, COOLING, AND PULLING. TWENTY-ONE RECIPES FOR CANDY.

THE great danger in candy-making is that of burning the sugar. To properly cook the candy requires a heat of about two hundred and fifty degrees. Less than that heat will leave the candy soft and sticky. A very little more than two hundred and sixty degrees will burn it. Here, then, is the need of care in candy-making.

In the cooking, allow the heat to reach the bottom of the pan only. Have a quick fire that the work may be done in the shortest possible time. When cooked for about fifteen minutes, test a spoonful of the mass upon a cold plate. If it form a viscid, tenacious mass, which forms a long, adherent thread when drawn out, then it is nearly done, and it needs special care lest it burn before the work be completed. Test frequently now, dropping a little in cold water. When the hardened portion is crisp as a pipestem, the cooking has gone far enough. Then comes the flavoring and coloring.

When the mass has cooled on a stone or buttered plate, so that it can be handled, it is ready for *pulling*, rolling into sticks, shaping into forms, etc. The pulling process is simply a mechanical means of whitening the candy. It is literally a *pulling*, the candy being thrown on a hook and pulled out from it, then being thrown on it again and again pulled, and so on, as may be desired. the longer pulling giving the whiter candy.

For home-made candies use pure materials and good fruit. Enough of earths and starch and decayed fruits are bought in the cheap candies of the stores.

CANDIES.

RECIPES.

Molasses Candy.—Three cupfuls of brown sugar, one-half cupful of molasses, one cupful of water, one-half teaspoonful of cream tartar, butter the size of a walnut. Bring to a boil, and when crisp by testing in cold water, flavor; pour out on a buttered plate, and pull to whiteness if desired.

Butter Scotch.—Two cupfuls of sugar, two tablespoonfuls of water, a piece of butter the size of an egg. Boil without stirring, until it hardens on a spoon. Pour out on buttered plates to cool.

Ice-cream Candy.—Take two cupfuls of granulated sugar, half a cupful of water, and add one-quarter of a teaspoonful of cream tartar dissolved in a teaspoonful of boiling water. Put it in a porcelain kettle, and boil ten minutes without stirring it. Drop a few drops into a saucer of cold water or on snow. If it become brittle, it is done; if not, boil till it is. Add a piece of butter half as large as an egg while it is on the fire, and stir it in. Pour into a buttered tin, and set on ice or snow to cool enough to pull it white. Flavor with vanilla just before it is cool enough to pull. Work into strands and cut into sticks.

Cream Candy.—One pound of white sugar, three table-spoonfuls of vinegar, one teaspoonful of lemon extract, one teaspoonful of cream tartar. Add a little water to moisten the sugar, and boil until brittle. Put in the extract, then turn quickly out on buttered plates. When cool, pull until white, and cut in squares.

Cocoanut Candy.—Grate very fine a sound cocoanut, spread it on a dish, and let it dry naturally for three days, as it will not bear the heat of an oven, and is too oily for use when freshly broken. Four ounces will be sufficient for a pound of sugar for most tastes, but more can be used at pleasure. To one pound of sugar, take one-half pint of water, a very

MEMORANDUM
ON
FRIENDS' RECIPES

MEMORANDUM ON FRIENDS' RECIPES

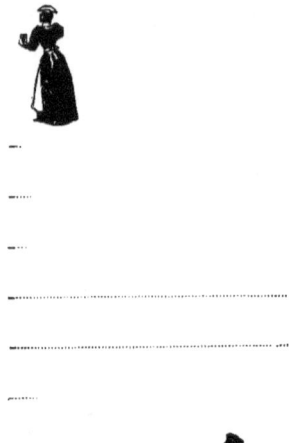

DOMESTIC COOKERY.

little white of egg, and then pour over the sugar; let it stand for a short time, then place over a very clear fire, and let it boil for a few minutes; then set it one side until the scum is subsided, clear it off, and boil the sugar until very thick; then strew in the nut, stir and mix it well, and do not quit for an instant until it is finished. The pan should not be placed on the fire, but over it, as the nut is liable to burn with too fierce a heat.

Almond Candy.—Proceed in the same way as for cocoanut candy. Let the almonds be blanched and perfectly dry, and do not throw them into the sugar until they approach the candying point.

Candied Nuts and Fruits.—Three cupfuls of sugar, one cupful of water; boil until it hardens when dropped in water, then flavor with lemon. It must not boil after the lemon is put in. Put a nut on the end of a fine knitting needle, take out, and turn on the needle until it is cool. If the candy gets cold, set on the stove for a few minutes. Malaga grapes, and oranges quartered, may be candied in the same way.

Chocolate Caramels.—Two cupfuls of sugar, one cupful of warm water, one-half cupful of grated chocolate, three-fourths of a cupful of butter. Let it boil without stirring until it snaps in water.

Chocolate Caramels, No. 2.—One cupful of rich, sweet cream; one cupful of brown sugar; one cupful of white sugar; seven tablespoonfuls of vanilla chocolate; one tablespoonful of corn-starch, stirred in the cream; one tablespoonful of butter; vanilla flavoring; soda, the size of a pea, stirred into cream. Boil all the ingredients, except the chocolate and vanilla extract, half an hour, stirring to prevent burning. Reserve half of the cream, and wet up the chocolate in it, adding a very little water if necessary. Draw the saucepan to the side of the range, and stir this in well; put back on the fire and boil ten minutes longer, quite fast, stirring constantly. When it makes a hard, glossy coat on the spoon, it is done. Add the vanilla after taking it from the range. Turn into shallow dishes, well buttered. When cold enough to retain the impression of the knife, cut into squares.

Lemon Taffy.—Two cupfuls of white sugar, one cupful of boiling water, one-quarter cupful of vinegar, one-half cupful of butter; flavor with lemon; pour in buttered plates to cool.

Butter Taffy.—One tablespoonful of vinegar, one cupful of sugar, two tablespoonfuls of molasses, and a piece of butter the size of an egg. When done, add a little soda.

Cream Chocolates.—For the *creams*, boil two cupfuls of white sugar and one-half cupful of milk for five minutes; add one teaspoonful of vanilla, then beat until stiff enough to handle and make into drops.

For the *chocolate*, take three-quarters of a half-pound cake of Baker's chocolate, grate and steam over the teakettle. Drop the creams when hard, one at a time, into the hot chocolate, using two forks to take them out quickly; set the drop on one fork on the bottom, using the other fork to scrape the chocolate off the cream; gently slip the drop upon a buttered dish. If, when cool, the drops stick to the dish, hold it over the steam of the teakettle for an instant.

Chocolate Creams.—*Inside:* Two cupfuls of sugar; one cupful of water; one and a half tablespoonfuls of arrow-root; one teaspoonful of vanilla. Mix the ingredients, except the vanilla; let them boil from five to eight minutes; stir all the time. After this is taken from the fire, stir until it comes to a cream. When it is nearly smooth, add the vanilla and make the cream into balls.

Outside: Melt a half pound of Baker's chocolate, but do not add water to it. Roll the cream balls into the chocolate while it is warm.

MEMORANDUM
ON
FRIENDS' RECIPES

MEMORANDUM
ON
FRIENDS' RECIPES

DOMESTIC COOKERY.

Cream Walnuts.—Two cupfuls sugar, two-thirds cupful water. Boil without stirring until it will spin a thread; flavor with vanilla. Set off into a dish with a little cold water in it; stir briskly until white and creamy. Have the walnuts shelled; make the cream into small, round cakes with your fingers; press half a walnut on either side, and drop into sifted granulated sugar.

Cream Dates.—For cream dates, take fresh California dates, remove the stones, and fill the centre of dates with the same cream as used in cream walnuts. Drop into sugar.

Peanut Candy.—Boil one scant pint of molasses until it hardens in cold water. Stir in two tablespoonfuls of vanilla, then one teaspoonful of soda, dry. Lastly, the shelled peanuts, taken from four quarts measured before shelling. Turn out into shallow pans well buttered, and press it down smooth with a wooden spoon.

Philadelphia Groundnut Cakes.—Boil two pounds of light brown sugar in a preserving kettle, with enough water to wet it thoroughly and form a sirup. Have ready a quarter of a peck of groundnuts (peanuts). When the sugar begins to boil, throw in the white of an egg to clear it. Skim and try by dropping a little into cold water to see if brittle or done. When it is brittle, remove from the fire, and stir in the nuts. Drop on wet plates, free from grease. The white of egg may be omitted.

Gum Drops.—Dissolve one pound of gum arabic in one and a half pints of water; strain and add one pound of refined sugar; beat until the sugar is entirely dissolved. Flavor to taste, and add coloring if desired. Then evaporate with a slow heat until the mass is thick as honey. Have a shallow box, or dish of fine starch; in this make a series of dents with a rounded stick, the size desired for the gum drops. Into each of these indentations drop from a spout, or a spoon, just enough of the thickened mass to fill the cavity, then set away in a warm place till the drops become sufficiently set to allow handling. This may require several days.

Jujube Paste.—Dissolve gum arabic, and add sugar as for gum drops. Evaporate till very thick, and while still warm flavor and pour out into shallow tin pans to cool.

Fig Paste.—Chop up one pound of figs, and boil in a pint of water till reduced to a soft pulp. Strain through a fine sieve, and add three pounds of sugar. Evaporate over boiling water till the paste becomes stiff, then pour it into a mold of wooden strips tied together. When cool, cut into squares; sugar each well, and put away for use. Flavors may be added to taste, or fresh fruits may be mingled with the paste.

Peppermint Drops.—Mix granulated sugar with enough water to form a paste, and put it to boil in a saucepan having a lip from which the contents can be poured or dropped. Allow it come almost, but not entirely, to a boil. Stir continually. Allow it to cool a little, and flavor to taste with strong essence of peppermint. Then drop the mass on sheets of tin or of white paper. To drop it properly, allow just enough to gather at the lip of the saucepan, and then stroke it off with a piece of stiff wire. They should dry in a warm place.

MEMORANDUM
ON
FRIENDS' RECIPES

MEMORANDUM
ON
FRIENDS' RECIPES

XX.—INVALID DIET.

INVALIDS NEED THE BEST OF DIET; WHAT INVALID DIET SHOULD FURNISH; "SICK-DIET KITCHENS;" HOME COOKING FOR THE SICK. THIRTY RECIPES FOR SICK-ROOM DIET.

WHAT is more disgusting to an invalid than to be served with a liberal supply of food adapted to a laboring man or to a person in robust health? Delicate appetites need to be delicately appealed to with dainty dishes, nicely served. But these dishes must be nourishing and easily digested. In short, the problem in sick-room diet is, how to furnish the patient the most valuable nutrition in the pleasantest form, and with the least tax upon his enfeebled powers.

To meet this need, organized movements have been made in many cities in the line of "Sick-Diet Kitchens." Benevolent contributions and skilled work are the corner-stones of these institutions. The foods are well prepared by competent hands. The sick who choose to purchase delicacies which can be relied on, can find them at these places. Those who are too poor to purchase, but who are deserving, can have them free. Instruction concerning diet for the sick is given also.

But many cannot reach such establishments, and do not care to if they can; hence the chapter of directions given below. If anywhere in cookery good materials and skillful manipulation are of value it is in cooking for the sick.

RECIPES.

Beef Tea.—One pound of lean beef, cut into small pieces. Put into a jar without a drop of water, cover tightly, set in

MEMORANDUM
ON
FRIENDS' RECIPES

a pot of cold water. Heat gradually to a boil, and continue this steadily for three or four hours, until the meat is like white rags and the juice all drawn out. Season with salt to taste, and when cold, skim. The patient will often prefer this ice-cold.

Beef Tea, No. 2.—Take lean, juicy beef, chopped very finely; cover with cold water, and set on back of the range for two hours; then draw forward, allowing it to heat gradually; then boil for five minutes. Season and strain.

Mutton Broth.—One pound of lean mutton, cut small; one quart of water, cold; one tablespoonful of rice or barley, soaked in a very little warm water; four tablespoonfuls of milk, salt and pepper, with a little chopped parsley. Boil the meat, unsalted, in the water, keeping it closely covered, until it falls to pieces. Strain it out, add the soaked barley or rice; simmer half an hour, stirring often; stir in the seasoning and the milk, and simmer five minutes after it heats up well, taking care it does not burn. Serve hot, with cream crackers.

Chicken Broth.—Proceed precisely as above, but substitute chicken for mutton.

Chicken Jelly.—Half a raw chicken, pounded with a mallet, bones and meat together; plenty of cold water to cover it well, *about* a quart. Heat slowly in a covered vessel, and let it simmer until the meat is in white rags and the liquid reduced one-half. Strain and press, first through a colander, then through a coarse cloth. Salt to taste, and pepper if you think best; return to the fire, and simmer five minutes longer. Skim when cool. Give to the patient cold—just from the ice—with unleavened wafers. Keep on the ice, or make into sandwiches by putting the jelly between thin slices of bread spread lightly with butter.

Soft Boiled Eggs.—Put in a pan of *boiling* water, and set on a part of the range where they will not boil for several min-

MEMORANDUM
ON
FRIENDS' RECIPES

utes. At the end of that time they will be like jelly, perfectly soft, but beautifully done, and quite digestible by even weak stomachs.

Egg Gruel.—Beat the yelk of one egg with one tablespoonful of sugar; pour one teacupful of boiling water on it; add the white of the egg beaten to a froth, with any seasoning or spice desired. To be taken warm.

Raw Egg.—Break a fresh egg into a glass, beat until very light, sweeten to taste, and add two tablespoonfuls of port wine, then beat again.

Egg Cream.—Beat a raw egg to a stiff froth; add a tablespoonful of white sugar and a half wineglass of good blackberry wine; add half a glass of cream; beat together thoroughly, and use at once.

Indian-meal Gruel.—One tablespoonful of fine Indian-meal, mixed smooth with cold water and a saltspoonful of salt; pour upon this a pint of boiling water and turn into a saucepan to boil gently for half an hour; thin it with boiling water if it thickens too much, and stir frequently; when it is done, a tablespoonful of cream or a little new milk may be put in to cool it after straining, but if the patient's stomach is weak it is best without either. Some persons like it sweetened and a little nutmeg added, but to many it is more palatable plain.

Oatmeal Gruel.—Soak a handful of oatmeal over night in water, in order that the acid gases which oatmeal contains may be withdrawn. Pour off the water, and add a pint of fresh; stir it well, add salt, and boil an hour and a half. This is much used, prepared in this way, by dyspeptics.

Sago.—Soak and wash it well; add a pint of water, a little salt, and boil till clear. Add lemon-juice or wine, if permitted.

Arrow-root Jelly.—Boil a pint of water with a few bits of cinnamon or yellow rind of lemon; stir into it two tablespoonfuls of arrow-root, dissolved in a little water; boil ten minutes; strain, salt, and season with sugar, wine, and nutmeg, if proper.

Arrow-root Broth.—Put half a pint of water into a saucepan; add a little lemon-juice, sugar and nutmeg, and a very little salt. Boil it up, and stir in a teaspoonful of dissolved arrow-root; boil five minutes. It should be taken warm and be very thin.

Cracked Wheat.—To one quart of hot water take one small teacupful of cracked wheat and a little salt; boil slowly for half an hour, stirring occasionally to prevent burning. Serve with sugar and cream or new milk.

Cracker Panada.—Six Boston crackers, split; two tablespoonfuls of white sugar, a good pinch of salt, and a little nutmeg; enough *boiling* water to cover them well. Split the crackers, and pile in a bowl in layers, salt and sugar scattered among them. Cover with boiling water and set on the hearth, with a close top over the bowl, for at least an hour. The crackers should be almost clear and soft as jelly, but not broken. Eat from the bowl with more sugar sprinkled in.

Bread Panada.—Set a little water on the fire in a very clean saucepan; add a glass of wine, if allowed, some sugar, nutmeg, and lemon-peel. The moment it boils up stir in a few crumbs of stale baker's loaf. Let it boil very fast for five minutes. It should be only thick enough to drink.

Chicken Panada.—Boil a chicken; take a few bits of the breast and pound fine in a mortar. Season it with a little salt, a grate of nutmeg, and a bit of lemon-peel; boil gently till a little thick, but so that it can be drank.

Soft Toast.—Some invalids like this very much indeed, and nearly all do when it is nicely made. Toast well, but not

MEMORANDUM
ON
FRIENDS' RECIPES

MEMORANDUM
ON
FRIENDS' RECIPES

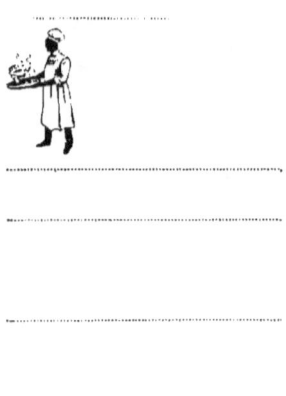

too brown, a couple of thin slices of bread; put them on a warm plate and pour over *boiling* water; cover quickly with another plate of the same size, and drain the water off; remove the upper plate, butter the toast, put it in the oven one minute, and then cover again with a hot plate and serve at once.

Milk Porridge.—Two cupfuls of best oatmeal, two cupfuls of water, two cupfuls of milk. Soak the oatmeal over night in the water; strain in the morning, and boil the water half an hour. Put in the milk with a little salt, boil up well, and serve. Eat warm, with or without powdered sugar.

Thickened Milk.—With a little milk, mix smooth a tablespoonful of flour and a pinch of salt. Pour upon it a quart of boiling milk, and when both are thoroughly mingled put all back into the saucepan and boil up once, being careful not to burn, and stirring all the time to keep it perfectly smooth and free from lumps. Serve with slices of dry toast. It is excellent in diarrhœa, and becomes a specific by scorching the flour before mixing with the milk.

Toast Water.—Toast stale bread until quite brown, but do not burn it; put it into a large bowl, and pour over it boiling water; let it stand for an hour or so, strain, and put in a piece of ice before drinking.

Barley Water.—Soak one pint of barley in lukewarm water for a few minutes; then drain off the water. Put the barley in three quarts of cold water and cook slowly until the barley is quite soft, skimming occasionally. This barley water, when cold, flavor with a little jelly or lemonade.

Rice Milk.—Pick and wash the rice carefully; boil it in water until it swells and softens; when the water is partly boiled away, add some milk. It may be boiled entirely in milk, by setting the vessel in which the rice is in boiling water; sweeten with white sugar and season with nutmeg. It also may be thickened with a little flour or beaten egg.

INVALID DIET.

Flaxseed Tea.—One-half pound of flaxseed, one-half pound of rock candy, and three lemons pared and sliced; pour over this two quarts of boiling water; let it stand until very cold; strain before drinking. This is good for a cough.

Appleade.—Cut two large apples in slices, and pour on them one pint of boiling water; strain well and sweeten. Ice it before drinking.

Apple Water.—Roast two large, tart apples until they are soft. Put them in a pitcher, pour a pint of cold water on them, and let them stand in a cool place for an hour. No sweetening is needed. This drink will be found very refreshing if the patient have fever or eruptive diseases.

Roast Apples.—Good-sized, juicy, tart apples are best for roasting. Wipe them clean, and put in a slow oven, allowing an hour for the work of roasting. When entirely done, sift fine, white sugar over them, and serve warm or cold, as desired.

Wine Whey.—Sweeten one pint of milk to taste, and when boiling throw in two wineglassfuls of sherry; when the curd forms, strain the whey through a muslin bag into tumblers

Blackberry Sirup.—One quart of blackberry juice, one pound of sugar, one-half ounce of nutmeg, one-half ounce of cinnamon, one-fourth of an ounce of cloves, one-fourth of an ounce of allspice.

MEMORANDUM ON FRIENDS' RECIPES

MEMORANDUM
ON
FRIENDS' RECIPES

ADVICE TO HOUSEKEEPERS

BY

MARION HARLAND

HOW WE MAKE HOUSEKEEPING HARDER.

By way of establishing a frank and friendly understanding between writer and reader, we will admit at the beginning of our talk that nothing can make American housekeeping easy. At the same time, it is comforting to bear in mind that the easiest things are seldom the best things. There are many reasons why the woman who "runs a house" in this land and at this day should have more and severer duties to perform than a housekeeper in the same station and with the same means in Great Britain, or on the continent of Europe. It may reconcile our housewife to her lot and clear away a difficulty or two if we consider a few of these reasons.

The newness of our nation runs through every department of life and labor. Nothing is firmly and definitely settled. The English farmer's wife cooks in the same kitchen and in the same sauce-pan that her mother used, and occupies exactly the same position filled by her grandmother. She has little new to learn, and she knows the old things well. If both ends meet and a tidy sum goes into the savings bank every year, she is contented. No thoughts of building a house twice as fine as that

254

MEMORANDUM ON FRIENDS' RECIPES

over her head keep her awake at night. So long as her boys have steady work, and she sees her girls well-behaved, industrious, and like the Scottish cottier's Jeannie, "respectit like the lave," her ambition for them is gratified.

We hear a vast deal said of the evil effects of American worry upon American women in crippling their energies and shortening their lives. Comparatively little is written or spoken of the element of restlessness that sets worry a-going. The wife of the farmer, or mechanic, or clerk, or small storekeeper, never settles in her own mind just where she belongs. To use a slang phrase—"she never gets there." Consequently, she never finds a resting-place for mind and body. By the time her house is decently furnished she begins to contrive how it can be made "smart" as the English women would say. The American uses a more objectionable word when she calls it "genteel." The girls take music-lessons, and a piano must be bought. Her children have playfellows who dress well, and she would not have her little ones seem mean or shabby. Everybody who is anybody has two parlors. Our housewife would do her own washing and ironing, and take in "shop-work" privately, yes! and sit up late at night to do it, rather than not have the pair of useless, dreary rooms on her first-floor that go by that name.

She lives, for the most part, in the basement. Her work is there, and the semi-cellar used as a dining-room is the family parlor when there is no company. It keeps the children's dirt in one place instead of letting it be strewed all over the house; it is cool in summer and warm in winter, and from her afternoon sewing-chair by the front windows she can have an eye on "the girl" and the girl's company.

I wonder, sometimes, what would be the effect upon

MEMORANDUM
ON
FRIENDS' RECIPES

ADVICE TO HOUSEKEEPERS.

our bustling, worried housewife, were she to determine, once for all, just what her sphere in life is, and make up her mind to fill the station to which God has called her, full, before straining and panting to climb to a higher. When will we study the old, sadly-true, and neglected lesson that it is not the duty or trial to-day that wears us out, but planning and hoping and dreading for to-morrow.

Again, our housekeeper, living, as she does, always a little ahead of her actual position and of her strength, if not ahead of her means, does not keep enough servants, considering the size of her house and family. While it is true that the more " help " one has of the kind furnished by intelligence-offices and the " wants " columns of the daily papers, the worse off she is apt to be, there is cruelty to herself in undertaking to do all the work of a household that must be kept abreast of the neighbor's. It is cruelty of a kind that kills wives and mothers oftener than poverty and want. Here, again, the English housewife who lends a hand in her own work is more sensible than the American. If she live in a three-story house, containing kitchen, dining-room, two parlors, six bedrooms with bathroom, cellar, and ten closets, the British matron would have two stout maids to assist her in keeping the premises in order. Our ambitious countrywoman prides herself upon getting along with one girl, " engaged for general housework," and not infrequently employs no regular servant. A woman " comes in " to do washing and ironing every week, and a semi-occasional day's cleaning. The mistress of the establishment takes all the rest upon her single pair of hands. Nothing is neglected that could contribute to the material comfort of her family. They have enough to eat, drink, and wear, and are well lodged in a respectable, often a luxurious house, clean from top to bottom. Of this you may make sure. No other domicile is so spick-and-span as that where "mother does for herself."

(How often the phrase may be otherwise and mournfully applied, cannot but occur to one familiar with the limitations of flesh and blood).

Her house gets to be as truly a part of herself as the shell is of the snail. No cloudy windows, no dusty corners, no drifts of "fluff" under beds and tables while she is up and around. She may be the soul of kindness to others, she is unmerciful to herself. There is never a moment in the day when she does not believe that she could take one more step if it were necessary. She has a way of saying that she "doesn't mind work" and "knows better than anybody can tell her what she can do and bear." Her thumb and finger are (figuratively) never off the screw that regulates her nervous system, and she is always ready to give it one more twist.

This is, strictly speaking, not housewifery, but slavery, and of a worse sort than ever disgraced San Domingo, or found its way into "Uncle Tom's Cabin." The nominal slave was an irresponsible machine whose care for his work ceased when he dropped his hoe in the field, or washed up the last dish at night. He carried no anxiety to his pillow, and ate his meat in careless security. Providing, paying for what was provided, and looking out for the future were the master's business. The American house-mother plans and performs, and takes consequences in her single self. Her brain works, her heart palpitates, her nerves are as terse as violin strings, while she toils up to the full measure of her strength through tasks that should be done by coarser hands. She is a maid-of-all-work, wife, mother, business manager, and housekeeper; she hears the lessons her children learn at home for the salaried school-teacher; she belongs to the church sewing-society; she teaches in the Sunday-school; she pays and

MEMORANDUM
ON
FRIENDS' RECIPES

ADVICE TO HOUSEKEEPERS.

receives calls, and is ambitious to see her husband a rich man some day. Then, she will keep her carriage, ride where she now walks, and rest instead of slaving. The vision is sometimes fulfilled. Oftener, her rest is in the tomb, and another wife, younger, more attractive, and more daintily bred, enters into her labors.

It was a woman of this stamp who hoped that "Gabriel would toot softly when he passed her grave, if the end of the world should come in less than a thousand years. She couldn't get rested out in less time."

The American matron is a wonderful creation and not to be found out of our favored country; but bones, blood, muscle, and nerve were never made that could bear, without injury, the life she sets for herself when she undertakes to do all the work of such an American home as she will have.

Another thing that makes her load grievous and hardly to be borne, even when she "tries to favor her strength" by means of hired help and modern conveniences, is lack of proper training for the housekeeper's business.

The life led by our girls up to the time of marriage is accountable for much of this deficiency. If mothers were bent upon disqualifying their daughters for what probably lies before them, they could not go more zealously to work to secure the evil end. Our public and private schools and colleges "keep up the standard" so fiercely that she who would rank well in her class has not time to make a pudding or to hem a handkerchief during nine months of the year, and needs the other three for recuperation. After graduation, the girl's harness is stripped off, and she is turned into the social pasture for a run that lasts until she is caught and noosed for life.

"Work and trouble will come soon enough. Let the young things have their day," is talk that finds as much favor among the poor as among the wealthy classes.

"What do you mean to do with that nice girl of yours?" I asked of my washerwoman, who had worked hard during ten years of widowhood to bring up her boy and girl respectably. "She must be about fifteen—isn't she?"

"Sixteen, mem. She's small, an' not strong for her years. But she's a smart scholar at the school, they say, an' as handy with her fingers as you could wish to see."

"She would make a capital lady's maid," proceeded I. "Or would you prefer to apprentice her to the milliner's or dressmaker's trade?"

The mother looked hurt and wistful.

"Indade, mem, an' it's sorry I'd be to see her a servant to anybody, or in anything but a ladylike business, where she could be her own mistress. She's wishful to be a music-teacher, or the loikes o' that. She's never had to put her hand to dirthy wurrk,—I'd a' rubbed me own fingers to the bone first."

She had lived in this free country eighteen years, quite long enough to imbibe national ideas as to kitchen and housework. Her daughter left school at sixteen. She had a smattering of algebra, history, rhetoric, chemistry, and English literature. She could bound every country in Asia and in Africa, and give the capital city of every European nation; could draw maps and recite chronological tables, and "had had three quarters on the piano." She could not have made a loaf of bread or a gown for herself to save her soul, but was slim of figure, with a complexion like a paraffine candle. At seventeen she married a journeyman carpenter, who took to drink in half a year's time because he "couldn't have things as a man had a right to expect when he comes home after a hard day's work." At twenty, a sickly, unhappy slattern, with two puny children, was more than half supported by the daily earnings of her faithful mother.

MEMORANDUM
ON
FRIENDS' RECIPES

MEMORANDUM
ON
FRIENDS' RECIPES

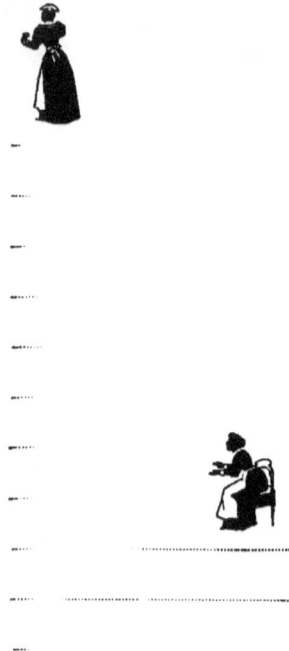

260   *ADVICE TO HOUSEKEEPERS.*

The wife of a well-to-do mechanic told me in the presence of her daughter, who was to be married the next week, that "Lucy doesn't like to have me say it, but she has never done a day's wash in her life. Ever since she left school four years ago, it's been go, go, go! all the time. Up late at night, and sleeping half the day, and then getting ready to go out again in the evening! It's to be hoped she'll sober down when she has a home and husband to look after."

A young woman who had such home training should have been able to employ a corps of competent servants and a housekeeper to look after them. Lucy went to live in a neat flat, furnished by her father, put out her washing, and valiantly undertook to do her own work. Without meaning to be extravagant she wasted her husband's income, and worried him and herself with continual mistakes and expensive failures. He grew savage and intolerant of the inefficiency which cost him dear. She grew wretched, peevish, and "delicate" under the pressure of tasks too heavy for her soft muscles, and cares that excruciated her nerves. The doctors—another expense—said she "had no stamina;" gossips shook their heads over "the way girls have of breaking down early." Eighteen months ended the unequal struggle. She and her baby were buried together.

The untaught child had done her best to repair the fatal blunders in her education. So sure am I of this in her and that of a thousand others that my indignation expends itself upon the inconsiderate, or weakly indulgent, or ambitious mothers who let daughters waste in useless follies time that should be given, in part, at least, to diligent preparation for the calling to which they were directed by nature and public sentiment. Not one girl in ten thousand expect or is expected to pass all her life in the home of her girlhood. What censure is too harsh for the parent who, ignoring this solemn truth, fails to instruct her in the practical details of the profession she is almost certain to enter?

WAYS AND WAYS OF WORK.

Mrs. Harriet Beecher Stowe, in a witty disquisition, in The Minister's Wooing, upon the New England housewife's "faculty" strengthens the fallacy that this same "faculty" of accomplishing work without fussiness and waste of time is altogether a natural gift. If a woman is so unfortunate as not to have been born with it, Mrs. Stowe implies, and popular opinion assents, that there is no use in attempting to acquire it.

ONE WAY.

"If I only had your knack of turning off work, I should not be forever in the suds!" exclaimed one woman enviously to another. "As it is, I never get ahead of what I am actually compelled to do. My work drives me continually with a cat-o'-nine-tails. I think it will whip me into my grave!"

I watched this scourged sister with compassionate curiosity, and made up my mind that faculty and fate had nothing to do with her chronic state of backwardness, any more than destiny branded a certain unstable king of Britain as "Ethelred the Unready." She worked without forecast or management. As the old-fashioned people would put it, she did not make her head save her heels. She had a general idea when she got out of bed in the morning that such and such pieces of work were to be grappled with during the day, but none as to the order in which they were to be attacked. She "went for them" as they presented themselves, as a wrecker, up to his knees in the surf, snatches at flotsam and jetsam as they float

MEMORANDUM ON FRIENDS' RECIPES

MEMORANDUM
ON
FRIENDS' RECIPES

262   ADVICE TO HOUSEKEEPERS.

toward him. To change the figure—she knit the sleeve for the day's wear loosely, dropping stitches every now and then, and letting them run down all the way to the bottom. Her duties did not "dovetail" into each other. Such a woman, after kindling the kitchen-fire, would linger to watch it, take off the lids and open the front of the range to make sure that it burned, until it was under full headway; then fill the kettle, and try three or four places on the stove before satisfying herself that it was in the best position; it would never occur to her, if she had three dishes to prepare, that she could divide her attention so judiciously between them that none would suffer. She would take time to set the table while the water was heating, and the potatoes boiling, and the biscuits baking, and plates getting safely warmed in the open oven, she keeping, meanwhile, her temper steady, her head cool, and her wits on the alert for something else she could clip into any chance crevice of time. She made one journey to the linen-shelves for the table-cloth and another for the napkins, and, instead of lifting the silver-basket from the buffet to the table when the silver was to go on, went backward and forward until she had all she wanted. In leaving one room in her housewifely rounds, she did not bethink herself to glance around to see if there were anything to be carried to another apartment, thus saving her a second journey to this part of the house.

She counted time by hours; the systematic economist of strength and time reckons by minutes, and knows what becomes of each.

ANOTHER WAY.

A mother who had the habit of commiserating herself for being hunted incessantly by duties, changed the order of her life, and probably added years to it by an ingenious scheme for correcting the foible. She hung a tablet by her side and recorded on it the hour and minute at which she completed each task, and the time at which she began the next, with a memorandum of how she spent the intervening space.

I give her conclusion in her own language:

"I found that sometimes ten minutes, sometimes half an hour, would elapse, and adding up these odd minutes, I found that, on some days, the time I lost was really longer than the time employed. I would let myself be attracted, after I finished a piece of work, by a few words in a newspaper, pick it up and read it standing, or, looking through the window, I lingered to watch anything that caught my eye, or I would run out to gather a flower or a bouquet. I envied women who could give an occasional hour to work among the flowers. If I snatched the time to do it out of season and place, it gave me no pleasure. It only added to my driven feeling.

"I kept my memorandum for a month. By that time I had learned to guard against the little foxes that had stolen my leisure."

A good definition of "dirt" was that given by the school-boy, who said it was "something that ought not to be where it was." Wasted time may be defined as that spent in doing nothing in particular.

From the other side of the water we get a word descriptive of one way of not getting work done. I have an excellent matron in my mind who never has a minute's rest all day long, and leaves more undone by night than seemed to lie before her when she awoke in the morning. She is always on the run,—and never gets anywhere. If she sets out to dust a room she espies a book that ought to be in the library. On her way downstairs she lays down the book on the landing to wipe off a streaked window-

MEMORANDUM
ON
FRIENDS' RECIPES

264   *ADVICE TO HOUSEKEEPERS.*

pane. A finger-smear on the window-seat attracts her notice, and off she goes to the kitchen for water, cloth and sapolio. These once in hand, she is in for an hour's "good scrubbing," for one discovery leads to another. And so the time slips by.

She and her sister "potterers" have no sense of the right proportion of duties. That which starts up right under their noses, however unimportant, drives all the rest out of the field. Represent to her that this or that could wait until her hands and mind are freer, and you are told that her "rule is never to put off until to-morrow what can be as well done to-day," that "whatsoever the hand finds to do should be done with might," and that she "cannot reconcile it to her conscience to slight anything; what is worth doing at all is worth doing well." Thanks to her subjection to these mouldy and one-sided saws, she is never on time, and the loose ends of duties begun and never done are carelessly flapping in other people's faces.

Happy is the working-force that does not enroll a "potterer" among its members.

AND STILL ANOTHER.

What do I mean by "systematic housekeeping!" Briefly this—that our housewife should think over and classify what she has to do each day, and decide before beginning the tasks when and how they would best be done. That, having set about them, she should go right on, "without haste and without waste," until the tale of labor is finished. If a clash of duties or hours befall her, let her not be dismayed, but bring to her help the business principle of "profit and loss." When she has done her best, nothing more is required by conscience, or Him to whom conscience gives in her report.

MEMORANDUM
ON
FRIENDS' RECIPES

I had a peep once at the memorandum-book of a systematic woman. One page stood thus:

"8–9 A. M. While washing breakfast dishes, remember to hear Rob's history-lesson. Put on bones for soup. Tapioca to soak. Speak to man about cleaning cellar. Look over table-linen.

"9–10. Dust parlors; water flowers. Look up quotation in Ruskin. Remind Annie of mantel-mirror.

"10–11. Write letters. Mend John's overcoat.

"11–12. Make blanc-mange and cake.

"12–1 P. M. Appointment at Industrial School."

She was an exceptionally busy person; actively engaged in philanthropic work and church societies, besides being a devoted wife and mother, and much sought after in society. The quantity of work she "turned off" was proverbial, but less remarkable than the ease with which she appeared to accomplish it. I objected to the memorandum-book on the ground that dependence upon it might weaken the memory.

"On the contrary," I was told, "it leaves memory free for better things. Every entry there saves me a wrinkle or a gray hair. I bestow ten minutes hard thought upon the list every morning, while I am dressing. Then my brain is at liberty. If I did not do this, something would be jostled out of the right place, some Peter robbed to pay Paul."

Comparing daily work to wall building, we may say that she suits her stones one to another, and lays them in cement, while our potterer is all the while pulling down the wall she has raised, to get at a stone she has put in the wrong place, or which she fancies she could dispose more advantageously.

MEMORANDUM
ON
FRIENDS' RECIPES

THE FAMILY PURSE.

THE gossips at a noted watering-place, where I once spent a summer, found infinite amusement in the ways of a married heiress, whose fortune was settled so securely upon herself by her father that her husband could not touch the bulk of it with or without her consent. Her spouse was an ease-loving man of fashion, and accommodated himself gracefully to the order of things. She loved him better than she loved her money, for she "kept" him well and grudged him nothing. It was in accordance with her wishes that he made no pretence of business or profession. "Why should he, when she had enough for both?" she urged, amiably. His handsome allowance was paid on the first of every month and she exacted no account of expenditures. Yet she contrived to make him and herself the laughing-stock of the place by her naive ignorance of the truth that the situation was peculiar. She sportively rated her lord in the hearing of others, for extravagance in dress, horses, and entertainments; affected to rail at the expense of "keeping a husband" and, now and then, playfully threatened to "cut off supplies" if he did not do this or that. In short, with unintentional satire, she copied to the letter the speech and tone of the average husband to his dependent wife.

"Only that, and nothing more." Her purse-pride was obvious, but as inoffensive as purse-pride can be. She lacked refinement, but she did not lack heart. She would have resented the imputation that she reduced her good-looking, well-clothed, well-fed, well-mounted "Charley" to a state of vassalage against which any man of spirit would have rebelled. He knew that he could have whatever it was in her power to bestow, to the half of her kingdom. Her complaints of his prodigality meant as little as her menace of retrenchment, and nobody comprehended this better than he. The owner of the money-bags is entitled by popular verdict to his or her jest. Her pretended railing was "clear fun."

I had not thought of this odd couple, and their odd ways in twenty years, until I read "A Painful Problem," in a weekly publication.

There are certain subjects upon which each of us is afraid to speak for fear of losing temper, and becoming vehement. This matter of "The Family Purse" is one of the few topics in all the range of theory and practice, concerning which I feel the necessity of putting on curb and bridle when I have to deal with it, and conscience urges just dealings with all parties. In the published volume which bears the same title as these informal "Talks," I put upon record two paragraphs which I crave leave to repeat here:

"If I were asked, 'What, to the best of your belief, is the most prolific and general source of heart-burnings contentions, harsh judgment, and secret unhappiness among respectable married people who keep up the show, even to themselves, of reciprocal affection?" my answer would not halt for an instant.

"'The crying need of a right mutual understanding with respect to the right ownership of the family income.'"

The example of the good old Friend, cited in "A Painful Problem," who in giving his daughters in marriage stipulated that each should be paid weekly, without asking for it, a certain share of her husband's income, is refreshing as indicating what one husband had learned by his own experience. It goes no further in the absence of proof that the sons-in-law kept the pledge imposed upon them as suitors, or that, in keeping it, they did not cause their respective wives to wish themselves dead, and

MEMORANDUM
ON
FRIENDS' RECIPES

MEMORANDUM
ON
FRIENDS' RECIPES

out of the way of gibe and grudge, every time the prescribed tax was doled out to them.

Nor do I admit the force of E. W. B.'s implication that the crookedness in this matter of family finances is "separation and hostility between the sexes, brought about by the advancement and equality of woman." Wives, in all ages and in all countries, have felt the painful injustice of virtual pauperism, and struggled vainly for freedom. The growth toward emancipation in the case of most of them amounts merely to the liberty to groan in print and to cry aloud in women's convocations. If the yoke is easier upon the wifely neck in 1897 than it was in 1840, it is because women know more of business-methods, and are more competent to the management of money, and some husbands, appreciating the change for the better, are willing to commit funds to their keeping. The disposition of fathers, brothers, and husbands to regard the feminine portion of their families as lovely dead-weights, was justified in a degree by the Lauras and Matildas, who clung like wet cotton-wool to the limbs of their natural protectors. Dependence was reckoned among womanly graces, and insisted upon as such in Letters to Young Ladies, The Young Wife's Manual, A Father's Legacy to his Daughters, and other valuable contributions to the family library, a half-a-century ago. Julia assured wooing Adolphus that absolute dependence, even for the bread she should eat, and breath she should draw, would be delight and privilege. Julia, as wife, fretted and plained and shook her "golden chains inlaid with down," when married Adolphus took her at her word.

It is surprising that both parties were so slow in finding out how false is the theory and how injurious the practice of the cling-and-twine-and-hang-upon school.

From my window, as I write, I see an object-lesson

that pertinently illustrates the actual state of affairs in many a home. At the root of a stately cedar sprang up, twenty years ago, a shoot of that most hardy and beautiful of native creepers, the wild woodbine, or American ivy. It crept steadily upward, laying hold of branch and twig, casting, first, tendrils, then ropes, to make sure its hold,—a thing of beauty all summer, a coat of many colors in autumn, until it reached the top of the tree. To-day, the only vestige of cedar-individuality that remains to sight, is in the trunk, the bare branches, stripped of all slight twigs, and at the extremity of one of these, a few tufts of evergreen verdure, that proclaim "This was a tree."

In the novels and poems which set forth the eternal fitness of the cling-twine-and-depend school, the vine is always feminine, the oak (or cedar?) masculine. Not one that I know of depicts the gradual strangling of the independent tree by the depending parasite.

Leaving the object-lesson to do its part, let us reason together calmly upon this vexed subject. When a man solemnly, in the sight of Heaven and human witnesses, endows his wife at the altar with his worldly goods, it is either a deed of gift, or an engagement to allow her to earn her living as honestly as he earns his, a pledge of an equal partnership in whatever he has or may acquire. That it is not an absolute gift is proved by his continued possession of his property and uncontrolled management of the same; furthermore, by his custom of bestowing upon his wife such sums, and at such periods as best suit his convenience and pleasure—and that she will be properly grateful for lodging, board, and raiment. If he be liberal, her gratitude rises proportionably. If he be a churl, she must submit with Christian resignation.

The deeper and juster significance of the much-derided clause is the second I have offered. "Live and let live,"

MEMORANDUM
ON
FRIENDS' RECIPES

ADVICE TO HOUSEKEEPERS.

is a motto that should begin, continue, and be best exemplified at home. The wife either earns an honorable livelihood, or she is a licensed mendicant. The man who, after a careful estimate of the services rendered by her who keeps the house, manages his servants, or does the work of the servants he does not hire; who bears and brings up his children in comfort, respectability, and happiness; who looks after his clothing and theirs; nurses him and them in illness, and makes the world lovely for him in health, does not consider that his wife has paid her way thus far, and is richly entitled to all he has given or ever will give her, is not fit to conduct any business upon business principles. If he be sensible and candid, let him decide what salary he can afford to pay this most useful of his employees—and pay it as a debt, not a gratuity. The probability is that he will find that the sum justifies her in regarding herself as a partner in his craft or profession, with a fair amount of working capital.

There is but one equitable and comfortable way of relieving the husband from the charge and the fact of injustice, and the wife from the sorer burden of conscious pauperism. She ought to have a stated allowance for household expenses, to be disbursed by herself, and, if he will it, to be accounted for to the master of the house, and a smaller, but sure sum which is paid to her as her very own, which she may appropriate as she likes. He should no more "give" her money, than he makes a present of his weekly wages to the porter who sweeps his store, or to the superintendent of his factory. The feeling that their gloves, underclothing,—everything that they wear, and the very bread that keeps life in their bodies, are gifts of grace from the husbands they serve in love and honor, has worn hundreds of spirited women into their graves, and made venal hypocrites of thou-

MEMORANDUM ON FRIENDS' RECIPES

sands. The double-eagle laid in the palm of the woman whose home duties leave her no time for money-making, burns, sometimes, more hotly than the penny given to her who, for the first time, begs at the street-corner to keep herself from starving.

The strangest of anomalies that have birth in a condition of affairs which everybody has come to regard as altogether right and becoming, is that the wife whose handsome wedding-portion has been absorbed into her husband's business is as dependent upon his favor for her "keep" as she who brought no dot. She does not even draw interest upon the money invested. Is it to be wondered at that caustic critics of human nature and inconsistencies, catalogue marriage, for the wife, under the head of mendicancy? Would it not be phenomenal if women with eyes, and with brains behind the eyes, did not gird at the necessity of suing humbly for what really belongs to them?

I have known two, or at most three women, who averred that they "did not mind asking their husbands for money." Out of simple charity, I preferred to believe that they were untruthful to discounting their self-respect and delicacy to the extent implied by the assertion. Yet, the street-beggar gets used to plying his trade, and I may have been mistaken.

Ella Marston of "A Painful Problem" is a type of a class, with whom injustice begets defiance. The woman who considers herself defrauded by present privations and what seem to her needless economies, loses sight, sometimes, of what John keeps before him as the loadstar of his existence and endeavor; to wit, that toil and economy are for the common weal. He is not a miser for his individual enrichment, nor does he plan with deliberate design for the shadowy wife. It is not to be denied that No. 2 often lives like a queen upon the wealth which No. 1

MEMORANDUM
ON
FRIENDS' RECIPES

272 *ADVICE TO HOUSEKEEPERS.*

helped accumulate, killing herself in so doing. But John does not look so far as this. Much scrimping and hoarding may engender a baser love of money for money's self. In the outset of the task, and usually for all time, he means that wife and children shall have the full benefit of what he has heaped up in the confident belief that he knows who will gather with him. Men take longer views in these matters than women. To " draw money out of the business " is a form of speech to a majority of wives. To him whose household expenses overrun what he considers the bounds of reason, this " drawing " means harder work and to less purpose for months to come; clipped wings of enterprise, and occasionally, loss of credit. He who has married a reasonably intelligent woman cannot make her comprehend this too soon. If he can enlist her sympathies in his plans for earning independence and wealth, he has secured a most valuable coadjutor. If he can show her that he is investing certain moneys which are due to her, in ways approved by her, which will augment her private fortune, he will retain her confidence with her respect.

Each of us likes to own something in his or her own right. The custom and prejudice that, since the abolition of slavery, make wives the solitary exception to the rule that the laborer is worthy of his hire, are unworthy of a progressive age. The idea that such having and holding will alienate a good woman from the husband who permits it, degrades the sex. He whose manliness suffers by comparison with a level-headed, clear-eyed wife capable of keeping her own bank-account, makes apparent what a mistake she made when she married him.

"MADE-OVERS."

To a large and interesting class of women the Fashion Department of the family paper must be a mockery, often a source of vexation and pain. The glib descriptions of street, home, and party costumes, in which brocaded velvet trains, tabliers of passementerie, cloths heavy with applique embroidery or braiding, are mentioned as articles which every creature of feminine mold can procure, are worse than tantalizing to the girl whose last winter's costumes must be varied by the few yards of new material she can afford to buy, and the matron who has not lost the desire to keep up with the prevailing mode, yet has one-tenth to spend upon her attire that she had before her marriage.

It is altogether possible for either or both of these to have better taste in all details of costume than the rich men's daughters and wives, whose magnificent imported toilettes are copied by artists of repute for such periodicals as can pay for the "show." The inability to indulge correct taste, and gratify the love for the beautiful which is a part of her personality, is the cause of actual suffering to a sensitive woman. Cheap, ill-fitting garments are to her positive humiliation; a fetter upon freedom of action, grace of look and language. Reason as we will of the duty of the strong mind to rise above such trifles, there is moral strength in the consciousness of being well-dressed, while dowdyishness and dampened spirits are inseparable in one who knows how to dress well, and would do it if she had the opportunity and means.

We cannot all be rich enough to array ourselves exactly as we would, but many a bright girl, or deft-fingered matron, might keep within easy range of elegance and fashion, by making the best use of her eyes, fingers, and

MEMORANDUM
ON
FRIENDS' RECIPES

ADVICE TO HOUSEKEEPERS

the materials already at hand,—provided these were in other shape than they appear to her discouraged senses when she unpacks and overhauls last winter's relics. The display is always unlovely, and worse than this, unlikely. Woolens are creased, velvets are crushed, silks are shiny, satins are wrinkled, and bonnets hopelessly out-of-date. This last item is invariable. A gown made in the height of an unremarkable fashion may do duty for two seasons without alteration—a bonnet never. The milliners see to that. They "must live."

Before the heap of creased, wrinkled, crushed, shiny tangled, and antiquated Impracticables, even a brave spirit shrinks. Yet the dressmaker is due next week, and the overstrained allowance admits of just one new gown, with perhaps a cloak or jacket in place of the aged and utterly unpresentable wrap.

Our Girl has a good social position. Whatever may be Miss Nouveau Riche's views as to the presumption of poor people pretending to be "in society," such things are, even in America. Our Girl will be invited to places where her elbows will touch the bared forearm of Miss Nouveau Riche; she will eat at the same table, and dance in the same set with her and her jeweled compeers. It is natural, it is inevitable that, foreseeing this, Our Girl should shrink from the thought of shabbiness, and grow sick at the suggestion of cheap finery,—the imitations which she cannot be deluded into imagining "look just as well as the real article."

In the hope that action may be a present relief from depression, and that, from renovation of material, may spring courage and hope, I ask serious consideration from my not rich reader of the simple directions herewith given for the crucial period of looking-and-making-over for the coming winter.

The initial stage of the business is

RIPPING.

The outfit for this operation is a pair of sharp-pointed scissors and a generous stock of patience. Each stitch must be clipped, that the seams may come apart without being pulled. The sharp tug at the material that parts the breadth for half-a-yard at once, stretches the biased edges beyond remedy, if it does not tear selvages. Even skirt braids should be ripped off carefully. If the garment is to be trimmed, separate every piece, no matter how small, from the rest. Careless rippers often reject the waist-front in which are the button-holes, as unavailable. With your keen scissors, pare away carefully the ridged edges that are the feature of the "button-hole stitch," then, pick out the threads, one by one. Button-holes thus treated may be worked over again, or darned up so neatly that buttons or hooks can be sewed upon the places they occupied.

The several portions of the garment ripped apart must be brushed free of dust and rid of all threads before any attempt is made to scour or press them. Neglect of this precaution makes grease-spots and other blemishes the worse by the addition of mud when they are dampened, while stray threads are ironed into the fabric.

In removing trimming from hats, special pains must be taken not to stretch the edges of velvet, silk and satin.

TO CLEAN WOOLEN GOODS.

Unless the stuff be very much soiled, do not plunge it into the washtub. It may look well for a while after it is washed, but it will "take dirt" more easily, and roughen in wearing as it did not before it was cleaned. It is

MEMORANDUM
ON
FRIENDS' RECIPES

MEMORANDUM
ON
FRIENDS' RECIPES

ADVICE TO HOUSEKEEPERS.

sound economy to buy material which is the same on both sides, but even when the two sides are not alike, the reverse is often presentable as a "make-over."

Lay each breadth and bit, singly, upon a table covered with a clean, folded sheet; wash the spots hard with a sponge dipped in warm water, then rubbed with fine, hard hand-soap. Wash out the suds thoroughly with clean, warm water; lastly, sponge the whole surface with a mixture of two parts warm water, one part ammonia. Shake well, hang on the line evenly, until half-dry; roll up each piece closely by itself, and iron, while still damp, on what is to be the wrong side, folding the breadths as they were in the original bulk, and laying smaller bits smooth.

TO RENEW VELVET.

Let an assistant hold the velvet taut, the wrong side up. Go all over this with a sponge wet in clean water, not letting the right side touch anything while you do this. Have ready a hot iron; turn it upside down, resting your arm and wrist on a table to hold the iron firmly in position. The wet back of the velvet must be drawn slowly and smoothly over this hot plane, slipping the velvet along as the "pile" on the right side rises slowly in the steam. Handle it carefully, as every finger-mark will show if touched when damp. Lay upon a table, right side up, and leave until entirely dry.

BLACK CRAPE.

Hold straight and level, but not too tightly over a kettle of boiling water. Let it get almost dry upon a cloth before folding and laying it under a light weight.

TO TURN SILK.

Sponge what is to be the wrong side with household ammonia, or with ammonia and water in the proportions already prescribed. Black silk is freshened and made firmer by being treated, after the ammonia has cleaned it, to a second sponging with hot water, in which three or four potatoes have been boiled, but not to breaking. The water should be strained free from specks. While still damp, each breadth should be laid upon a folded sheet and covered with fine old cambric or linen. Iron upon this covering, hard and quickly, the wrong side of the silk being uppermost. The cambric prevents the shine of the iron from appearing on the silk. The gloss left by it would ruin the silk for future turning or for use as trimming.

Satin may be sponged on the wrong side with potato-water, and ironed quickly, also on the back, without the cambric covering.

Ribbons are treated like velvet, silk, or satin, each according to its kind, and when nearly dry, should be rolled evenly, not too tightly, upon blocks.

FEATHERS.

Some women have the patience and dexterity to curl ostrich tips with a dull knife, and to bring about satisfactory results. Practice is requisite to success in this undertaking. The novice would better make experiment upon a "tip" which is decidedly past worthy before running the risk of tearing to pieces a valuable feather.

Feathers may be curled more easily and quickly (although they will be more easily undone by dampness) by holding them for a minute over a pot of boiling water, then shaking them over the hot top of the range, or, setting them in a stone-china plate in a moderate oven for a few minutes. If caught in a rain-storm or wet through by fog, the "tips" may be renovated again and again by this last process.

WHITE LACE.

Mend securely every rent, and fasten loose threads. Then leave the lace to soak over-night in tepid water, in which were dissolved, while it was boiling hot, half a teaspoonful of borax and the same quantity of shred white soap (sweet) for each pint of water. In the morning, wash gently in pure, tepid water, rubbing cautiously all soiled edges, and leave in clear, cold water for an hour. Squeeze hard without wringing, and lay between two dry towels for ten minutes to take up the wet. With clean, dainty fingers pull straight every mesh, figure, and "pearling," and while it is still damp, baste the lace upon a jar with straight sides, covered with several thicknesses of muslin or linen, laid perfectly smooth. Begin sewing the lace to the muslin at the bottom of the jar, and winding it around and around, the edges just touching one another, baste carefully each scollop and point to keep the figures even, and keeping the lace smooth. If you have much, or wide lace, you will need several large jars or bottles.

Set them in the sun when all the lace is on, selecting a window where there is not much dust. Leave them out all day, wetting several times, the more frequently if the lace is badly discolored; take in at night, but do not rip off the precious fabric until next day. Clip every thread carefully, unwind with equal care, and fold upon a card or in lengths. Lay under a weight until you are ready to use it.

If these directions are followed exactly, the lace will

look as well as if you had paid a big price to have it done by a professional cleaner.

RUSTY BLACK THREAD LACE.

Boil a black kid glove an hour in a quart of water, take out the glove, and let the water get blood-warm. Rinse the lace in it, shaking it up and down, but not rubbing. Dry off the wet between two towels, and while it is damp, pull it out and straighten with your fingers.

Afterwards, proceed as with white lace—sewing it upon the jars, but not wetting it again, and drying it in the shade. The hot sun would fade it.

All lace should be skillfully mended before it is cleaned. It is worth every woman's while to learn how to do this.

This matter of "made overs" is full of pleasurable excitement if one goes into it with the determination to consider it as a fine art, rather than a task—one full of graceful inventions, although born of necessity. Some women have the happy, nameless touch that imparts grace and style, and makes a combination of color and shape which in another would be audacious, look like a stroke of genius. For the average worker, a safe rule is not to attempt startling effects. Study such fashion-plates, and the directions appended to them as may be depended upon; select a model that is approved by your taste and is within each of your materials, and follow it—not slavishly, but with respect to general design. Set before your mind distinctly what you want to do, and what you can do. Skilful manipulation must effect the rest.

There is solid satisfaction which rich people never know in wearing a "made-over" that has lost identity in the process and "looks like new." I commend the sensation as consolation to those whose ideals outreach their means.

MEMORANDUM
ON
FRIENDS' RECIPES

HOT-WEATHER DISHES.

BY MARION HARLAND.

THE query, hateful to the weary housewife's soul, "What shall we eat three times a day?" increases in irksomeness in direct ratio as Old Sol becomes more assiduous in his attentions to the inhabitants of this insignificant sphere. The first meal of the day, eaten before the heat has a chance to sap energy and destroy appetite, is not the bugbear that the noon and evening repast prove. Boiled eggs and toast, fried or boiled fish and potatoes, a tender piece of steak or a tender French chop, can easily be "coaxed down" in the morning, especially when aided by the invaluable breakfast stand-by—oatmeal and cream, and freshly made and stimulating coffee or tea. The husband and father will confess that while he likes a good breakfast, he can, if necessary, "keep" until lunch-time if fortified by a cup of excellent coffee and a roll.

"It is when the enervating noon and afternoon sun has power over the world that the jaded appetite turns with a feeling akin to disgust from hot meats and smoking vegetables. This is also the time when the mother sighs to herself a wish that "things grew ready-cooked," and that someone "would invent a new flesh, fish or fowl, for hot weather."

For her sake, as well as for her family's, I give some recipes for "plains and sweets," which, while not new or ready-made, may be prepared before the heat of the day, or in so few minutes as not to test the strength and patience, and will, I hope, offer a little variety to the usual bill-of-fare. Every household gets into the habit of having certain things to eat once in so often, and over and over again, until a new dish proves a positive blessing.

My readers will notice that there is not a single recipe for a hot viand among these I give, as I have tried to have them especially suited to the requirements of the heated term.

Dressed Eggs.—Boil eight eggs hard, and throw into cold water. When quite cold, take off the shells, cut the eggs in half lengthwise, from end to end, and remove the yolks. Put the yolks into a bowl, and with the back of a silver spoon rub smooth, adding, as you do so, a table-spoonful of chopped ham or chicken, one of butter, one of salad-dressing, a half-teaspoonful of French mustard, pepper and salt to taste. When these ingredients are blended to a paste, mold with the hands into oblong balls, which will fit into the halved whites. As the two sides are not to be put together again, the yolks may be moulded neatly instead of being smoothed off flat. Lay on a platter, garnish with a quantity of water-cress, and serve very cold.

Beet Salad.—Three heads of lettuce; six large red beets, boiled, and sliced when cold; two small cucumbers sliced and laid in iced water; one bunch of water-cress; one cup of mayonnaise dressing. Line a salad-bowl with lettuce leaves, lay upon it the sliced beets alternately with the cucumbers, pour over all the mayonnaise, and dot here and there with sprigs of water-cress. This should be prepared just before the meal for which it is intended, or the cucumbers will wither and the cress droop.

Cold Golden Buck.—Boil six eggs hard, and after they have been in cold water for half an hour, peel and slice.

MEMORANDUM
ON
FRIENDS' RECIPES

282   ADVICE TO HOUSEKEEPERS.

Spread very thin slices of crustless bread with two cupfuls of dry, grated cheese, worked to a creamy paste, with half a teaspoonful of made-mustard, a pinch of cayenne, a half-teaspoonful of salt, two teaspoonfuls of cream, and two tablespoonfuls of butter. Cut the pieces of bread in half, lay on top of the cheese mixture the sliced eggs, and put the two halves of bread together,—sandwich-wise,—the mixture inside.

Beef Cakes.—Cut enough meat from your cold roast of beef to make two cupfuls when chopped fine with two small onions. Add to this two tablespoonfuls of tomato-catsup, one cup of fine bread-crumbs, and half a cup of gravy. Mix well and mould into cakes, sprinkle with bread-crumbs, and bake to a delicate brown. When cold lay the cakes on a platter, pour a tablespoonful of mayonnaise over each, and stick a sprig of parsley in the center of every cake.

Rusk and Milk.—Two cups of milk: one-half cup of butter; one-half yeast-cake, dissolved in warm-water; one quart of flour; two eggs; one even teaspoonful of salt. Mix milk, butter, yeast, and a pint of flour into a sponge, and let it rise until light. Beat in the eggs, salt and the rest of the flour, roll out the dough into a paste more than half an inch thick, cut into round biscuits, set rows of them in a baking-pan, rub the top lightly with butter, and put another row on these; let them rise for half an hour before baking. Remove from the oven, and let them get nearly cold before dividing the upper from the lower stratum; pile lightly in pans, and leave them in a cooking-oven all night to dry. Hang them in a bag in the kitchen closet, or other dry, warm place. In two days they will be ready for use. Set a bowl at each place at table, lay a rusk cracked in several places in it, a piece of ice on this, and pour over all enough milk to cover the rusk well. The rusk will soon become soft, and will then be ready to eat.

Beef-Loaf.—Two pounds of lean beef chopped fine, with two cups of bread-crumbs, and seasoned highly with pepper, salt, nutmeg, sweet marjoram, and a little minced onion, and wet up with half a cup of good gravy; two eggs beaten light, and mixed with the meat. Press firmly into the mould, fit on the cover, and set in a dripping-pan of boiling water to cook slowly for an hour and a quarter. When done, let it get perfectly cold before turning out. It must be cut in thin slices at table.

Red Raspberry Float.—One quart of ripe red raspberries; one pint of cream; one cup and a half of powdered sugar; white of six eggs, beaten to a meringue, and slightly sweetened. Press the berries until they are quite dry. To their juice add the powdered sugar, and stir into the pint of cream. Pour this into a glass bowl. Stir lightly into the meringue the squeezed berries, and pour carefully, not to mix, on top of the cream in the bowl. Serve at once. This is, if properly made, not only a delicious but a pretty dish. The pink cream at the bottom of the glass vessel, and above this the white meringue dotted with red fruit, please the aesthetic taste as well as the palate.

Peach Ice Cream.—One quart of rich cream : one pint of milk; two and a half cups of sugar; one quart of peeled and chopped peaches. Sweeten the cream with one cup of sugar, mix with the milk and freeze. When half frozen, stir in the peaches, over which you have strewed the remaining cup and a half of sugar. Grind until hard-frozen; pack in pounded ice until you are ready for it.

Coffee Ice-Cream.—Four eggs; one quart of milk; two cups of sugar; one pint of cream; one cupful of hot,

MEMORANDUM
ON
FRIENDS' RECIPES

MEMORANDUM
ON
FRIENDS' RECIPES

284   ADVICE TO HOUSEKEEPERS

clear, strong coffee. Put a pinch of soda in the milk, and heat to the boiling point. Beat the eggs until light, add the sugar, and pour little by little the hot milk over them. Return to the fire and cook, stirring all the time, until the custard coats the spoon. Remove from the fire, and add immediately the hot coffee. When cold, add the cream and freeze.

THE PREPARATION OF "FOODS" FOR INFANTS.

BY MARION HARLAND.

A LARGE proportion of women who bring up babies by hand honestly believe it to be impossible to do otherwise. It would be perhaps uncharitable to undertake to decide with how many of these the wish is father to the belief. Nurses and neighborly gossips have a busy finger in this ugly pie. Mrs. Gamp is quick to suspect that her "lady" is lively and fond of company, or likes her own ease and comfort, and she comes to the front with doubts as to whether or not the dear young mother will have food enough for the child or, if she has, if her health can endure the strain and drain. Every one who has observed such matters intelligently knows how much depends upon encouraging the flow of the milk-vessels, and how trivial a cause will dry them up before the habit of milk-giving is established.

There are born mothers, and there are mothers who are made mothers by their children, and there are wives who bring children into the world who never become mothers at all. Not until the blessed baby, an acknowledged entity,—"alive and warm upon her arm,"—unseals her tongue, can the *real* mother live out the best part of her.

The other two classes of women have no new desires and hopes to repress. They rise, not sink, in the opinion of their compeers when they declare after the children come, that as women, they were made up without mater-

MEMORANDUM
ON
FRIENDS' RECIPES

MEMORANDUM
ON
FRIENDS' RECIPES

ADVICE TO HOUSEKEEPERS.

nal instinct, but they will try to do their duty toward the "poor little creatures, now that they are here." Poor little creatures, indeed! God and His angels must name them thus in sorrowful pity. Heaven only can ever tell why they are sent where they are not wanted. Nor can human wisdom pronounce why the highest vocation committed to mortals should be the one for which no special preparation is made by law or public opinion, and, stranger still, none by natural affection. All that our born mother can do is to atone by special and intelligent effort, for others' sins of omission to be visited upon her and her guiltless baby.

Now, if never before, she must watch her own health, grow strong and cheerful, be active without over-fatiguing herself, partake freely of strengthening beverages, such as milk and cocoa, eat nutritious food, and secure enough sleep. She is taking care of BABY'S MOTHER. Her own life has become suddenly invaluable, herself an object of interest hitherto undreamed of. One useful hint may serve her well should she become discouraged that Baby's supply is, for a while, insufficient. The more active her habits, the more apt this is to increase, and the more Baby takes, the more satisfactory will be the coveted "filling up." Any dairymaid can tell you this.

This kind of Infants' Food outranks all others in value as real flowers outrank artificial. Still, there are babies who must be brought up upon something else, and it is an important question what that shall be. Speaking, as St. Paul says, of mine own judgment, I give the preference above all manufactured foods, to what our mothers called "cambric tea." Of fresh cow's milk take one-third, and two-thirds hot water, sweeten slightly, and as soon as it is blood-warm, give it to the baby. This proportion of milk and of water is for an infant a month old. As he gains in age and strength, increase the quan-

MEMORANDUM ON FRIENDS' RECIPES

tity of milk and lessen the quantity of water. Do this gradually, and watch the effect upon him. Should he show signs of distress, weaken the supply somewhat. By the time he is three months old, if he be healthy and vigorous, put half and half. At six months, reverse the order of the orginal mixture, putting two-thirds milk, one-third hot water. Be careful, always, not to put in too much sugar. This too-common blunder produces acidity of stomach and colic. There can be no better home-made imitation of mother's milk than this old fashioned food.

But—and the "but" is a big one—cow's milk is of as many brands as "prepared foods," and subject to changes many and grievous. The sweet fluid which is fresh and nutritious in the morning is "on the turn" by evening, or, if not actually "touched," has altered materially, chemically. Illness so often follows these chemical changes that mothers are timid and artificial food-makers get rich. Within the last ten years, a benefactor of his species has made known a means of "sterilizing" and holding milk at the right stage, for twenty-four hours, and moreover, of killing certain hurtful germs that sometimes lurk in the bowl, especially when the "turn," which is fermentation, has begun. The simple process removes all objections brought against cow's milk as the base of infants' food.

For awhile, mothers attempted, with more or less success, to sterilize milk by putting it into a double boiler, filling the outer vessel with water and bringing the contents of both kettles almost to scalding point. The operation was attended with several difficulties. To boil milk robs it of certain valuable properties possessed by raw, and the skin that rises to the top of the milk that is barely scalding hot proves that some to the virtue has gone out of the liquid. Unless the milk were

MEMORANDUM ON FRIENDS' RECIPES

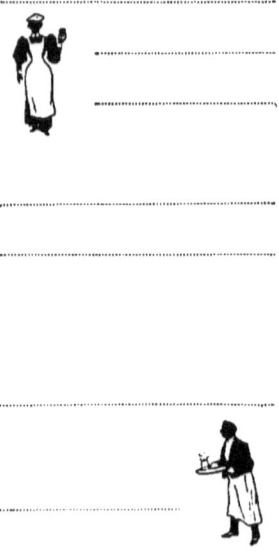

removed instantly from the fire at exactly the right second, and cooled instantly, the experiment was a partial or total failure. At a later date, a utensil called a "sterilizer" was put into the market, which, those who have tried it affirm, does away with the risks of the primitive process. Every nursery should be furnished with one of these. They are simple and inexpensive, and require little care to keep them in order.

It is folly to contend that any made food is superior to good milk, thus treated and combined, in proper proportions, with boiled water. If it does not suit your baby, nothing will. Change your cow, or milkman, and try a different combination, leave out the sugar—do anything sooner than discard food made by the Creator for that turned out by a mill. At ten months, a healthy baby should be weaned from the breast or bottle. He ought to be able, by now, to digest sterilized milk unmixed with water.

In my own nursery, prior to the discovery of the sterilizing principle, I had much respect for a preparation of food (for a weaned child), of farina soaked for several hours, then boiled to a thin gruel in water, very slightly salted and slightly sweetened, and cooked for a few minutes in milk, I still think it good where the strong child appears to require somewhat substantial substance.

As to the legion of artificial foods, good, indifferent, and good for less-than-nothing—apart from the evident truth that if milk agrees with a child and he is nourished thereby, it is folly and a danger to change his diet,—one prominent objection applies to them all. One baby's broth is another baby's bane, and it is impossible to distinguish between broth and bane without experimenting upon baby's stomach.

Let me give examples drawn from the three nurseries in which I am most interested.

One hapless baby, whose natural supply was cut off by unnatural causes, could not digest any preparation of cow's milk, although peptonized by the home-made apparatus, the sterilzer not having been invented. In close succession were tried four kinds of artificial food, all recommended by friends of experience and trustworthiness. Each agreed with the suffering innocent less than the one discarded for it. Condensed milk was confidently prescribed by a physician who made a specialty of children's diseases. One meal of it was followed by agonizing colic, culminating in convulsions. In sheer desperation, the mother tried a sample of food brought in by a visitor whose child "had lived on it from birth." For the first time in months, the feeding-time was not succeeded by contortions and screams, and when the baby dropped into the natural slumber of a satisfied child, the mother, with grateful tears, thanked heaven for the end of the long agony she had shared with her darling. After this, the little girl was fed on nothing but "The Food," and throve happily under the regimen. In time, a baby brother appeared on the scene, and the mother's milk waning when he was six months old, he was also nourished upon the inestimable prepared Food, with equally gratifying results. The tale went far and near, the parents cheerfully commending what they honestly believed was the discovery of the age for suffering infancy.

In nursery No. 2, "The Food" was a signal failure, the stomach of the baby for whom it was introduced usually rejecting it within a few minutes after it was swallowed, and, when the diet was persisted in, in the hope of mastering the idiosyncrasy, wasting away to a mere skeleton. Convinced reluctantly, against inclination, that "The Food" was subject to like vicissitudes with others, the mother, by advice of the same doctor who had given condensed milk to No. 1, resorted to it,

MEMORANDUM
ON
FRIENDS' RECIPES

MEMORANDUM
ON
FRIENDS' RECIPES

but with small hope of benefit for the puny baby-daughter. She retained the few spoonfuls she had strength to swallow, and rallied visibly. After this, she was nourished upon condensed milk until she was eighteen months old, and a fine, plump child.

In the third nursery, "The Food" and condensed milk were alike calamitous to Baby's capricious stomach. Both had a fair trial, and were discarded as absolutely perilous to the child's life, and arrow-root gruel was introduced by a relative who had fed three children upon it. Another relative present exclaimed shudderingly that she had ignorantly starved a baby to death upon what the best writers of dietetics pronounce, nowadays, to be no better than starch. The arrow-root was administered by the almost despairing mother and brought the baby back from the very mouth of the grave.

Who shall decide when babies disagree as to the merits of various "substitutes"? The tender parent shrinks from testing the qualities of three or perhaps a dozen by the degree of pain they inflict upon her unoffending darling; yet something must be found that can be assimilated by the digestive organs. Thirty odd years ago, a colored woman gave me a golden bit of counsel that has been put out at interest many times since.

"Don't you *prodjick* wid you' baby's stummock, chile! Dar is dem what can't let chillen 'lone, but mus' be all de time pourin' things down dey t'roats, same like dey was jugs. Listen to what yer ole mammy tells you—an' let *prodjickin'* alone!"

Mammy was in advance of her generation. Her advice, sound always, borrows pertinence from the hundred only safe and perfect foods for infants advertised in every column of every newspaper, and thrust upon us in sample packages in street-cars and by mail.

Give the baby *boiled* water to drink until he is over

two years old, particularly when he is carried from one place to another. The change of water affects the bowels more surely than change of milk. There are salts and other minerals in solution in some regions, in others putrid vegetable and animal matter that lend gaseous sparkle to the fluid. Boiling causes a precipitate of some elements, and makes others harmless. Iced water should never be given to the children. It chills the stomach and checks digestion, to say nothing of germs and larvæ which cold does not kill, that are thus taken into the system.

If you desire to give Baby pleasure, do not fall into the mistake of introducing variety into his bill-of-fare. While the simple diet enjoined by nature and common sense agrees with and satisfies him, be you likewise content. Bear in mind Mammy's caution as to "prodjickin'," and leave to others doubtful projects upon a delicate organ. Neither is it kind to create in him desires for what may be an unlawful indulgence. Up to the age of three or four years, give him little meat,—rare beef, steak or roast, tender roast mutton, and roast chicken. Prohibit fried foods of all kinds, also stews and rich soups. Broths—well-skimmed—will not hurt him, but he ought not to know the taste of gravy. Plain puddings may be a holiday luxury, also custards, blanc-mange, and ice-cream in small quantities. Ripe, fresh fruits, partaken of in moderation, should take the place of most sweets, but these he should not eat until after his weaning is some months old. Make haste slowly with all innovations.

Thomas Carlyle called the human stomach "that most diabolical of all machines." It depends largely upon the mothers of the rising generation to decide whether in the next century the biting epigram shall be truth or falsehood.

MEMORANDUM ON FRIENDS' RECIPES

MEMORANDUM ON FRIENDS' RECIPES

POTTED PROVISIONS.

BY MARION HARLAND.

FIFTY years ago, desiccation (or drying) was the one method practiced for the preservation, for winter use, of green vegetables, while preserving in syrup, vinegar, and spirits was resorted to for keeping fruits in palatable form for the table. Sweet corn was dried when nearly hard, and had to be soaked over night, then boiled for a long time before it could be eaten. After all, it was hardly an improvement upon the coarser hominy. Tomatoes, peaches, plums, cherries, and pears lost most of their distinctive flavor through long exposure to the sun, and subsequent soaking and stewing.

The housekeeper who complains of the stale monotony of "canned goods," would do well to bear in mind the privations of a former day, and be thankful. She would do better to make good things excellent by judicious treatment. While the demand for potted provisions may not have lessened throughout the country, it is undeniable that there is a growing disrelish for them in the minds of people of dainty and cultured tastes. There is danger of relegating to boarding-house and hotel-keepers what are, really, delicacies, and wholesome assuasives of bile and satiety. People who can ill afford it, pay high prices for forced vegetables, rather than set before guests the contents of cans purchased for little money at the corner grocer's. It is the purpose of the present "Talk" to lift the reproach from the serviceable "can," and show the cause of disrelish to be not in the nature of the thing preserved so much as in the cook's determining to regard it as an end, not a means, a finished product, instead of semi-raw material. The wrong way to serve all potted provisions is to "dump" them from the can or jar into the saucepan, and from the saucepan into the platter or root-dish, with no attempt at seasoning or enrichment.

Here let me say, once for all, that canned meats, fruits, vegetables, soups, etc., should be turned out of the vessels in which they were preserved, at least one hour before they are cooked, or sent to table, and left in open dishes to rid them of the close airless smell which disgusts many with the entire class. I remark, furthermore, that the prejudice against potted corned beef would never have gained prevalence and strength, had this precaution been taken in every case.

Still, furthermore, I drop as a word of warning, that your cook will not obey your orders in this respect unless you watch her. Brains, and the ability to use brains, are required to see the wisdom of the simple safeguard.

I set, first, because most abundant and useful among potted provisions,—

Tomatoes.—Of these, there are brands and brands. Some tins turn out a superfluity of liquid, many unripe lumps, and bits of skin mingled with the pulp. Note the name and address of the manufacturer, and avoid the "make" in future. The housewife who takes advantage of the height of the season, and puts up her own tomatoes, rejecting cores and hard pieces, and draining off half the juice, will fare best on this score.

Stewed Tomatoes.—Mince a quarter of a small onion, and put with the tomatoes over the fire. Cook, after the boil is reached, fifteen minutes. Add, then, three tablespoonfuls of dry, fine crumbs, a tablespoonful of butter, and salt and pepper to taste. Stew gently for five minutes more, stir in a teaspoonful of sugar, and pour into a deep dish.

MEMORANDUM ON FRIENDS' RECIPES

MEMORANDUM ON FRIENDS' RECIPES

Scalloped Tomatoes.—Drain off all the liquid that will come away. (Salted and peppered, it can be kept for a couple of days to be made into tomato sauce for chops, etc.) Sprinkle the bottom of a buttered pie or pudding-dish with dry crumbs, salted and peppered. Cover with a layer of the drained tomatoes; stick bits of butter in this, and sprinkle lightly with sugar. Fill the dish in this order. The top layer should be fine crumbs, seasoned and buttered. Cover closely, and bake half an hour. Then brown slightly upon the grating of the oven.

Scalloped Corn and Tomatoes.—Empty a can of each, and drain, separately, in a colander. Chop the corn fine, and treat as directed in last recipe, substituting chopped corn for crumbs, until you reach the top, when a coating of the latter, seasoned with pepper, salt, sugar, and butter, may be used to facilitate browning. Bake forty-five minutes (covered) then brown.

This is a most palatable dish, and an elegant one when baked in scallop-shells.

Cream Tomato Soup.—Put a cupful of (aired) tomatoes into a sauce-pan with half a small onion, chopped fine, and cook half an hour after the boil begins. Strain and rub through a colander, and return to the fire. Season with pepper, and salt, and a teaspoonful of white sugar. Stir in, by degrees, two tablespoonfuls of butter, cut up and rubbed into two tablespoonfuls of flour. Have ready in another sauce-pan a pint of boiling milk, in which has been dissolved a bit of soda, not larger than a pea. Let the soup simmer for three minutes after butter and flour go in, stirring well and often; pour into a tureen, add the boiling milk, mix well, and send to the table. If milk and tomatoes are boiled together, they will be apt to form a curdled compound, in spite of the soda.

Creamed Tomato Toast.—Take a pint of tomatoes, with pepper and salt, and cook gently for fifteen minutes.

Rub through a colander, and return to the fire. In another sauce-pan heat a cupful of milk,—with the tiny bit of soda,—add two teaspoonfuls of butter, cut up in flour, and stir for one minute; put a teaspoonful of sugar with the tomato; take from the fire, and mix with the boiling milk. Pour at once upon slices of crustless bread, toasted and buttered, and laid upon a hot platter. Cover, set for a minute in the oven, and send to the table.

This is a pleasant adjunct to fish, poultry, or mutton.

Canned Corn Pudding.—Drain the corn and chop very fine. Make a raw custard of four eggs, well beaten, two teaspoonfuls of sugar, three cups of milk, and a dessert-spoonful of melted butter. Season the corn with salt and a little pepper. Mix all well together, and bake, covered, forty-five minutes then brown.

Canned Corn Cakes.—Drain and chop the corn fine. Beat three eggs very light; add a pint of milk, a little salt, a teaspoonful of melted butter, a teaspoonful of sugar, and, when all are thoroughly mixed, three tablespoonfuls of sifted flour,—or just enough to hold the corn together. Bake on a griddle, as you would buckwheat cakes, and eat as a vegetable.

Canned Corn Soup.—Chop the corn very fine; add a scant quart of boiling water, and a teaspoonful of minced onion. Stew steadily for three-quarters of an hour after it reaches the boil. Rub through a colander into a sauce-pan; add salt, pepper, three tablespoonfuls of butter, rolled in as much flour, and a tablespoonful of chopped parsley. Heat in another vessel a pint of milk, and when the corn purée has simmered five minutes longer, turn first one, then the other into a tureen, stir well, and serve.

This soup is nice if veal or chicken stock be substituted for boiling water. If the stock be strong, omit the butter.

Canned Pea Soup.—Make according to the recipe just

MEMORANDUM
ON
FRIENDS' RECIPES

296   ADVICE TO HOUSEKEEPERS.

given. The peas should not be chopped, but boiled soft, and then rubbed through the colander.

Canned peas should always be drained, and left to lie in very cold water, slightly salt, for half an hour before they are cooked. This takes away the smoky flavor which people are apt to consider inseparable from American peas. These, by the way, are as good for soup as the French, which are double the price.

American peas may also be made into

Pea Pancakes.—Drain the peas; lay in slightly salted ice-water for half an hour. Pour off the water, and boil soft. Rub through a colander, and while hot work in pepper, salt, and two teaspoonfuls of butter. Let them get cold. When ready to cook them, stir in, gradually, two beaten eggs, a pint of milk, and a very little flour, just enough to bind the mixture. Cook as you would griddlecakes.

Sardines au Gratin.—Most people know of but one way of using sardines. That is to eat them just as they come from the box, with or without lemon-juice.

So far as I know, it was reserved for the caterer of my modest household to discover, under the whip of necessity, that they could be "treated" into a tolerable likeness of the toothsome things they are when fried fresh upon the shores of the Adriatic. A carriage-load of guests arrived unexpectedly, one June noon, at our mountain cottage. It was one of the days when the butcher "did not happen to call." There were berries and lettuce galore in the garden, milk, and cream in the cellar, eggs and canned bouillon, crackers, cheese, and olives in the storeroom, but not a morsel of anything "hearty" as rural housewives call it—in the house.

Sardines au gratin were evolved from the mortification of the dilemma. The inspiration came midway

MEMORANDUM ON FRIENDS' RECIPES

MARION HARLAND.

between storeroom and kitchen. I opened two boxes, removed the fish without so much as breaking the skin of one, and laid them upon soft paper to drain and air. When the oil had dripped away, I peppered each charily with cayenne, and squeezed a few drops of lemon-juice upon it. Next I rolled them in pounded crackers, arranged them carefully within a buttered bake-pan, and set them in a quick oven. In ten minutes they were smoking hot and delicately browned. They were transferred to a hot-water dish, garnished with parsley and sliced lemon, a piece of which went with each "help."

Hot bouillon preceded them; and egg-and-lettuce salad, with mayonnaise-dressing, came next; then crackers, cream-cheese, and olives; lastly, strawberries and cream, cake and coffee; but my "fresh sardines" were the favorite dish of the simple feast.

Sardine Salad.—Drain them well of oil. Lay fresh, crisp lettuce upon a dish, and upon each leaf a fish. Reserve two to be skinned and rubbed fine, then mix with your mayonnaise.

Sardine Sandwiches.—Drain and skin the fish, and rub into a paste, working in gradually a teaspoonful or so of melted butter, pepper, salt, lemon-juice and a little French mustard. Butter thin slices of bread; spread with the paste and double each slice upon the mixture.

Mock Turtle Soup.—Add four hard-boiled eggs, cut into eighths, a glass of claret (or whatever substitute you use, if you object to wine), the juice of half a lemon, or a lemon peeled, then slice thin (this last to be laid on the surface after the soup is dished), a teacupful of boiling water, and such additional salt and pepper as your taste adjudges to be needful. If you care to take the trouble, omit the whites of the eggs; pound the yolks into a paste, work in melted butter, a pinch of mustard,

MEMORANDUM
ON
FRIENDS' RECIPES

pepper and salt, and bind with the yolk of a raw egg. Flour your hands, make the paste into small balls, and drop into the boiling soup. Simmer three minutes after they go in.

Still another way.—Drain a cupful of juice from a can of tomatoes; strain through mosquito netting; put over the fire, and boil fast ten minutes. Skin, add a tablespoonful of butter, rolled in browned flour, and when the soup has boiled, stir into it. After this, drop in the hard-boiled eggs (or the egg-balls) and the sliced lemon.

Consomme may be the base of a dozen different soups—such as tomato, Julienne, rice-broth, tapioca, sago, barley, potato, turnip, etc., etc., each of which will repay you for the additional trouble it costs you.

A can of chicken, minced fine and stirred, with half as much fine crumbs, well seasoned, into boiling consomme, makes delicious bisque. A good spoonful of butter, and a few spoonfuls of cream improve this.

Mutton Broth.—Add three tablespoonfuls of rice and the water in which it was boiled. With the rice may be cooked a small onion, and this, minced, go into the broth, also a tablespoonful of chopped parsley. Season to taste.

Chicken Soup.—This makes a delightful bisque when a cupful of cold veal or a can of chicken, chopped, is stirred in, with a half a cupful of dry, seasoned crumbs. A finer soup can be based upon chicken-broth by making egg-balls, such as I have described, and putting them into the boiling broth. Have ready a cupful of scalding milk, stir in a tablespoonful of butter rolled in one of flour, cook one minute, and pour, a little at a time, upon two beaten raw eggs. Turn into the tureen, and add the soup and balls.

MEMORANDUM
ON
FRIENDS' RECIPES

HOUSEHOLD MANAGEMENT.

NEXT to good domestic cooking stands good household management. It would be hard to say which is entitled to precedence. There are houses which are kept to a nicety, in which the cooking is execrable. There are others where good cooking is the one thing that makes them endurable. But all good things should be happily combined if a really model home is sought. "I am no cook," said a newly established housekeeper, "but I am a good manager." If her capacity to manage extended to managing her cook, and her cook happened to be a good one, then things might move smoothly; but for the best results the year through, housekeepers should be queens in every part of the home.

Somebody manages the domestic affairs of almost every house. Occasionally it is the man of the house. Sometimes it is his mother, or his wife's mother. Oftener it is the cook. There are homes where the rightful heads are not heads, but are more like tails. Another makes the decisions, and they wag assent, or submissively curl themselves up with ill-concealed disgust. There are some houses where there is no management whatever. Affairs go as a log goes down stream. Now one end leads; again the other. Now it goes

MEMORANDUM
ON
FRIENDS' RECIPES

302   *HOUSEHOLD MANAGEMENT.*

broadside; again it does not go at all. Alas for those who dwell in such a house, and call it home!

There are private as well as public resting places, where those who travel much occasionally stop, where wonderful contrasts are visible. One of these was a luxurious home in a Southern city. There was no stint because of straitened circumstances nor on the score of parsimony. The gentleman and lady were wealthy, generous, and refined. Their cook had served long in a restaurant, and was fully competent to do any culinary work. The meals were superb. They were cooked to a nicety and served to perfection. There was plenty, and that, too, of the best sort.

But, oh! the condition of the house! The best guest-chamber was laden with odors so offensive that a chance lodger there began an exploration. Stowed in the bottom of the clothes press of the room was accummulated rubbish, musty, moldy, mouse-infested, and disgusting. Having no means to correct the evil, the guest left this closet door wide open in the morning, hoping thereby to attract attention to its condition and secure its cleansing. But when he re-entered the room he found, to his dismay, that the door had been carefully closed upon its unsightliness and unwholesomeness, the skeleton-maker, if not the "skeleton in the closet," being scrupulously retained.

Such gross mismanagement is to be severely condemned. No excuse for it suffices. Common sense and common decency demand better management in every home. But the "happy-go-easy" inmates of that home saw nothing amiss. Of course, management may run to the other extreme. A house may be so orderly that a man instinctively gathers himself together when in it, lest he be caught in some of its machinery and be ground to powder; or, what is equally to be dreaded, be the means of disarranging some part of that intricate family machine.

A golden mean in management must be observed

Enough of it is necessary to compel complete and unceasing supervision at every point, so that everything shall be just as it should be. But when it becomes an overshadowing and awe-inspiring presence—subduing the laugh, suppressing the smile, restraining the steps, fettering the words—then it is a bane and not a blessing.

Executive ability is in great part a natural endowment. Some are born to rule. Command is natural and easy for them. They can organize and execute. But the rarest genius in this art will be the better for practice. Experience will improve his natural aptitude. And he will gather valuable lessons from the experiences of others. Where others fail he will shun to tread, unless the reason of their failure he so clearly sees that he is sure of mastery over it. What the person of ability sees in others and experiences in himself is capital on which he trades, and from which he derives his revenues of advancement.

If geniuses in executive ability grow by what they learn, surely those less gifted need to learn the more, that they, too, may grow, though their advantages be less. Therefore it is that in this department of household management directions are given on many practical points of home duty. These directions are the results of experience. They may seem unimportant, and possibly excessive, but they will help the most competent, as well as the least competent, by suggesting both what to do and what not to do. The old maxim, "Prove all things; hold fast that which is good," may well be sounded in the ears of all housekeepers. The best housekeepers have reached their proud eminence by this wise course.

As housewives press on to higher and still higher attainments, let the words of one of the noblest of their company, Mrs. Sigourney, inspire them. She says: "The strength of a nation, especially of a republican nation, is in the intelligent and well-ordered homes of the people."

MEMORANDUM
ON
FRIENDS' RECIPES

MEMORANDUM
ON
FRIENDS' RECIPES

I.—MARKETING.

OPPORTUNITIES vary so in different localities, that general rules about marketing are hard to frame. In rural places the butcher drives to the door, and the customer must be content with what is found in the wagon. In villages and small cities, the butcher shops and stores, denominated "Markets," afford a variety more or less excellent. Some of the large cities have their market stores, and green-grocers, and butcher shops, and great central markets, where qualities vary with the prices, and where customers of all grades and conditions can be supplied.

In marketing, as in all other business transactions, it may be accepted as a rule, that goods will bring their value. The best usually costs most, and in the long run it is the cheapest. In such perishable goods as meats, fruits, fish, vegetables, etc., there are innumerable chances for fluctuations in price and for variation in quality. A judge of these commodities may "pick up bargains," but the inexpert and uninitiated are more frequently fleeced than favored in catch operations at the markets.

General hints as to the selection of meats, fish, vegetables, etc., have already been given in this volume, under the department of Cookery, but no hints, and no rules, will suffice absolutely. Keen and continuous observation, growing into a large and varied experience, are essential to a good marketer. There is not a family which has not suffered from a want of the knowledge that would enable them to judge the quality of meats offered them. Often at the market an expert is waited on from the best quality and the best cuts, while another, with less knowledge, is served from

MARKETING. 303

a poorer quality and less desirable cuts. Many a housekeeper has been censured for poor cooking, when the fault was back of that, and in the quality of the meats; and again, the market man has often been censured for furnishing poor meats, when the fault was in the cooking. A good piece of meat may be spoiled in cooking and a poor piece may be made palatable.

To know the parts of the animals sold in the markets, and to understand their relative value and most economical uses, is the first requisite in successful marketing. Cutting of animals varies somewhat among butchers of different places, but the chart given below will fairly set forth the usual methods of cutting, and the ordinary designations of the several portions.

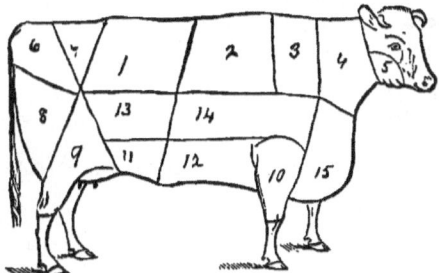

CHART ILLUSTRATING THE CUTTING OF BEEF.

In explanation of the illustration of the cutting of beef the following notes will suffice:

No. 1.—The choice cut of the beef, the *Sirloin*, containing the kidneys and the tenderloin. These are the finest pieces of roasting and steak meat.

No. 2.—The *Standing Rib* piece, also a choice roasting portion, which includes about eleven of the ribs.

MEMORANDUM
ON
FRIENDS' RECIPES

MEMORANDUM
ON
FRIENDS' RECIPES

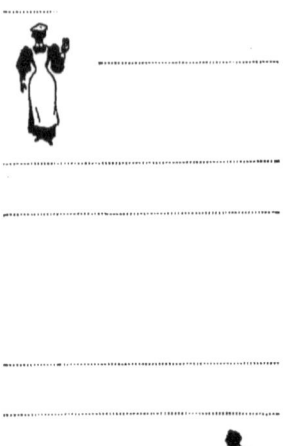

306   *HOUSEHOLD MANAGEMENT.*

No. 3.—The *Chuck Ribs*, also used for roasting, but of a less desirable quality and usually sold at a lower price.

No. 4.—The neck, with considerable bone, used generally for stewing and for pot roast.

No. 5.—The *Cheek*, or jowl, a fleshy part, used for stewing or for boiling.

No. 6.—The *Rump*, sometimes cut differently from the manner shown in the diagram, which is the usual cutting at the East, for domestic purposes. This part has very little bone and is generally used for choice steaks, and the portion next the tail, left from the steak cutting, is a choice piece for corning.

No. 7.—The *Pin-bone*, a choice piece for roasting, being very tender.

No. 8.—The *Round*, which furnishes common steaks, and is the choice cut for dried beef or for corning.

No. 9.—The *Leg*, the choice soup piece.

No. 10.—The *Shin*, also used for soup.

No. 11.—The *Thin flank*, used for boiling and for corning.

No. 12.—The *Brisket*, used for corning.

No. 13.—The *Plate*, used for family boiling and for corning.

No. 14.—The *Plate* (thick end), extending under the shoulder, used for corning and family boiling.

No. 15.—The *Breast*, or butt end of the brisket, also called the "sticking piece." Used for corning and soup-meat.

If the cutting vary materially from this plan, it is still true that the essential parts of the animal continue to exist and are for sale under some name and in some shape. A polite inquiry of any reputable butcher will secure the desired information as to any part. By this means a person may secure intelligent skill in purchasing beef. Some special points concerning beef need a moment's attention.

The *Tongue* is used fresh, salted, or smoked. It is a very

desirable and delicate portion, suitable for table use at almost any time. The *Tail*, which affords some meat and much gelatinous substance, is prized for soups, ox-tail soup especially being founded upon it. The *Heart* and *Liver* are used for food—the former being stuffed and roasted, the latter being fried, usually with onions. The *Tripe*, which is the lining of the large, or receiving stomach of the beef, is used for souse, for pepper-pot, etc. It is a cheap article. The *Kidneys* of beef are sold separate from the sirloin, from which they are cut. They are used for stewing, etc. *Suet*, used for pie-crust, plum-puddings, mince-meat, etc., is the solid, clear fat, which incloses the kidney. When pure it is a very desirable article. The *Feet* are used for jellies, though not so delicate as the calf's foot. The *Head* is refuse. The *Marrow-bones* are those of the shin, leg, and round. Any of the round, hollow bones contain marrow. The other remains of beef are refuse, except as available for manufacturing purposes.

VEAL.

Veal is a favorite meat. Consult the points concerning it made upon page 76. Veal is cut as shown below.

No. 1.—*Loin*, the best end. It is the favorite roasting piece, and furnishes the choice chops. It commands the best price.

No. 2.—*Fillet*, or cutlet piece. This too is a choice part, being excellent for steaks and for roasting and filling. It is also very fine for a cold cut.

CHART ILLUSTRATING THE CUTTING OF VEAL.

No. 3.—The *Leg*, called knuckle also, used chiefly for stewing and for soup.

No. 4.—The *Rack*, used for chops, and for roasting; less

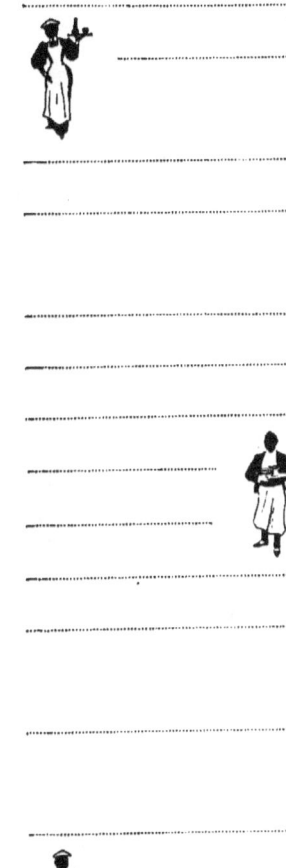

MEMORANDUM
ON
FRIENDS' RECIPES

MEMORANDUM
ON
FRIENDS' RECIPES

308   *HOUSEHOLD MANAGEMENT.*

desirable and lower priced than the loin, having more bone.

No. 5.—The *Neck*, used for stewing, pies, etc. The best end is quite desirable, that nearer the head being of less value.

No. 6.—*Head*. The brains and tongue are prized by many, the former for frying as a delicacy, the latter for boiling. The head, as a whole, is used in mock turtle and some other fancy soups.

No. 7.—The *Shoulder*, used for roasting, for which it answers a good purpose. It is valuable for a stew also.

No. 8.—The *Breast*. This is the second choice piece for stuffing and roasting. It is too valuable for pies, stews, etc.

No. 9.—The *Shin*. This usually goes with the shoulder, with which it is often roasted. If used separately, it answers fairly well for stewing.

The *Sweetbread*, a very delicate portion, belongs with the breast. It is often sold separately, however. The *Kidneys* are sold with the loin, in the fat of which they are imbedded. The *Heart* and *Liver* are great delicacies for frying, or the heart for stuffing and roasting. The *Feet* are the basis of genuine calves-foot jelly, and are much prized for this purpose. The *Entrails*, cut open and well cleaned, are made into souse by some persons.

MUTTON.

Next to beef, the most profitable and healthful meat is mutton. In all markets this meat is cut substantially in the same manner as shown in the following chart. The names and ordinary uses of the parts are as follows:

No. 1.—The *Loin*, best end. This is the choice piece for filling and roasting and for prime chops. Of course, it commands the best price.

No. 2.—The *Leg*. This joint is nearly always used for roasting and chops, sometimes also for boiling. It has but little bone, as compared with the other parts of the animal, and is, therefore, an economical piece to select, though the price per pound be greater than that of any other cut. It is common to find a good leg weighing from seven to twelve pounds.

No. 3.—The *Loin*, second choice. This furnishes "French

CHART ILLUSTRATING THE CUTTING OF MUTTON.

chops," a favorite dish in eating-houses, and is specially good for a roast.

No. 4.—The *Loin*, rump end. Good for roasting and boiling. It contains considerable bone.

No. 5.—The *Shoulder*, used for boiling and for filling and roasting. It is less in price and nearly as good as the leg, but it has more bone.

No. 6.—The *Breast*, used for stews and for meat pies. A savory, juicy part.

No. 7.—The *Flank*. A continuation of the breast, but somewhat thinner. This with the breast makes a cheap roast, which may be split and filled.

No. 8.—The *Rack*. The best end of the rack is used for second-rate chops. The neck end of the rack is good for stewing only.

No. 9.—The *Neck*. This, with the neck end of the rack, is for stewing only.

MEMORANDUM
ON
FRIENDS' RECIPES

310   *HOUSEHOLD MANAGEMENT.*

No. 10.—The *Head.* The tongue only is used, the remainder being refuse.

It is customary to split mutton down the back, and then to split each half into parts called hind and fore quarters. The saddle is the middle portion before this quartering is done. Part of it goes with each quarter.

The hind quarter of mutton, consisting of the leg and the loin, is the choice quarter. It makes a very superior large roast, while either of its parts, the leg or the loin, suffices nicely for a small company. A hind quarter from an animal in good condition will weigh from twenty to thirty pounds. The *Kidneys* are used as in beef, so also the heart and liver. The other parts are refuse.

LAMB.

Lamb is cut as mutton, but it is usually dressed with more care, so as to present a more attractive appearance. Lamb proper is in market in the spring only. As the season advances older lamb is in market, but what is called "lamb" in the winter months is usually poor mutton dressed lamb style. The butcher indulges in a quiet smile when his customer, in the winter season, asks for and pays for "lamb." Of course, the superiority and rarity of lamb demand for it the best prices. Indeed, "fancy prices" reign in lamb. For tests, see p. 82.

PORK.

Fresh pork and salt pork are much used. General facts on pork are given on page 85.

CHART ILLUSTRATING THE CUTTING OF PORK.

The usual method of cutting for domestic use is shown in the accompanying cut. For packing a somewhat different method is pursued.

No. 1.—The *Ham,* the most valuable part of the hog.

When nicely cured it is a very great delicacy. It is a great article of commerce also.

No. 2.—*Sirloin*, furnishing chops and the finest roasting pieces.

No. 3.—*Rack*, used for second-rate chops and roasts, the meat being as sweet, but the bone being greater than in the sirloin.

No. 4.—*Neck*, used for inferior roasting, and for boiling when fresh, and also for corning.

No. 5.—The *Shoulder*. A fair roasting piece, but chiefly used, like the ham, for pickling and curing, though it is greatly inferior to ham in juiciness and flavor. Either fresh or corned it is a fine boiling piece.

No. 6.—The *Jowl*. Useful for smoking. Sometimes cured with the tongues remaining in them.

No. 7.—The *Head*. Used for puddings and head cheese.

No. 8.—The *Belly* or *Flitch*. A good boiling piece either fresh, salted, or smoked.

No. 9.—*Feet*. These are much used for souse and for pickling. They contain so much gelatinous matter that they are exceedingly desirable.

The *Ears* also are used for souse and head cheese. The *Liver*, *Heart*, and *Kidneys* are used for liver pudding. The *Entrails*, nicely cleaned, are used for sausage skins. The *Fat* about the kidneys furnishes leaf lard. The other fat furnishes common lard. The other parts are refuse.

VENISON.

If the marketer desires venison, it is well to remember that buck venison is best from August 1st to November 1st; and that doe venison is best from the latter date to January 1st, after which no deer should be killed. It is quite common, however, to freeze deer meat, and to keep it for months in that state. This adds to the cost, but it also improves the fibre of the meat.

Venison is cut into parts respectively designated haunch

MEMORANDUM ON
FRIENDS' RECIPES

MEMORANDUM
ON
FRIENDS' RECIPES

saddle, leg, loin, fore-quarter, and steaks. The latter should not be cut until ready for use. Venison should be fat. It cannot be too fat. Its flavor is better after hanging a few days, but it should not become rank. To test this, pierce it with a skewer and notice the odor. Shun tough venison.

For roasting, choose the haunch, the saddle, the neck, or the shoulder. Cut steaks from the leg. Stew the shoulder, or any part which is too thin for satisfactory roasting.

POULTRY.

Tests of poultry are given on page 61. But the expedients resorted to in order to mislead purchasers are so numerous that even experts are not wholly safe. Technically, the term *chickens* belongs to fowls under a year old, but actually, the entire tribe is included in the name. *Capons* are young roosters, gelded and carefully fed so as to secure the utmost delicacy of flesh. *Pullets* are young hens.

Turkeys reach their maturity in eight or nine months, and hence young, but well-grown turkeys, are in market about the fall and winter holidays. Young hen turkeys are regarded as best, being fatter and more juicy; but the male turkeys will be larger for the same age. The legs of young turkeys are black; of old ones reddish and rough. Young cocks have small spurs; old ones large spurs and very rough legs. Fat turkeys, with broad, full breasts, are preferable. Soft, pliable feet indicate fresh-killed birds.

Wild turkeys are deemed to be finer in flavor than tame ones. They are in season in November, December, and January. They are usually sold with their feathers on. Small birds have their well-defined seasons, as have other kinds of game, but they admit little choice except as fresh.

VEGETABLES.

Every good marketer will supply his table with a variety of vegetables all the year round. There is hardly a vegetable that cannot be had in our markets at any season, either fresh or canned. Railroads and steamers connect the different climates so closely that one hardly knows whether he is eating fruits and vegetables in or out of their natural season. But it takes a long purse to buy fresh vegetables at the North while the ground is yet frozen. Still, there are so many vegetables that keep through cold weather that if we did not have new ones from the South, there would be, nevertheless, a variety from which to choose. Late in the spring, when the old vegetables begin to shrink and grow rank, we greatly appreciate what comes from the South.

If one has a good, dry cellar, it is wise to procure in the fall vegetables enough for all winter. But if the cellar is warm, vegetables will sprout and decay before half the cold months have passed. Those best adapted for winter keeping are onions, squashes, turnips, beets, carrots, parsnips, cabbages, and potatoes. Squashes and onions should be kept in a very dry room. The others will keep readily in a cool, dry cellar, or bedded in sand beneath the reach of frost.

If vegetables be bought as needed, care must be used to get them in good condition. In season, they should never appear wilted, but should be fresh and crisp. At no time should they be used if suffering from decay. The utmost prudence is needed at this point. A very little waste will more than counterbalance all you save by purchasing large quantities, and by storing for the winter.

The luxuries of the world are spread at the feet of the customer in our markets; still, extravagant expenditure is by no means necessary. Many delicacies are within the reach of all. Those who content themselves with sending to the markets, miss many golden opportunities. Those who go, see for themselves, and embrace many a favoring chance. Personal observation ripens into experience also, and the experienced purchasers command the situation.

These remarks apply with equal force to purchasing of the grocer, the baker, the milkman, and all, in short, who supply us with the necessaries of life. There are reliable

MEMORANDUM
ON
FRIENDS' RECIPES

314   HOUSEHOLD MANAGEMENT.

dealers and those of doubtful integrity; but in every case the hope of the household is in its provider. Cultivate power in this line.

It is best to deal steadily with persons whom you have tried and found reliable. Do not relinquish your independence, so as to suggest to them the idea that they may impose on you. Be ready to go elsewhere, if the old service falls off; but usually those who are regular dealers at a place get the best attention, and errors or failures can be rectified with ease.

In all marketing and dealing with storekeepers keep your temper. To lose one's temper and scold or threaten, is undignified and worse than useless. State your grievances calmly and plainly. If they are redressed, all right; if not redressed, you can quietly go elsewhere and bestow your patronage. A little suspension of trade with a dealer often works wonders. He does not want to lose customers; but such is the waywardness of human nature, that all of us need reminders to keep us fully up to duty. Let the dealer have these when he needs them, but never at the expense of your own self-possession and courteous dignity.

MEMORANDUM
ON
FRIENDS' RECIPES

II.—CARVING.

THE ART OF CARVING; REQUISITES; CARVING TURKEY, CHICKEN, DUCKS, GEESE, SMALL BIRDS, BEEF, MUTTON, LAMB, VENISON HAM, PIG, RABBIT, STEAKS, FISH, TONGUE, AND CALF'S-HEAD.

EVERY person who travels or visits much sees numberless illustrations of the varied capacities of carvers.

Hotel and restaurant life does not make much display in this line, as the carving is done out of sight. And yet even here the marvelous thinness of the slice, which is so immense in its area, demonstrates that somebody is on hand who is expert in this line. In private houses the meat and the poultry are sometimes carved before they come to the table. By whom done, or with what accompaniments of perspiration and emphatic words, the guests know not. But meat served thus is chilled and juiceless, and generally damaged. It is worthy of better treatment.

Many amusing and not a few irritating examples of clumsy carving occur under everybody's eyes. Meat is condemned as tough, knives as dull, dishes as too small, there is too much gravy, skewers are not drawn, and a thousand other reasons are blurted out by the clumsy carver, as he outwardly sweats and inwardly swears at his task. He slops gravy on to the cloth; he drops part of the meat from the dish; he cuts himself by an unfortunate slip of the knife; and sometimes, like a distinguished wit of whom the story tells, he lands a fowl in the lap of a lady beside him, though probably, unlike that wit, he will not have the grace to say, "I will thank you, madam, to return that chicken."

Every housekeeper should learn to carve. Carving should be done at the table by the gentleman of the house, or, in his

MEMORANDUM
ON
FRIENDS' RECIPES

316 HOUSEHOLD MANAGEMENT.

absence, by the lady, unless some other of the family be an expert carver. Unless a guest is known to be an expert, or unless he volunteers for the duty, he should not be expected to carve. He may be a clumsy hand, and the courtesy of hospitality should protect him from exposure at this point.

The carver at a private table should retain his seat while carving and serving. To facilitate this, his chair should be high, so that he can reach readily to his work. The dish should be large enough to prevent soiling the cloth, except by some unusual accident. The centre of a carving-dish for roast meats should be raised nearly as high as the surrounding edge, so that a horizontal movement of the knife in slicing may be made without interference from the edges. No man can slice meat neatly if the meat is in the bottom of a deep dish, into which he must scoop with his knife as best he may. Elevate the meat, but have a surrounding depression between the centre and the edge, where the rich juices of the meat may accumulate, and where they may be served readily.

Not all knives are suitable for carving, nor is any one knife just the thing for all work in this line. For slicing, a long, thin, broad blade is essential. With a fine roast, elevated on the dish, and with a good, sharp slicing knife in hand, a cool-headed man can hardly help doing neat and rapid work.

But such a knife is not the one for poultry or rib carving. For these uses a shorter blade, which is both narrower and stiffer, must be employed. All knives for carving must be sharp. There should be a good steel at hand to touch up the edge—nothing more, for a dull knife should be ground, or whet up on an oil-stone. Any large fork, with a guard to prevent accidents, will do. A rest for the knife and fork when not in use is desirable. The carver's requisites, therefore, are as follows: A high chair, suitable serving plates, two sharp knives, a good fork, and a knife and fork rest. With these he is ready for work. Without them he is at serious disadvantage.

CARVING.

Carving a Turkey.—Nothing delights an expert carver more than the opportunity to cut up a fine roast turkey. Such a man is in doubt whether the eating of the meat even is the greater luxury.

Whether the head of the bird shall lie to the carver's right or left is an open question. Better to the right, as more work is required on the head end, and in this position the knife-hand works less over the hand which holds the fork.

The fork should be inserted astride of the breast-bone, just back of its most prominent point. It should be sunk deep enough to penetrate the encasing bone below the white meat. This secures full command of the bird. If the company be small and the bird fairly large, better do all the cutting from one side, reserving the other in as perfect a form as possible.

TURKEY PROPERLY TRUSSED FOR ROASTING.

Remove all the limbs first unless half the bird is to be reserved. The neat cut is to remove each drum-stick, or lower leg, by a single stroke of the knife, which must exactly hit the joint. To remove the thigh, or upper leg joint, make a V-shaped cut, wide enough at the point whence the drum-stick has been cut to include all the meat, but converging at the joint, which can always be distinctly seen near the back. Two strokes of the knife do this work, each of them cutting down to the carcase. A slight outward pressure of the knife-blade, applied between the carcase and the upper point of the thigh joint, will cause it to drop off neatly on the plate. Outside the lines of these cuts, flakes of dark meat will remain adhering to the carcase, which should now be cut off. They help to meet demands for dark meat.

MEMORANDUM ON FRIENDS' RECIPES

MEMORANDUM
ON
FRIENDS' RECIPES

318   *HOUSEHOLD MANAGEMENT.*

In carving the wings, the neat stroke removes the lower part, which contains the two bones, by cutting at the inner part of the joint, and so turning the blade of the knife as to throw that part off in the direction opposite to its natural movement. The first joint of each wing then follows, the cut being deep enough to fully reach the ball and socket joint. A slight motion of the pinion toward the head of the bird will suffice usually to detach this part. If it does not, the point of the knife may be thrust into the socket of the joint to sever the cartilage. This will free it.

When this dismembering is accomplished, proceed to slice the breast meat in thin, broad slices. Clean off all the white meat, unless part only is needed. Placing your knife close to the front of the breast-bone, and cutting toward the neck, you will dislodge the V-shaped bone, corresponding to the "merrythought" or "pull-bone" of chickens. To dislodge the collar-bones is to many a hard task. But cut the cartilages which bind them to the frame of the bird. These cartilages are in the cavity between the neck and the breast-bone. Through this cavity, thrust your knife outwardly under one of these bones; make a fulcrum of the front part of breast-bone, and a lever of the knife, its edge resting on the fulcrum. You can then easily pry up the troublesome bone and turn it off to the side. This movement takes the bone at the best mechanical advantage. It must come, and come at once, if this movement be made.

Now attend to the other end of the bird. Shave off all superfluous meat from the carcase. Turn the carcase on its side, the back toward you. Insert your knife beside the oil-bag and thrust it forward parallel to the spine. It will cut its way very easily. A slight outward movement of the knife will then throw off these side bones, which are choice pieces, yielding the juiciest of the dark meat. The ribs may now be cut through with ease from front to rear, about midway from breast to back. The breast-bone is incapable of further division, but the back easily divides into six parts. Turn it back up and hold with the fork; separate the oil-bag, about an inch of the spine with it; lift the projecting spine with the knife back and it will break readily, carrying one rib with it. Cut off from each side of the remaining spine the rib parts adherent to it; then divide the remaining spine just back of the neck.

An entire drum-stick, or second joint, need not be served to any one person, but had better be divided among several. A fair-sized turkey divided on the above method will furnish a good supply for twenty people.

BACK OF A FOWL.

It will be asked, however, how can one become so expert in hitting these joints? Frequently the carver tries, and tries again, but tries in vain, to strike the right place for his knife. There is one way only to succeed in this art. The anatomy of the turkey or chicken, or any other animal, must be carefully studied. Do it in this way. Whenever a turkey is brought into your house and is made ready for the roasting, place it on its back, as it will lie on the plate when it comes to the table. Carefully manipulate it, and note exactly where every joint lies. Imagine yourself about to carve it. Where would you put the knife to throw off that drum-stick? How would you cut to throw off the thigh bone. Read the preceding directions; apply them in fancy to the bird as you see and handle it; then carry it all out at the table when the bird is cooked.

[*a, b,* line of easy breakage. *a, c, e,* and *b, d, f,* lines of separation of side-bones. *a, g, h, h,* rib portion.

No surgeon could do his work except he had thus practiced on actual subjects in dissection. He must know by actual trial just what to do and how to do it. So must the carver know. Chickens, ducks, geese, small birds, meat, roasting pigs, every article, in short, which he expects to carve must be understood beforehand; then success will be his.

MEMORANDUM
ON
FRIENDS' RECIPES

MEMORANDUM
ON
FRIENDS' RECIPES

Carving Roast Chicken.—The same course precisely as has been prescribed for carving turkey must be followed with chickens. The only difference is in the formation of the "pull-bone" or "merrythought," but this makes no difference whatever in the cutting of the bird.

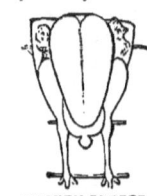

CHICKEN PROPERLY TRUSSED FOR ROASTING.
[Feet may be removed at option.]

Carving Roast Ducks and Geese.—These are more difficult than turkey or chickens, for the reason that they are constitutionally more sinewy in the joints and they have far less flesh proportionately.

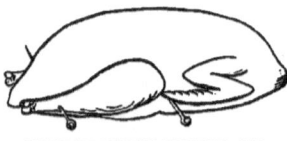

GOOSE PROPERLY TRUSSED FOR ROASTING.

They are barrel-shaped, with thin layers of meat instead of the fine masses of flesh found on the turkey or on fine chickens. The leg joints lie farther to the rear, and higher on the side than in land fowls. They are not so easily reached, therefore.

Their anatomy must be studied, however. It is the only way to obtain command of the carcase. In carving, dismember the bird as in other cases. Then cut the meat in long, narrow strips, along the sides and breast of the bird, and use these as the choice cuts. The legs and wings

BREAST OF DUCK PROPERLY TRUSSED.
[The lines show the direction of cutting the breast meat.]

BACK OF DUCK PROPERLY TRUSSED.
[Feet twisted to lie on the back.]

may be given out if desired or if the supply be short. Duck is but a side dish, however; it is supposed to be served with

Carving Broiled Chickens.—Chickens for broiling are presumably young and tender. If not, thorough steaming before they are broiled will do something for them. They are trussed in such shape usually that joints are not easily struck. But study the bird when trussed. See where joints do lie and cut them. If the birds are really young and tender, however, they may be halved or quartered, cutting through the bones directly and so serving them.

Carving Smaller Birds.—Smaller birds which need carving, may simply be split longitudinally, just beside the breast-bone and the spine. Their bones can be cut easily. This will apply to pigeon, partridge, prairie hen, pheasant, etc.

SMALLER BIRD PROPERLY TRUSSED FOR ROASTING.

Carving Roast Beef.—Pieces of roast beef vary so that no one rule covers all. A safe general direction, however, is to study carefully just what is in the piece before it is cooked. Know your meat before you attempt to carve it. Another general rule, applicable to all meats indeed, is to cut across the grain in all cases. Meat cut with the grain is stringy and fibrous. If cut across the grain, all the longitudinal flakes of flesh and the minute sinews are cut so short that any toughness existing in them is wholly concealed. The first slice, by this process, will always be a brown, outside cut. Slices should always be thin, but not so as to seem ragged. In carving ribs of beef the knife may be thrust along close to the ribs, so as to separate the meat from them. The cuts then made across the grain will separate the slices with ease and neatness. Never cut beef across the bone. It is the easiest way, but also the poorest.

MEMORANDUM
ON
FRIENDS' RECIPES

322   *HOUSEHOLD MANAGEMENT.*

Carving Roasts of Mutton.—A leg of mutton is carved as a ham, by cutting down to the bone, from the outer edge, making the cuts converge on the bone, so freeing each slice as it is cut.

A shoulder of mutton should be carved as the leg. In each case, when the choice cuts are exhausted, clip off the remaining meat as best you can, always across the grain.

Saddle of mutton is carved in several ways: 1st, in longitudinal slices along the backbone; 2d, by transverse slices, each taking in a rib, which makes thick and clumsy portions; 3d, by oblique slices, not taking in the bones, but forming a slight angle with them. The latter method is deemed preferable by most carvers.

In all roasts which include the ribs the backbone should be well and cleanly cut through by the butcher, between every pair of ribs. Otherwise no satisfactory carving can be done.

Carving Roasts of Lamb.—The cut shows a fore-quarter of lamb with its outer side uppermost. This joint is first to

FORE-QUARTER OF LAMB.

be cut so as to divide the shoulder from the rest of the quarter, which is called the target. For this purpose, put the fork firmly into the shoulder joint, and then cut underneath the blade-bone, beginning at *a*, and continue cutting all around in the direction of the circular line, and pretty close to the under part of the blade-bone. Some cut the shoulder large, while others take off no more meat with it than is barely necessary to remove the blade-bone. It is most convenient to place the shoulder on a separate dish. This is carved in the same way as the shoulder of mutton. When the shoulder is removed, a lemon may be squeezed over that part of the remainder of the joint where the knife has passed; this gives a flavor to the meat which is generally approved. Then proceed to cut completely through from *b* to *c*, following the line across the bones as cracked by the butcher, and this will divide the ribs (*d*) from the brisket (*e*). Tastes vary in giving preference to the ribs or the brisket.

Other parts of lamb are carved as mutton. The fat is very delicate and should be served to all the guests.

Carving Roasts of Venison.—These resemble roasts of mutton so closely that no different directions for their carving need be given.

Carving Ham.—Boiled or baked ham may be served either side up. The inner edge of the ham, which lay adjacent to the body, is rather more tender than the edge, which lay toward the tail. Slices should be cut directly from the edge to the bone, cutting out the middle portions first. Let the cuts converge upon the bone every time, so that each slice is set free at once. When the choice cuts are gone, trim up the remaining parts neatly as possible, and always across the grain. The knuckle end of a ham furnishes the leaner and drier cuts. Some prefer carving hams with a more slanting cut, rather than a direct, right-angled cut upon the bone, beginning at the thick end, and so continuing throughout. This mode is, however, apt to be very wasteful, unless the carver be careful to take away both fat and lean in due proportion.

Carving Roast Pig.—The cut below represents a pig roasted whole and served in the most approved style. Many, however, separate the head before serving, and garnish the body with the ears, jaw, etc. The head may be severed by a neat cut around the neck, and a little sideward motion, but this is not necessary, as the cheek or jaw can be removed

WHOLE ROAST PIG.

MEMORANDUM
ON
FRIENDS' RECIPES

without removing the head. The shoulder should then be taken off from the body, by passing the knife under it in a circular direction, and the leg separated as shown in the line *d, e, f*. The ribs may then be divided into two or more parts, helping at the same time an ear or jaw with it, with some of the sauce also. Pieces may be cut from the legs and shoulders. Some consider the neck end the finest part, while others give the ribs the preference.

Carving Roast Rabbit.—Begin by cutting longitudinally from head to tail near to the backbone, then make a corresponding cut on the other side of the backbone, leaving the back and the head in one distinct piece. Cut off the legs at the hip-joint, and take off the wing, or fore leg, nearly as you would the wing of a bird, carrying the knife round in a circular line. The ribs are of little importance, as they are bare of meat. Divide the back into three or four equal portions. The head is then to be cut off, and the lower jaw divided from the upper. By splitting the upper part of the head in the middle, you have the brains, which are prized by epicures. The comparative goodness of different parts of a rabbit will depend much on the age, and also upon the cooking. The back and the legs are always the best parts.

RABBIT, OR HARE, PROPERLY TRUSSED FOR ROASTING.

Carving Steaks, etc.—Where there is a tenderloin in a beefsteak, it should be divided among the party with the other portion. If there are too many persons to allow each a share, give ladies and guests the preference. Epicures eat the tenderloin at the last. As a bright boy said, "You ought always to eat the best last; then you feel as if you have had all best."

Carving Fish.—This is more a serving than a carving. The meat of fish is usually so tender that cutting is unnecessary. Skillful separation of the flakes is what is needed.

A silver knife, or fish slice, and a silver fish fork, broad at the tines, are desirable. Steel tools impart a disagreeable odor to fish. Fish should be served in neat, unbroken portions, never in scraps and bits.

In many kinds of fish the backbone may be taken out entire, as in all the mackerel family as served for the table. This is a neat proceeding for company; but for home uses the backbone is preferred with the fish, because of the very savory morsels which adhere to it.

The skin and fins of the turbot are regarded as very delicate. It, therefore, should be split along the backbone, at its side, and then cut into cross sections so that part of a fin shall go with each portion. This is the neatest method of serving.

Carving Tongue.—The juicy and fatter part of the tongue is at its thick end or root. Some prefer the smaller and drier end, however. If the whole tongue is not likely to be needed, cut off its tip in one piece, and on the main portion work backward toward the butt end. Do not cut squarely across, as it leaves the slices unduly small; but cut on an angle, so doubling the area of the slices.

Carving a Calf's Head.—Cut the external meat in strips from the nose to the back of the head. Some deem the eye a delicacy. It may be removed with the point of the knife, if requested, but do not puncture it with the fork or the knife. The palate is a choice part. It may be cut from under the head, with its surrounding parts, all of which are delicate morsels. The jawbone may be removed also, and will disclose fine meat.

MEMORANDUM
ON
FRIENDS' RECIPES

MEMORANDUM
ON
FRIENDS' RECIPES

III.—SERVING MEALS.

METHODS OF SERVING MEALS; RUSSIAN, ENGLISH, FRENCH, AND AMERICAN STYLES; TABLES, TABLE-CLOTHS, NAPKINS, AND DECORATIONS; FINGER-BOWLS; DUE CEREMONY; WHAT TO AVOID; GARNISHES; ROYAL DISPLAYS.

METHODS of serving meals differ widely. The items of conveniences and pecuniary ability always become important elements in the case. Taste, too, enters largely into it. Some people need the formal and the ceremonious. Others despise these and prefer the free-and-easy plan. There are national methods also, which largely rule among the refined and elegant.

One of these methods, the Russian, decorates the centre of the table elaborately with flowers, and surrounds it at the outset with the dessert tastefully displayed. This secures a delightsome central object. The several dishes are then brought to the table carved and ready for use, each dish being served as a separate course, one vegetable only being allowed to appear with it.

The English method sets the whole of each course at once, no matter how many dishes it may contain. This, it is objected, allows the dishes to cool, and one often vitiates another. The dishes which require carving are by this method first placed on the table, and then removed to a side table for cutting and serving.

The French method serves everything as a separate course, even each vegetable, unless it be simply a garnish for another dish. The American plan, however, serves at least one vegetable with each substantial dish. At the more formal meals among us, carving is done at the side tables, but in the genuine home dinners the work is done at the table by the host himself. If, however, he cannot do the honors of the serving with ease, let the work be done by another, at the side table.

When the general plan of the dinner management is settled, those who are to do the various parts of the work must be thoroughly instructed. A servant not sufficiently intelligent to learn the required part well, and to do it properly, is too stupid for satisfactory service with company or at a purely family gathering.

Square end tables are now the proper style. They should be sufficiently roomy to wholly avoid crowding. A spotlessly white table-cloth should be spread, with another under it to deaden sound and make a softer appearance. The cloth should not be very stiffly starched, but it should be nicely polished and beautifully glossy. It should hang two feet from the top edge, the corners gathered up, if needs be, to prevent their drooping on the floor. Napkins should be large and heavy. Such texture does not need much starch. The glass and silverware should be perfect in brightness. It may be of inexpensive kind, but it must be scrupulously clean.

Colored table-cloths of ornamental patterns are allowable for luncheon or tea. They are not in place where hot meats are served. Nor are colored napkins. Too often these deep tinted articles are used "to save washing," which means " to conceal dirt." Not unfrequently covers and napkins of this kind are kept in use when their rank odor cries out for the wash-tub, even though their soiled appearance does not. The doily, or *D'Oiley*, as some will have it from the proper name of its first reputed maker, is a small, colored napkin used with fruits and wines. Stains will not show so readily upon these, but they must always be scrupulously fresh and clean. To conceal filth under rich coloring is sacrilege of the worst sort, but to bring it to the table, and ask guests to wipe their lips with it, is a crime.

MEMORANDUM
ON
FRIENDS' RECIPES

HOUSEHOLD MANAGEMENT.

A great variety of ornaments and adornments are admissible on a table, but nothing is so pure and so appropriate as a handsome display of ferns or flowers. The flowers should not be just such as ladies wear so profusely and so beautifully in their belts and on their dresses. Larger blooms are preferable for the table, especially those of the pure white and fine texture belonging to the lily family.

It is quite the proper and beautiful thing to place a neat bouquet beside each plate, in tasteful bouquet-holders. For gentlemen the little bunching suitable for the button-hole is desirable. For ladies the belt bouquet will meet the case. The floral centre-piece may be composed of small bouquets, which at the end of the meal may be distributed.

Fruit pieces and handsome confectionery pieces may be disposed to advantage in ornamenting the table. Tasty folding of spotless napkins is so important a decoration that the subject will be treated fully farther on. These may be perched in polished goblets, while bouquets, or small rolls of bread nestle amid their snowy folds. Little arts like these embellish a table, and delight the guests.

But these embellishments must not be overdone. What will be correct for a large table will be too much for a small one, and what will be just right for a small table will look thin and meagre on a large one. Study the proprieties of every occasion. What suits once does not suit forever.

Embellishments may be liberally bestowed upon the dining-room itself. In addition to its permanent decorations, flowers are always admissible. At the great ball on March 20th, 1883, at the Vanderbilt Mansion in New York, the decorations of the supper-room were absolutely regal. The walls were completely hidden with palms and ferns, from which a countless number of orchids were suspended. Two large fountains were introduced into the far corners of the room. The doors of the main entrance to the supper-room were in an open position and were completely covered with roses and lilies of the valley. In the centre of the room a large palm towered almost to the ceiling, and about it from the dome was suspended an immense Bougen Villa vine, the tendrils of which drooped in bunches from the branches of the palm. Throughout the room there were many stands and vases filled with flowers, the entire effect more resembling fairyland than an earthly home. Few can rival such a display, of course, but all enjoy at least a pen-peep upon such princely splendor.

No ornament should be so large as to obscure to any great extent a view of the entire table, or to conceal any of its guests. As many knives, forks, and spoons as will be needed for the various courses may be placed at each plate, though, to avoid the display of so much cutlery, a better style is to supply these accessories as needed. Goblets and wine-glasses, if the latter be used, should be on the table at the start. Large spoons, with salt and pepper casters, should be on the table also. The dessert-plates, finger-bowls, etc., should stand ready on the sideboard, awaiting the time when they shall be needed. The hot closet should be well stocked with dishes needing to be used warm.

Finger-bowls should be half filled with water. In Paris they are served with warm water scented with peppermint. A slice of lemon in cold water answers the purpose entirely, as it removes any grease from fingers or lips. A geranium leaf may float in the water. Its fragrance on the fingers, if it be pressed, will be agreeable. It is customary to place a fruit napkin, or doily, on the dish on which the finger-bowl rests, to avoid the rattle of the bowl, and to protect the dish from injury if it be highly ornamented. Little openworked mats will, however, answer better. Do not summon your company to dinner by a bell. Country hotels and cheap boarding-houses may do that, but not a refined home, especially when guests are present.

Soup is dished by the lady of the house at a home dinner

MEMORANDUM
ON
FRIENDS' RECIPES

330   HOUSEHOLD MANAGEMENT.

Meat is cut and dished by the gentleman of the house. Vegetables, bread, butter, water, etc., are served by the waiter, dessert by the hostess, except in the case of melons, requiring to be cut at the table, which is the work of the host.

Home meals should all be sufficiently ceremonious to dispense with haste and confusion. On the other hand, they should not run into stiffness and frigidity. Bright, cheery, pleasant chat should enliven every meal. If the leading dish be nothing but hash, let it be served in good style and amid a profusion of genial, social sunshine.

WHAT TO AVOID.

1st.—Never use table-linen which is open to the suspicion of being soiled. The napkin-ring business is of questionable propriety. Why not, as at hotels, furnish a clean napkin to each person at every meal?

2d.—Crockery with an abundance of nicks and splints and cracks is not unsightly merely, but, where the glazing is broken, the porous material absorbs grease and dish water, making these spots dense with unsavory and unwholesome matter.

3d.—Partly emptied dishes become unsightly, and sometimes positively repulsive. They look like refuse and scraps. At the great State dinners at the Tuileries, no guest saw a partly emptied dish. A full, beautifully garnished dish was presented for his approval, upon expressing which, his personal plate was taken to a side table and supplied from another serving dish.

4th.—An overloaded table or plate satiates appetite rather than stimulates it. A gracious expectancy of what is to come is a great help at the table.

5th.—A stinted supply is very discouraging. To the apprehension of a lack of food, the moral sense of mortification is added in this case.

SERVING MEALS.

6th.—Beware of ill-assorted dinners or tea-parties. An occasion intended to be a pleasure is often a pest for lack of care in this regard. This caution applies to the selection of guests, and more strongly to the disposition of guests at the table. Secure fitness both in the viands presented and in the parties present.

7th.—Do not inaugurate new features at a dinner party, unless you are sure you have the mastery of them, and that when done in a masterly way they will certainly prove agreeable.

8th.—Beware of the delusion that hospitality is expressed by the weight of its beef and mutton, and the multitude and rarity of its viands.

9th.—Have no meddlesome, noisy, or slovenly service. Waiters should be attired neatly, and should wear light shoes or slippers. They should take no part in the social proceedings, not so much, indeed, as to smile at the best things. On formal occasions the man-servant should wear a dress-coat, white vest, and white necktie. The maid-servant should be attired in a neat, inconspicuous dress, with spotless white apron.

10th.—Both haste and slowness should be shunned. At the finished French dinners, the courses will not average more than five minutes each. French waiters are marvelously expert, however, in removing and replacing dishes.

GARNISHES.

Much of the attractiveness of a table depends on the *garnishes*, which are added to certain dishes to embellish or beautify them. A few hints on this subject will be of value.

Parsley is the almost universal garnish to all kinds of cold meat, poultry, fish, butter, cheese, etc.

Horse-radish is the garnish for roast beef, and for fish in general; for the latter, slices of lemon are sometimes laid alternately with heaps of horse-radish.

MEMORANDUM
ON
FRIENDS' RECIPES

MEMORANDUM
ON
FRIENDS' RECIPES

332 HOUSEHOLD MANAGEMENT.

Slices of lemon for boiled fowl, turkey, and fish, and for roast veal and calf's head.

Carrot in slices for boiled beef, hot or cold. They may be cut into ornamental forms if desired.

Barberries, fresh or preserved, for game.

Fried smelts for turbot.

Red beet-root sliced for cold meat, boiled beef, and salt fish.

Fried sausages or force-meat balls for roast turkey, capon, or fowl.

Fennel for mackerel and salmon, whether fresh or pickled.

Lobster coral and parsley for boiled fish.

Currant jelly for game, also for custard or bread-pudding.

Seville oranges in slices for wild ducks, widgeons, teal, and such game.

Mint, either with or without parsley, for roast lamb, whether hot or cold.

Pickled gerkins, capers, or onions, for some boiled meats, stews, etc.

A red pepper, or small red apple, for the mouth of a roast pig.

Spots of red and black pepper alternated on the fat side of a boiled ham, which side should lie uppermost on the serving dish.

Sliced eggs, showing the white and yellow parts, for chicken salad.

Sprays of celery top for salads, cold meats, etc.

ROYAL DISPLAYS.

A peep at some royal table displays is valuable as suggesting what may be done. Perhaps the grandest display ever made was by Baron Rothschild in honor of the last Napoleon when at the height of his power, some five years before his fall. The entertainment was given at Rothschild's regal pleasure-house of Ferrières, thirty miles out of Paris. The cost of the out-door decorations alone exceeded $100,000. Workmen were put on the road in vast gangs, and had it prepared with asphaltum every inch of the way. Chinese lanterns and Bengal lights rendered it brilliant as day. Forests of new trees in full growth were set out wherever the roadside happened to be bare. The imperial carriage, which left the Tuileries at five o'clock P. M., passed through continuous masses of jubilant spectators. Wine and edibles were given by the Rothschilds' orders to all along the route who bore decorations of any sort.

The chateau itself, which is as roomy as the Capitol at Washington, was a blaze of light and rich drapery. The dining-room and the feast were thus described in a leading journal:

"It was such a scene as the mind conjures in Aladdin's palace, built by the slaves of the gold and jewel caves. At a vast height from the floor a narrow gallery runs around the chamber. From this were suspended folds of golden drapery, in which some legend of Bonapartist glory flashed out in jeweled letters. The walls were encrusted with treasures that the house of Rothschild had been centuries collecting. The tables were a mass of glittering gold, even to the candelabra The dinner began at nine o'clock and was served by waiters in livery rivaling the imperial in sumptuousness. The knives and forks were of solid gold, and when the dinner was ended the head of the house solemnly directed them gathered together and in presence of the Emperor ordered them melted and the mass sent to the mint, declaring that, having been sanctified by imperial use, they should never be degraded to baser hands."

MEMORANDUM
ON
FRIENDS' RECIPES

MEMORANDUM
ON
FRIENDS' RECIPES

IV.—THE BILL OF FARE.

BILLS OF FARE NEEDED; EDIBLES IN SEASON; WHAT TO HAVE FOR BREAKFAST, DINNER, LUNCHEON, TEA, AND SUPPER; PLAIN LUNCHEONS; PLAIN DINNERS; QUANTITIES NEEDED; ODD BILLS OF FARE.

WHAT shall be served for a meal is in most homes a haphazard affair. Somebody wants a certain dish, or something happens to be in the house, or a huckster comes along offering a certain article at a low price, and so the diet for the day is determined. The religious customs of some persons decide the bill of fare for certain days, and so far their domestic management is controlled. Others, especially in cheap boarding-houses, have a bill of fare inflexible as the ancient laws of the Medes and Persians. You know when to look for that greasy vegetable soup, made out of—fortunately for the eater, he knows not what. Then comes cabbage day—regular as the week revolves it comes; and that beefsteak and onions—the house is odorous with it, and you are greeted with its fragrance as you clamber up the front steps. The desserts, too, are fearfully regular. Boiled rice, corn-starch pudding, huckleberry pie in its season, canned peaches both in season and out of season, apple pie or custard pie—these, with a few more of the same family, march on in their ceaseless round with the same old sequence as the figures follow each other in a cheap puppet show. These are travesties on a bill of fare. They burlesque the *menu*.

A housekeeper should plan out her table offerings with great care. Her dishes should suit the seasons. On a frosty day in midwinter substantial, well-seasoned food is needed. It renews a hungry man. It stays by him. It does him good. But the same dinner in midsummer will disgust rather than delight. On a hot, exhausting day, heavy soups, substantial meats, and rich desserts are out of harmony. Light meats, delicate vegetables, and cooling desserts are then in demand.

Dishes should suit the days of the week also. What can be furnished by one fire or wash-day or ironing-day is not the same as can be furnished conveniently on other days. The man who proposed dumplings for wash-day dessert because they could be boiled in the same kettle with the clothes was on the true line of progress, though his application was not a happy one. The idea is that harmony shall exist. The washing must not suffer for the dinner, nor the dinner for the washing. Plan the bill of fare to fit the movements of the domestic establishment.

A third point to be gained by planning is unity in each meal. Some articles of food, delicious in themselves, are unpalatable, and even unwholesome, in combination. Cucumbers or beets and milk, fish and milk, lobster and ice-cream, are combinations of this class; while peaches and cream, lamb and green peas, stewed chicken and waffles, catfish and coffee, are fitly wedded, and no man can put them asunder. To secure all the above-named happy coincidences and combinations is the mission of the well-digested bill of fare.

Of course, the pocket controls many of these things. He who cannot have his turkey and venison and plum-pudding on Christmas day, may, nevertheless, find satisfactory chewing on his boiled goose, and savory garnishing in his sour-krout or cabbage. But the poorest meals will be the better, like the artist's colors, when "mixed with brains." Think and plan. How can these things be best done? Settle that question and carry out your conclusion with a queenly grace. But be open for the teachings of experience. What does not work well be ready to change. Those who never change their plans are poor learners.

MEMORANDUM
ON
FRIENDS' RECIPES

MEMORANDUM ON FRIENDS' RECIPES

HOUSEHOLD MANAGEMENT.

When planning home meals, and especially company meals, it is of prime importance to know just what is in season. Particulars on this point vary with different localities, but New York is the metropolis, and its markets are on the grandest scale; its market is made the standard, therefore, in the following table of edible merchandise in its various seasons.

SPRING:—MARCH, APRIL, AND MAY.

Shell Fish.—Clams, hard crabs, lobster, mussels, oysters, prawns, scallops, shrimps, terrapins, turtle.

Fish.—Bass (black, striped, and sea), bluefish, cod, eels, haddock, halibut, herrings, mackerel, muscalonge, pickerel, pompan, prawns, salmon, shad (North River), sheepshead, shrimps, skate, smelts, soles, turbot, trout (brook, lake, and salmon, May to July).

Meat.—Beef, lamb, mutton, sweet-breads, veal.

Poultry.—Capons, chickens, ducks, geese, and turkeys.

Game.—Ducks and geese until May 1st, pigeons, plover, snipe, squabs, after April.

Vegetables.—Asparagus, Jerusalem artichokes, lettuce, potatoes (sweet and white), radishes, spinach, sprouts, watercresses, and all the vegetables of the winter list.

Fruit.—The winter list, with the addition of pie-plant, pineapple, strawberries.

Nuts.—The winter list, with the addition of Brazil nuts.

SUMMER:—JUNE, JULY, AND AUGUST.

Shell Fish.—Clams, soft crabs, lobster, turtle in August.

Fish.—Bass (black and sea), bluefish, eels, flounders,

MEMORANDUM ON FRIENDS' RECIPES

THE BILL OF FARE.

haddock, herring, mackerel, muscalonge, salmon, sheepshead, turbot, trout (brook, lake, and salmon).

Meat.—Beef, lamb, mutton, and veal.

Poultry.—Chickens, ducks.

Game.—Snipe, woodcock (after July).

Vegetables.—String beans, beets, cabbage, cauliflower, carrots, corn, cucumbers, eggplant, lettuce, macaroni, okra, onions, green peas, potatoes, rice, radishes, summer squash, tomatoes, turnips.

Fruits.—Apples, apricots, cherries, currants, gooseberries, grapes, lemons, oranges, peaches, pears, pineapples, raspberries, strawberries, imported dried fruits.

AUTUMN:—SEPTEMBER, OCTOBER, AND NOVEMBER.

Shell Fish.—Clams, soft crabs, lobster, mussels, oysters, scallops, turtle, terrapin.

Fish.—Black bass, bluefish, flounders, mackerel, muscalonge, perch, pickerel, pike, salmon, sheepshead, skates, smelts, soles, sturgeon, trout (brook, lake, and salmon), white fish.

Meat.—Beef, lamb, mutton.

Poultry.—Capons, chickens, ducks, geese, turkeys.

Game.—Brant, duck, goose (September to May), prairie-chicken, ruff-grouse (September to January), venison until February, quail and rabbits (October 1st to January 1st), snipe, woodcock (July 3d to February 1st).

Vegetables.—Artichokes, beans (lima and other shell beans), beets, broccoli, cabbage, cauliflower, carrots, celery, corn, cucumbers, eggplant, lettuce, macaroni, okra, onions, potatoes (white and sweet), rice, squash, tomatoes, turnips

MEMORANDUM ON FRIENDS' RECIPES

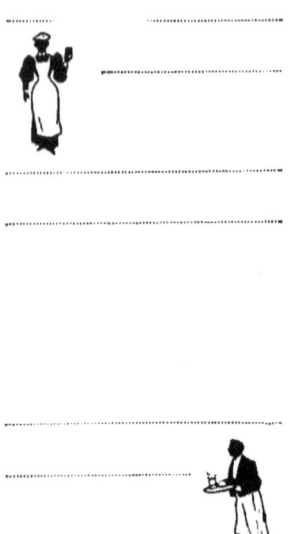

HOUSEHOLD MANAGEMENT.

Fruits.—Apples, bananas, blackberries, dates, figs, grapes, lemons, oranges, peaches, and pears.

Nuts.—Black walnuts, chestnuts, hazelnuts, shellbarks.

WINTER:—DECEMBER, JANUARY, AND FEBRUARY

Shell Fish.—Clams, mussels, oysters, scallops, terrapin, turtle.

Fish.—Bass (black and striped), bluefish, cod, eels, flounders, haddock, muscalonge, perch, pickerel, pike, salmon, skate, smelts, sturgeon, white fish.

Meat.—Beef, mutton, pork.

Poultry.—Capons, chickens, ducks, geese, turkeys.

Game.—Brant (until May), duck (wild, until May), wood-duck (until January), geese (until May), prairie-chickens, ruff-grouse, snipe, venison (until February), quail, rabbits (until December), woodcock (until February).

Vegetables.—Artichokes, beets, dried beans, broccoli, cabbage, carrots, celery, macaroni, onions, parsnips, potatoes (sweet and white), rice, salsify, turnips, winter squash, all canned vegetables.

Fruit.—Apples, bananas, cranberries, dates, figs, ginger, lemons, oranges, pears, prunes, raisins, all kinds of canned fruits, and compotes of dried fruits.

Nuts.—Almonds, black walnuts, butternuts, cocoanuts, English walnuts, filberts, pecan nuts, shellbarks.

With such a range accessible, surely, good meals can be selected in abundant variety. But what shall be selected for ordinary use in the family? To suggest answers to this question, standard bills of fare for each season are appended. Remember, however, these are only to *suggest* happy combinations. Try one or more of them entire, or in part, and see whether they suit you or not. At least they will lead toward good results.

FAMILY BREAKFASTS FOR SPRING.

No. 1.—Oatmeal and milk; stewed apples; rolls, butter, coffee, chocolate, broma, or tea; beefsteak, broiled oysters; Lyonnaise potatoes, poached eggs on toast; rice cakes, sirup.

No. 2.—Cracked wheat and milk; stewed prunes; bread or rolls, butter, coffee, etc.; broiled ham with fried eggs; mutton and potato hash, browned; baked potatoes; flannel cakes, powdered sugar.

No. 3.—Fried hominy; stewed dried peaches; rolls or bread, butter, coffee, etc.; mutton-chops, fried bacon; broiled eggs, potatoes, Saratoga style; waffles, cinnamon, and sugar.

FAMILY BREAKFASTS FOR SUMMER.

No 1.—Coarse hominy boiled; strawberries and cream; bread, butter, coffee, etc.; broiled chicken, stewed potatoes; dried beef dressed with cream; radishes, muffins.

No. 2.—Oatmeal and milk; fresh currants and sugar; buttered toast, bread, coffee, etc.; broiled blue or white fish; stewed potatoes; minced mutton served on toast; shirred eggs.

No. 3.—Cracked wheat and milk; fresh raspberries; rolls, butter, coffee, etc.; cold roast beef, sliced thin; frizzled ham with eggs; fried potatoes, sliced cucumbers; Graham gems, or pop-overs.

FAMILY BREAKFASTS FOR AUTUMN.

No. 1.—Oatmeal mush fried in slices; peaches and cream, or blackberries; brown bread, rolls, butter, coffee, etc.;

MEMORANDUM
ON
FRIENDS' RECIPES

MEMORANDUM ON FRIENDS' RECIPES

lamb chops, fried potatoes; mushrooms baked and served on toast; sliced tomatoes, dressed as a salad.

No. 2.—Hulled corn with cream; baked pears, grapes; bread, butter, coffee, etc.; veal cutlets, potato balls; omelette with grated ham; cornmeal pancakes.

No. 3.—Coarse hominy boiled and browned; peaches and cream; bread, butter, coffee, etc.; beefsteak, oysters on toast; stewed potatoes; muffins.

FAMILY BREAKFASTS FOR WINTER.

No. 1.—Fried mush; baked sweet apples; rolls, bread, butter, coffee, etc.; turkey hash, stewed potatoes; salt mackerel; buckwheat cakes, sirup.

No. 2.—Cracked wheat; baked pears; rolls, Graham bread, butter, coffee, etc.; sausages garnished with fried sour apples; quail on toast, baked potatoes; buckwheat cakes, sirup.

No. 3.—Fried hominy; stewed apples; bread, butter, coffee, etc.; venison steak, cold sparerib, sliced; potatoes, Saratoga style; buckwheat cakes, sirup.

FAMILY DINNERS.

In January.—Beef-soup with vegetables; bream with oyster sauce; boiled potatoes; corned beef with carrots, stewed kidneys; Spanish puffs.

In February.—Ox-tail soup; boiled chicken; fried parsnips, caper sauce; fillets of bass with pickles; mince patties.

In March.—Oysters with lettuce; roast sirloin of beef; potato croquettes; cabbage boiled with cream; baked lemon pudding.

THE BILL OF FARE.

In April.—Fried oysters, sliced cucumbers; smelts fried with fat salt pork; baked potatoes; lamb chops with baked macaroni; pumpkin pie and coffee.

In May.—Clam soup; boiled leg of mutton, tomato sauce; mashed potatoes; oyster-plant in batter; lettuce and green onions; raisin-pudding, sherry sauce.

In June.—Salmon; chicken-soup with barley; cold roast mutton with boiled cauliflower; lettuce with cives and olives mixed; Charlotte russe.

In July.—Beef soup with noodles; rock bass with fried potatoes; tomatoes with slices of chicken, dressed in mayonnaise sauce; peaches and cream.

In August.—Clams on the halfshell, pickles; broiled tenderloin steak; green peas and asparagus; strawberry-short-cake and coffee.

In September.—Oyster soup; broiled eels with cucumbers; braised fowl; string-beans; celery with capers; currant tart with whipped cream.

In October.—Beef soup; halibut with parsley sauce; the beef with the vegetables; potato salad; tapioca-pudding, sauce of sliced fruits; cream cakes.

In November.—Mock turtle; turkey, cranberry sauce; rice croquettes; egg-plant stuffed; snipe, fried oysters; water cresses with hard-boiled eggs; German puffs.

In December.—Puree of beans; broiled herring, Dutch sauce; ribs of beef; boiled potatoes; stewed tomatoes; pumpkin pie.

In many of the cities Tea has passed away. Late dinners are in order. Luncheon is served to those at home at midday, which includes a cold cut, bread and butter, cheese, a glass of milk or cup of tea, and possibly a light dessert.

MEMORANDUM ON FRIENDS' RECIPES

MEMORANDUM ON
FRIENDS' RECIPES

342   *HOUSEHOLD MANAGEMENT.*

A bowl of hot, light soup is very acceptable at luncheon also. Luncheons are sometimes made quite elaborate, and become very pleasant company occasions.

Late suppers are served by some who have the late dinners, but unless they sit up very much later, the practice must soon affect them very injuriously. For supper, or tea, given at the usual hours, say from six to eight o'clock, the bill of fare suggested for breakfast may serve in substance. The later the supper the lighter it should be. Strong tea or coffee should not be used near bed-time if sound sleep is desired.

Specimen bills of fare are given below. They are in suitable form for the hostess to follow, and also for the printer to follow if it be desired to produce either of them in type.

MENU.
BREAKFAST.

Fine Hominy		Buttered Toast
	Beefsteak	
French Rolls		Potatoes a la Creme
	Buckwheat Cakes	
Tea	Coffee	Chocolate

Or, in this form:

BREAKFAST.
Broiled Spring Chickens

Parker House Rolls		Saratoga Potatoes
Scrambled Eggs		Fried Oysters
	Rye and Indian Loaf	
Coffee	Tea	Chocolate

Or, in this form:

BREAKFAST

White Fish		Potatoes
	Muffins	
Fried Ham		Egg Omelette
Coffee	Tea	Chocolate

THE BILL OF FARE.

MEMORANDUM
ON
FRIENDS' RECIPES

For lunches, the menu may take either of the forms which now follow.

LUNCH PARTY

Beef-tea served in small porcelain cups
Cold Chicken, Oyster, and other Croquettes
Chicken Salad   Minced Ham Sandwiches
Scalloped Oysters
Tutti Frutti   Chocolate Cream
Cake-basket of Mixed Cake
Mulled Chocolate
Mixed Pickles   Biscuits, etc.
Ice-cream and Charlottes

Or, in this form:

LUNCH PARTY

Oyster-pie   Boiled Partridge   Cold Ham
Sweet Pickles   Sandwiches
Pound and Fruit-cake   Pyramids of Wine Jelly
Blanc Mange   Snow Jelly
Pineapple Flummery
Kisses   Macaroons   Ice-cream

For dinners either of the following forms will answer.

DINNER

FIRST COURSE

Oyster Soup with Celery

SECOND COURSE

Roast Turkey
Croquettes of Rice   Sweet and Irish Potatoes

THIRD COURSE

Quail on Toast
Vegetables   Pickles   Escalloped Tomatoes
Macaroni   Jelly

DESSERT

Mince Pie   Almond Pudding   Lemon Pie
Cheese   Fruits   Nuts
Coffee

MEMORANDUM
ON
FRIENDS' RECIPES

344   *HOUSEHOLD MANAGEMENT.*

Or, in this form:

DINNER

FIRST COURSE

Raw Oysters   White and Brown Soup

SECOND COURSE

Boiled White Fish with Sauce and Sliced Lemons

THIRD COURSE

Roast Beef

FOURTH COURSE

Roast Turkey   Ducks
Vegetables in Season   Croquettes of Rice or Hominy
Cranberry Sauce   Currant Jelly

DESSERT

Cream Custard   Lemon Pie
Fruit   Nuts
Coffee

For tea, the order below will be found valuable:

TEA COMPANY

Tea   Coffee   Chocolate
                      Biscuits
Oyster Sandwiches   Chicken Salad
                    Cold Tongue
                  Cake and Preserves
        [Ice-cream and Cake later in the evening]

Or, in this form:

TEA COMPANY

Tea, Coffee, or Chocolate
Scalloped or Fried Oysters   Muffins
Sliced Turkey and Ham
Cold Biscuits
Sardines and Sliced Lemons
Thin Slices of Bread Rolled   Sliced Pressed Meats
Cake in Variety

THE BILL OF FARE.

For more substantial supper serve as below:

SUPPER

Cold Roast Turkey   Chicken Salad
         Quail on Toast
Ham Croquettes   Fricasseed Oysters
    Charlotte Russe   Vanilla Cream
Chocolate Cake   Cocoanut Cake
        Mixed Cakes
          Fruit
     Coffee and Chocolate

Or, in this form:

SUPPER

      Cold Roast Partridges or Ducks
Oyster Patties   Cold Boiled Ham   Dressed Celery
      Oysters or Minced Ham Sandwiches
Raw Oysters   Chicken Croquettes or Fricasseed Oysters
   Wine Jelly   Ice-cream   Biscuit Glace   Cakes
     Fruits   Chocolate   Coffee
       Pickles and Biscuits

Another authority suggests for supper and luncheons the following suitable dishes from which to make choice, namely:

Soups, sandwiches of ham, tongue, dried sausage, or beef; anchovy, toast or husks; potted beef, lobster, or cheese; dried salmon, lobster, crayfish, or oysters; poached eggs; patties; pigeon pies; sausages; toast with marrow (served on a water plate), cheesecakes; puffs, mashed or scalloped potatoes, brocoli; asparagus, sea-kale with toast, creams, jellies, preserved or dried fruits, salad, radishes, etc.

If a more substantial supper is required, it may consist of fish, poultry, game; slices of cold meat; pies of chickens, pigeons, or game; lamb or mutton chops; cold poultry, broiled with high seasoning, or fricasseed; rations or toasted cheese, etc.

MEMORANDUM ON FRIENDS' RECIPES

MEMORANDUM ON FRIENDS' RECIPES

And now, what more on bills of fare does the good housewife need? Possibly she needs some hints as to cold lunches for wash-days, house-cleaning times, and other days of extra work. She shall have a few such hints:

PLAIN HOME LUNCHEONS.

No. 1.—Cold corn-beef, nicely sliced; baked potatoes; bread, butter, and pickles. Dessert—mince pie and cheese.

No. 2.—Chicken pie, baked potatoes; rolled bread or biscuit. Dessert—cake and custard.

No. 3.—First course: Raw oysters, with lemon and crackers. Second course: Cold veal, with jelly and Saratoga potatoes, bread, and butter. Dessert—pie with cheese.

No. 4.—Casserole of fish, with mushroom catsup; bread and butter. Dessert—cherry pie with cheese.

Possibly some hints as to economical dishes for dinner may be of service. Such hints, adapted to each day of the week, are added to render this needed service.

DINNER FOR EVERY DAY.

Sunday.—Roast beef, potatoes, and greens. Dessert—pudding or pie, cheese.

Monday.—Hashed beef, potatoes, and bread-pudding.

Tuesday.—Broiled beef, vegetables, apple-pudding.

Wednesday.—Boiled pork, beans, potatoes, greens, and pie, or rice-pudding.

Thursday.—Roast or broiled fowl, cabbage, potatoes, lemon pie, cheese.

Friday.—Fish, potato croquettes, escalloped tomatoes, pudding.

Saturday.—*A la mode* beef, potatoes, vegetables, suet-pudding and mince pie, cheese.

MEMORANDUM ON FRIENDS' RECIPES

THE BILL OF FARE.

As one who attempts to master the many dishes at the table of a great hotel finds himself worsted, so the housewife who attempts at once to master the foregoing suggestions will find herself. Patient and repeated attention, however, will master the whole.

QUANTITY OF PROVISION NEEDED..

What quantity of the standard articles must be provided for entertainments? This question is a practical one of no small importance. Nobody wishes to run short at a company, nor does a prudent person care to waste good food. How then shall estimates be made which can be fairly depended on? Experience shows the following general principles to hold good.

It is safe to assume that of one hundred and fifty invited guests, but two-thirds of the number will be present. If five hundred are invited, not more than three hundred can be counted upon as accepting. Smaller numbers will be more largely represented in proportion.

Allow one quart of oysters to every three persons present. Five chickens, or, what is better, a ten-pound turkey, boiled and minced, and fifteen heads of celery, are enough for chicken salad for fifty guests; allow one gallon of ice-cream to every twenty guests; one hundred and thirty sandwiches for one hundred guests; and six to ten quarts of wine jelly for each hundred.

For a company of twenty, allow three chickens for salad; one hundred pickled oysters; two molds of Charlotte russe; one gallon of cream, and four dozen biscuits.

CURIOUS DISHES AND BILLS OF FARE.

A recent French fancy is a deep dish of mashed potato filled with hot broiled plover or snipe, and then hidden in a grove of parsley sprigs and celery tops stuck into the

MEMORANDUM
ON
FRIENDS' RECIPES

potato. It comes to the table looking as green and fresh as a salad. But the salad is still to come; you have simply struck a fresh covey of birds.

A royal Chinese banquet was tendered Sir Thomas Brassey, M. P., at Macao, March 6th, 1877. The following was the *menu* of that entertainment:

BILL OF FARE:
Four Courses of Small Bowls, one to each guest, viz.:
Birds'-nest Soup, Pigeons' Eggs,
Ice-fungus (said to grow in ice), Sharks' Fins (chopped).

Eight Large Bowls, viz.:
Stewed Sharks' Fins, Fine Shell Fish, Mandarin Birds'-nest,
Canton Fish Maw, Fish Brain, Meat Balls with Rock Fungus,
Pigeons Stewed with Wai Shan (a strengthening herb), Stewed Mushroom.

Four Dishes, viz.:
Sliced Ham, Roast Mutton, Fowls, Roast Sucking Pig.

One Large Dish, viz.
Boiled Rock Fish.

Eight Small Bowls, viz.:
Stewed Pig's Palate, Minced Quails, Stewed Fungus (another description),
Sinews of the Whale Fish, Rolled Roast Fowl, Sliced Teals,
Stewed Duck's Paw, Peas Stewed.

A stylish Japanese dinner was served with the following

BILL OF FARE:
Soup,
Shrimps and Seaweed;
Praws, Egg Omelette, and Preserved Grapes;
Fried Fish, Spinach, Young Rushes, and Young Ginger;
Raw Fish, Mustard and Cress, Horseradish and Soy;
Thick Soup of Eggs, Fish, Mushrooms and Spinach, Grilled Fish;
Fried Chicken and Bamboo Shoots,
Turnip Tops and Root Pickled,
Rice ad libitum in a large bowl,
Hot Saki, Pipes, and Tea.

INDEX

	PAGE		PAGE
Advice to Housekeepers	254	Beef, Minced	73
Anchovy Sauce	108	Roast	71
Angel's Food	196	Savory	73
Apees	183	Soup	37
Appleade	253	Soup with Okra	38
Apple Butter	218	Spiced	72
Dumplings	165	Stew	74
Fritters	114	Tea	248
Pie	150	Beefsteak, Broiled	75
Snow	175	Pudding	76
Water	253	Stuffed	75
Apple Float	204	with Onions	75
Meringue Pie	150	with Tomatoes	75
Sauce	204	Beer, Ginger	240
Transparent	204	Quick	241
Apples, Baked	204	Spruce	241
Roast	253	Beets, Salad	281
Arrow-root Broth	251	Boiled	96
Jelly	250	Beverages	234
Artichokes, Boiled	99	Bill of Fare	334
Asparagus, Boiled	96	Bird Trussed for Roasting	321
Sauce	106	Biscuit	136
Bacon, Broiled or Fried	89	Cream	137
Bananas and Cream,	205	Light	137
Fried	205	Potato	137
Barley Bread	133	Tea	137
Water	252	Flavored	138
Beans, Baked	96	Glace	178
Boiled	95	Graham	138
Lima	95	Maryland	138
String	95	Short	138
Bean Soup	39	Soda	137
Beef	70	Yorkshire	138
à la Mode	72	Blackberry Mush	164
Cakes	282	Sirup	253
Corned	74	Blanc-mange	175
Curried	73	Chocolate	176
Cutting up	305	Corn Starch	176
Deviled	73	Neopolitan	176
Beef, Extract of	44	Tapioca	175
Hash	73	Boston Brown Bread	130
Loaf	283	Brandied Peaches	217

INDEX

	PAGE		PAGE
Brandy, Cherry	240	Cake, Farmer's Fruit	191
Raspberry	240	Fig	188
Sauce	110	Fruit	190
Bread	126	Gold	186
Brown	129	Hickorynut	189
Corn	130	Ice-cream	194
Fancy	132	Jelly	192
Graham	130	Lincoln	186
Milk	128	Loaf Dutch	180
Potato	128	Marble	194
Pumpkin	133	Molasses	181
Rice	130	Moravian	186
Rye	129	Neapolitan	195
Salt Rising	128	New Year's	189
Unleavened	130	One, two, three, four	185
Vienna	129	Orange	194
Wheat	127	Peach	192
Stuffing for Fish	60	Pinafore	186
Breakfast Cocoa	238	Pineapple	192
Breast of Veal	308	Plum	190
Brisket	306	Poor Man's	186
Broma	238	Pound	187
Broth, Chicken	249	Puff	185
Mutton	38, 249	Silver	186
Brown Betty	162	Snow	188
Browned Flour for Soups	45	Spice	188
Buckwheat Cakes	143	Sponge	187
Bun, Cinnamon	181	Tea	185
Buns	139	Tumbler	185
Hot Cross	139	Union	194
Butter, Apple	218	Walnut	189
Peach	218	Washington	187
Sauce	109	Watermelon	195
Scotch	243	Wedding	190
Cabbage a la Cauliflower	98	White Mountain	193
Boiled	98	White Pound	187
Salad	103	Wine	188
Cafe Noir	236	Cake Baking	179
Cake, Almond Sponge	187	Cakes, Buckwheat	143
Black	190	Cinnamon	183
Bread	181	Flannel	144
Chocolate	191	Groundnut	246
Cider	185	Hominy	145
Cinnamon	183	Indian Griddle	145
Citron	189	Knickerbocker	182
Cocoanut	189, 193	Lemon	183
Coffee	188	Potato	93
Cork	186	Seed	183
Cream	193	Shrewsberry	182
Cream Sponge	187	Sugar	182
Cup	186	Rice	144
Currant	189	Sour Milk	145
Delicate	193	Walnut	183

INDEX

	PAGE		PAGE
Calf's Liver or Heart	80	Celery Sauce	106
Tongue	81	Stewed	99
Candied Fruits	205	Charlotte Russe	177
Nuts	244	Cheek or Jowl	306
Candy, Almond	244	Cheese-cake Pie	152
Cocoanut	243	Chicken, Broiled	63
Cream	243	Broth	249
Ice-cream	243	Croquettes	112
Molasses	243	Fricasseed	64
Peanut	246	Fried	64
Canned Asparagus	223	Jellied	65
Beans	223	Jelly	249
Corn	223	Panada	251
Canned Corn Cakes	295	Pie	64
Corn Soup	295	Pot-pie	65
Corn Pudding	295	Pressed	65
Gooseberries	221	Roast	63
Grapes	222	Smothered	64
Pea Soup	295	Stewed	63
Peaches	221	Trussed for Roasting	320
Pears	222	Salad	104
Pineapple	222	Chili Sauce	106, 231
Plums	222	Chinese Bill of Fare	348
Strawberries	221	Choca	238
Tomatoes	223	Chocolate	237
Canvas-back Duck	66	Creams	245
Caper Sauce	107	Frothed	237
Capons	69	Chow-chow	230
Caramels, Chocolate	244	Chowder, Fish	51
Carving	315	Chuck Ribs	306
Calf's Head	325	Cinnamon Cakes	183
Turkey	317	Clam Chowder	59
Broiled Chickens	321	Fritters	115
Fish	325	Soup	50
Ham	323	Clams, Deviled	50
Roast Beef	321	Stewed	44
Roast Chicken	320	Cleaning a Shad	60
Roast Ducks and Geese	320	Cocoanut Steeples	198
Roast Pig	323	Cocoa Shells	238
Roast of Lamb	322	Cod, Baked	48
Roast Rabbit	324	Coffee	236
Roasts of Mutton	322	Ice-cream	283
Roasts of Venison	323	Iced	236
Small Birds	321	Meringued	236
Steaks	324	Cold Golden Buck	281
Tongue	325	Coldslaw	102
Catfish, Fried	51	Cookery Books, on	28
Catsup, Grape	231	History of	18
Green Tomato	230	Cookies	182
Mushroom	233	Soft	183
Oyster	232	Cocoanut	184
Tomato	230	Cooking, Art of	17
Walnut	231	Cooking, Object of	17
Cauliflower, Boiled	98	Schools of	28

	PAGE		PAGE
Cooking, Science of	17	Dinners, Every-day	346
Utensils, Ancient	24	Doughnuts	184
Corn, Baked	95	Drawn Butter	109
Boiled Green	95	Dressed Eggs	281
Fritters	113	Dressing, plain French	108
Soup	40	Dried Pea Soup	40
Corn Beef, Boiled	74	Duck, Canvas-back	66
Beef Soup	38	Properly Trussed	320
Cornstarch Blanc-mange	176	Roast	66
Costly Entertainments	25, 33	Dumplings, Apple	165
Crabs, Scalloped	59	Drop	45
Cracked Wheat	251	Lemon	165
Cracker Panada	251	Peach	165
Cranberry Sauce	107	Dutch Cake	180
Cream, Chocolate Bavarian	170	East India Pickle	229
Chocolates	245	Eclairs a la Creme	199
Dates	246	Eels, Fried	51
Fritters	115	Egg Balls	125
Italian	169	Baskets	122
Orange	170	Cream	250
Pink	170	Gruel	250
Puffs	197	Nog	238
Sauce	110	Raw	250
Spanish	169	Sandwiches	124
Tapioca	170	Toast	122
Turret	171	Eggs	117
Velvet	171	a la Mode	120
Walnuts	246	Baked	120
Whipped	169	Boiled	118
Cream and Jellies	166	Boiled, with Sauce	119
Creamed Tomato Toast	294	Curried	123
Croquettes and Fritters	111	Deviled	125
Chicken	112	Fricaseed	122
Hominy	111	Pickled	125
Lobster	113	Poached	119
Oyster	112	Scrambled	121
Oyster Plant	112	Soft Boiled	249
Potato	112	Steamed	120
Rice	111	Sur le Plat	121
Veal	112	Toasted	121
Crullers	184	Whirled	120
Crimpets	142	Eggplant, Baked	98
Cucumber Pickles	225	Fried	98
Cucumbers, Sliced	101	Family Breakfast in Season	339
Crystallized Fruit	205	Family Dinners in Season	340
Cup Custard	160	Fancy Breads	132
Curious Dishes	347	Fig Paste	246
Currant Fritters	114	Figs a la Genevieve	178
Custard, Chocolate	161	Filet of Veal	307
Rice	161	Fish Balls	52
Dates, Cream	246	Chowder	51
Deserts	166	in Season	60
Deviled Eggs	125	Omelet	124
Lobster	57	Oysters, etc.	46

INDEX

	PAGE		PAGE
Fish White	49	Griddle, Indian	145
Fishturner	285	Groundnut Cakes,	246
Flannel Cakes	144	Gruel, Egg	250
Flaxseed Tea	253	Indian-meal	250
Flint Pickles	228	Oatmeal	250
Floating Island	175	Gumbo Soup	41
Food in Season	336	Gum Drops	246
Forks	283	Halibut, Baked	48
French Fritters	115	Boiled	48
Pickle	229	Cutlets	47
Rolls	135	Ham and Eggs	88
Straws	184	Baked	88
Fritters and Croquettes	111	Boiled	87
Fritters, Apple	114	Glazed	88
Bread	113	Toast	88
Clam	115	Hard Sauce	110
Corn	113	Head of Veal	308
Cream	115	Heart of Beef	307
Currant	114	Heart, Baked	74
French	115	Hoe Cake	133
Fruit	114	Hominy, Boiled	100
Hominy	114	Cakes	145
Oyster	115	Croquettes	111
Parsnip	114	Fritters	114
Plain	113	Horseradish, Plain	105
Potato	113	Sauce	105
Rice	114	Hot Cakes	126
Spanish	116	Cross Buns	139
Venetian	116	Ice-cream, Chocolate	168
Frosting, Cocoanut	200	Freezers	295
Cooked	200	Lemon	167
Prothed Cafe au Lait	237	Orange	167
Fruit Crystallized	205	Peach	168
Fritters	114	Pineapple	168
Fruits, Candied	205	Raspberry	168
Frozen	169	Strawberry	168
Nuts, etc.	201	Vanilla	167
Game and Poultry	61	Icing, Almond,	200
in Jelly	68	Banana	200
How to Keep	69	Chocolate	199
Garnishes	331	Lemon	199
Gingerbread	181	Orange	199
Ginger Beer	240	Imperial	241
Snaps	182	Indian Griddle Cakes	145
Golden Buck, Cold	281	Invalid Diet	248
Goose, Roast	66	Irish Stew	84
Trussed for Roasting	320	Italian Cream	169
Grapes in Brandy	217	Jam, Barberry	213
Gravy	69	Blackberry	213
Green Pea Soup	40	Cherry	213
Greens, Boiled	99	Damson	214
Griddle Cakes	142	Green Gage	214
Graham	143	Raspberry	213

354 INDEX

	PAGE.		PAGE.
Jam, Strawberry	213	Lobster, Deviled	57
White Currant	213	Patties	58
Jams	207	Salad	105
Japanese Bill of Fare	348	Sauce	108
Jellied Chicken	65	Soup	43
Oranges	172	Stewed	57
Jellies	166, 207	Loin of Mutton	308
Jelly, Apple	173, 210	Veal	307
Barberry	211	Love Knots	185
Black Currant	210	Lunch Party Menu	343
Calf's Foot	172	Macaroni, Baked	100
Crab-Apple	210	Soup	42
Currant	209	Stewed	100
Grape	211	with Tomatoes	100
Lemon	174	Macaroons	196
Orange	174	Chocolate	197
Peach	173	Marketing	304
Raspberry	211	Marmalade, Apple	211
Roll	192	Grape	212
Wine	172	Orange	212
Wine Currant	210	Peach	212
Quince	211	Pear	211
Johnny Cake	133	Pineapple	212
Jujube Paste	247	Quince	211
Julien Soup	42	Maryland Coldslaw	103
Jumbles	183	Stewed Oysters	53
Currant	184	Mayonnaise Sauce	109
Kidney, Beef	307	Mead	241
Broiled	81	Meat Balls, for Soup	45
Kisses	197	Omelet	124
Kitchens	361	Menu, for Breakfast	342
Lady Fingers	198	for Dinner	343
Lamb and Mutton	82	for Supper	345
Lamb	310	for Tea Company	344
Chops, Breaded	85	Meringue, Peach	176
Broiled	85	Meringues	198
Roast	84	Milk, Porridge	252
Saddle of	84	Thickened	252
Steaks, Fried	85	Mince Pie	152
Stewed in Butter	84	Mint Sauce	106
Leeks, Boiled	97	Mock Fried Oysters	101
Leg of Beef	306	Terrapin	58
Lamb, Boiled	84	Turtle Soup	41
Mutton	308	Molasses Candy	243
Mutton, Boiled	83	Muffins	140
Pork, Roasted	87	Bread	141
Veal	307	Corn	141
Lemonade	238	Graham	141
Lemon Sauce	107	Hominy	141
Lettuce Salad	103	Rice	141
Lima Beans	95	Mushroom Sauce	107
Lobster, Boiled	57	Mushrooms, Broiled	99
Croquettes	113	Stewed	99

INDEX

	PAGE.		PAGE.
Mustard, Mixed	105	Parsnip Fritters	114
Mutton, Choosing	308	Parsnips, Boiled	97
and Green Peas	83	Fried	97
Broth	38, 249	Partridges, Roast	67
Chops, Broiled	83	Paste Shells	150
Dressed like Venison	83	Pastry	148
Roast	82	Pea Pancakes	296
New England Chowder	52	Peach Dumplings	165
Noodles, Home-made	45	Peach Ice Cream	283
Nursery Stove	273	Peaches, Fried	204
Nut Cracker	287	Frosted	203
Nutmegs	203	Preserved	214
Nuts	201, 206	Sliced	203
Oak Balls	165	Stewed	203
Okra in Beef Soup	38	Pears, Baked	205
Omelet, Baked	123	Canned	222
a la Mode	124	Peas, Boiled Green	96
Cheese	124	Pepper Hash	228
Meat or Fish	124	Peppermint Drops	247
Plain	123	Perch, Fried	50
with Oysters	124	Pheasants, Roast	67
Onion Soup	40	Piccalilly	229
Onions, Boiled	97	Pickled Beets	227
Fried	97	Peppers	228
Pickled	226	Eggs	125
Oranges	203	Garlic and Eschalots	226
Orange and Cocoanut	203	Mushrooms	227
Desert	174	Nasturtions	226
Trifle	174	Onions	226
Oyster, Cream	54	Oysters	55
Croquettes	112	Red Cabbage	227
Fritters	115	Salmon	50
Macaroni	56	Walnuts	226
Omelet	55, 124	Watermelon	226
Patties	56	Pickle, East India	229
Pie	56	French	229
Sauce	108	Pickles and Catsups	224
Toast	54	Cucumber	225
Oyster Plant Croquettes	112	Sweet	230
Stewed	101	Sweet Tomato	230
Oysters, Fish, etc.	46	Pie-crust	149
Broiled	54	Glace	149
Fried	54	Pie, Apple	150
Mock Fried	101	Apple Meringue	150
Panned	53	Cheese-cake	152
Roasted	54	Cherry	151
Scalloped	55	Cocoanut	152
Spiced or Pickled	55	Cream	152
Stewed	53	Custard	152
Ox-tail Soup	38	Gooseberry	151
Panada, Bread	251	Lemon	152
Chicken	251	Mince	152
Panned Oysters	53	Orange	152

		PAGE.			PAGE.
Pie, Oyster		56	Pudding, Arrow Root		157
	Peach	150		Baked Hasty	155
	Peach Meringue	150		Baked Indian	161
	Pumpkin	151		Batter	154
	Rhubarb	151		Bird's Nest	163
	Sweet Potato	151		Bread	159
Pigeons, Roast		66		Cabinet	163
Pig, Roast		86		Cherry	164
Pin Bone		306		Chocolate	161
Pineapples		203		Cocoanut	157
Pone		133		Corn	155
Pop Overs		140		Cottage	158
Pork		85		Delicious	163
	Boiled	90		Delmonico	160
	Cutlets	87		English Plum	162
	Roast	86		Farina	156
	Tenderloins, Baked	87		Fruit Bread	159
Porridge, Milk		252		Hasty	155
Potato Biscuit		137		Jelly	162
	Croquets	112		Lemon	158
	Fritters	113		Minute	155
	Salad	104		Orange	159
Potatoes, Boiled, Sweet		93		Paradise	162
	Fried	93		Plain Tapioca	156
	Fried, Sweet	93		Poor Man's Plum	162
	Mashed	92		Queen's	161
	Roasted, Sweet	93		Rennet	158
	Roasted, White	92		Rice	157
	Roasted with Meats	92		Sago	157
	Saratoga	93		Berry or Fruit	164
	Boiled, White	92		Snow	164
	Stewed	93		Spice	162
Potted Provisions		252		Suet	154
Pot-pie, Chicken		65		Tapioca and Apple	156
	Veal	78		Vermicelli	156
Poultry		312	Puff Paste		149
	and Game	61	Puffs, Cream		197
Preserved Cherries		216		German	165
	Citron	216		Indian	165
	Damsons	216		White	165
	Green Gages	216	Pumpkin Bread		133
	Peaches	214		Pie	151
	Pears	215	Punch, Milk		239
	Pineapples	215		Roman	239
	Quinces	215	Quail on Toast		67
	Strawberries	216	Quails, Roast		67
	Watermelon Rind	215	Quick Beer		241
Preserves		207	Quinces		205
Pressed Chicken		65	Rabbit, Fried		67
Provision for Guests		347		Roast	67
Pudding, Almond		160		Trussed for Roasting	324
	Apple	159	Raspberry Float		283
	Apple Batter	154		Vinegar	240

INDEX

	PAGE.		PAGE.
Raw Egg	250	Sauce, Horseradish	105
Rhubarb, Stewed	205	Lemon	107
Rice, Boiled	100	Mayonnaise	109
Cakes	144	Mint	106
Croquettes	111	Mushroom	107
Fritters	114	Oyster	108
Milk	252	Strawberry	107
Rockfish, Boiled	48	Tomato	105
Roley-poley	164	Vanilla	108
Rolls	134	Venison	108
Breakfast	134	White	110
English	134	Wine	110
French	135	Sauces in General	110
Geneva	136	Sausage, Fried	89
Parker House	135	Meat	89
Plain	134	Baked	89
Vienna	135	Scalloped Crabs	59
Royal Displays	332	Corn	294
Rusk	136	Oysters	55
Rusk and Milk	282	Tomatoes	294
Sweet	139	Scallops	60
Tea	138	Scrappel	90
Sago	250	Serving Meals	326
Salad, Cabbage	103	Slapjacks	145
Chicken	104	Smoked Salmon	49
Lettuce	103	Snipe, Roast	66
Potato	104	Shad, Baked	47
Salmon	105	Broiled	47
Salads and Sauces	102	Sherbet	240
Sally Lunn	132	Shin of Beef, Stewed	74
Salmon Baked	49	Veal	308
Broiled	49	Short-cake, Scotch	133
Steaks, Fried	50	Strawberry	153
Boiled	49	Shoulder of Veal	308
Pickled	50	Shrub, Currant and Raspberry	239
Salt Pork, Broiled	89	Soaking Salt Fish	60
Sandwiches, Egg	124	Soft-shell Crabs	59
Saratoga Potatoes	93	Soup, Bean	39
Sardine Salad	297	Beef	37
Sandwiches	297	Chicken	43
Sardines au Gratin	296	Clam	44
Sauce, Anchovy	108	Consomme	298
Asparagus	106	Corn	40
Boiled Egg	109	Corned Beef	38
Brandy	110	Cream Tomatoe	294
Butter	109	Dried Pea	40
Caper	107	Green Pea	40
Celery	106	Gumbo	41
Chili	106	Julien	42
Cranberry	107	Lobster	43
Cream	110	Macaroni	42
Drawn Butter	109	Mock Turtle	297, 41
Hard	110	Mutton Broth	298

INDEX

	PAGE		PAGE
Soup, Onion	40	Toast Soft	251
Ox Tail	38	Water	252
Portable	44	Tomatoes, a la creme	95
Southern Gumbo	42	and Beefsteak	75
Tomato	39	Baked Sliced	94
Turkey	43	Baked whole	94
Vegetable	38	Broiled	94
Vermicelli	42	Fried	94
White	43	Stewed	94, 293
Soups, Soup Stock, etc.	35	Tomato Catsup	230
Sour Milk Cakes	145	Sauce	105
Souse	90	Sauce, Green	106
Spanish Cream	169	Soup	39
Fritters	116	Soy	231
Spare-rib Roast	86	Tongue, Boiled	74
Spiced or Pickled Oysters	55	Calf's	81
Peaches	217	Trout, Fried	50
Spinach, Boiled	99	Stewed	59
Spruce Beer	241	Turkey, Boiled	62
Squash, Boiled	97	Boned	63
Fried	97	Roast	62
Strawberries in Wine	217	Soup	43
Strawberry Sauce	107	Turnips, Boiled	97
String Beans	95	Tutti Frutti	168
Stuffing, Oyster	69	Vanilla Sauce	108
Plain	69	Veal	76, 307
Potato	69	Boiled, Filet	77
Succotash	95	Croquettes	112
Sweetbreads, Broiled	81	Cutlets, Broiled	80
Stewed	81	Cutlets in Cracker	79
Sweet Pickles	230	Hash	78
Syllabub	169	Loaf	79
Table Ornaments	328	Minced	80
Taffy, Butter	245	Pie	78
Lemon	245	Pot-pie	78
Tapers	382	Pot-Roasted Fillet	77
Tarts	153	Pressed	80
Tea	235	Roast	77
a la Russe	236	Scallops	80
Baskets	153	Stew	77
Beef	248	Sweatbread	308
Flaxseed	253	with Oysters	79
Iced	235	with Rice	79
Iced, a la Russe	236	with Peas	79
Terrapin	58	Vegetables	91, 312
Toast	131	Vegetable Soup	38
Buttered	131	Venison	311
Cream	131	Sauce	108
Dry	131	Steaks, Broiled	67
Egg	131	Venetian Fritters	116
French	131	Vermicelli Soup	42
Milk	131	Vinegar, Raspberry	240
Oyster	54	Waffles	140

INDEX

	PAGE.		PAGE.
Waffles Raised	140	Wine, Raspberry	240
Rice	142	Sauce	110
Quick	142	Whey	253
Wafers, Scotch	182	Yeast and Yeast Cakes	145
Water Ices	168	Brewers	146
Watermelons	202	Compressed	147
What to Avoid	330	Hop	146
Wheat Bread	127	Patent	147
Whipped Cream	169	Potato	147
White Fish	49	Yorkshire Pudding with Beef	71
Wine, Currant	239		

www.ingramcontent.com/pod-product-compliance
Lightning Source LLC
Chambersburg PA
CBHW030256240426
43673CB00040B/985